ABOUT ITALY
Puglia to the Po

David D. Hume

PublishingWorks
Exeter, NH
2007

PublishingWorks, Inc.,
60 Winter Street
Exeter, NH 03833
603-778-9883

For Sales and Orders:
Revolution Booksellers, LLC
60 Winter Street
Exeter, NH 03833
1-800-738-6603 or 603-772-7200

Edited by Melissa Hayes
Front cover art: Devil's Bridge, Gargagnata, north of Lucca
Back cover art: Nineteenth century fishing boats in Leonardo's fifteenth century canal in Cesenatica.

LCCN: 2007920529
ISBN: 978-1-933002-43-7

Printed in Canada

ABOUT ITALY

Puglia to the Po

TABLE OF CONTENTS

For Cathy

INTRODUCTION

This collection of personal, geographic, social, and historical essays is somewhat hard to define. These visits to various parts of Italy were selected to be of interest to travelers who have already had some experience with the principal destinations of American and British tourists—especially Rome, Venice, Assisi, and Florence, which are scarcely mentioned here. Instead, we have attempted to introduce future travelers to some of the delightful parts of the country that the first-time visitor hasn't yet seen. The selections of historical description were chosen to connect these often smaller cities with the history of the Roman Republic, the Empire, the Church, the wars of conquest and liberation, and the great Risorgimento, which fashioned the mighty and beguiling nation that Italy has become today.

For the past several centuries, books about travels in Italy have been a popular genre. Goethe, Charles Dickens, Paul Yorck von Wartenburg, Arthur Symons, D. H. Lawrence, the incomparable H. V. Morton, and many others have tried their hand at this medium. I do not hope to emulate their mastery, only to join them in sharing their enthusiasm.

GERMANY

SWITZERLAND   AUSTRIA

FRANCE   DOLOMITES

ALPS   •Bergamo   •Trento   Treviso   SLOVENIA
    Vicenza

Milan   Verona Padua •Venice
Pavia• Piacenza   Mirandola   CROATIA
Turin   •Parma

Genoa   APENNINES   Bologna   ADRIATIC
•Chiavari   •Forli   SEA
Lucca•   •Rimini
•Pisa   BOSNIA-
LIGURIAN SEA   •Florence   •Urbino   HERZEGOVINA
    •Perugia
•Siena   •Ascoli Piceno
CORSICA   •Viterbo
    •Orvieto   APENNINES   Rodi
    Garganico
    •Rome
    •Trani
SARDINIA   Ostuni•
    •Naples   Lecce•
    Paestum

TYRRHENIAN   IONIAN
SEA   SEA

    Palermo• Mt. Etna
    SICILY
    Syracuse

ITALY

Hale

PART I

ANCIENT ITALY

I.

PUGLIA:
The Pregnant Princess

She was scarcely more than a girl, not yet twenty when she died: pregnant, greatly loved and treasured, buried with ceremony and grief, still bearing her unborn child. We do not know her name, but we do know that her husband and family tenderly placed her decorated body in the cave of Sant'Angelo in Ostuni. Her wrists bore bracelets of carefully perforated shell and bone. Her headdress was composed of more than a hundred *Cyclope neritea* shells covered with red ochre, still bright despite the passage of time.

She lies there still in the cave out of time, older than the Greek maidens that Keats mused upon. She is older than Helen of Troy, older than Cassandra or Nefertiti, older than Lillith or Eve, who was described by the Genesis writer thirty-five hundred years ago. She lived before Inanna of Sumeria or Ninlil, who followed her beloved into the netherworld. She lived before there was any written poetry or a pharaoh on the throne of Egypt or stone circles on Salisbury Plain. Were there songs or joyful chants of sprouting spring, dances where she and other young women displayed their perfect bodies?

Yet she is not a magic talisman of pregnancy such as her younger sister, the plump Venus of Willendorf; she is an athletic young woman who died before her delivery. The tiny, fragile bones of her baby are still carried inside her body, which evidences the love and esteem her family displayed when they decorated her after her death. She was laid to rest more than twenty-four *thousand* years ago!

She is not a Neolithic woman; she is more of the Old Stone Age, the Paleolithic, born at or even before the age of the cave painters of Altamira and Lascaux. I later learned that Italian archaeologists nicknamed her Delia, for a form of Diana the Huntress. But the Greek goddess is much later in time, and I prefer to think of this pre-mythic young woman as a princess from a period before any Greek divinities were named.

Ostuni in Puglia is an old town by its own or any measure. There is plenty of evidence of human habitation and even the beginnings of agriculture six or eight thousand years ago. The whole Salentine peninsula was inhabited early in the history of Europe. Neolithic and Copper Age people were exploiting the fertile, flat land that borders the Adriatic Sea in the millennia after the fragile princess of Ostuni was buried. Today the olive trees are everywhere, some slight and erect, some gnarled, twisted, and bent into caricatures of the fertility they promise. When we drove through this old land, we saw olive orchards carpeted with the bright yellow flowers of the broom in April. These fields climb the flanks of the low mountains that form the central spine of the Salentine known as the Murge, the low hills that are the southernmost remnants of the mighty Apennines that fill the center of the boot of Italy all the way from here north to the River Po. How many centuries of biting the miniature and bitter wild olives did it take before early men or women planted them and selected the plumpest to breed trees that gave sweet oil for cooking and lamp fuel? Ostuni is probably not the oldest settlement here, but it was carefully sited on the edge of an upland where its position on the hill protected it from marauders that could overwhelm and sack it, for war is as old a human institution as settlement. From the plain below, the picture-perfect whitewashed houses are situated above the serpentine road that mounts the hill.

It seems probable that the first language users and tool makers that migrated into Europe from the African continent came through Asia Minor and across the Dardanelles, passed through the wild Balkan country the ancients called Illyria, and came down to southern Italy from the North. They would have worked their way down the great Italian peninsula following the promise of a milder climate and the rich harvest of the sea. Eventually they would have come to this jutting, seagirt land now called the Salentine with its cave- and grotto-rent shore. Who can tell? Farther south they could not go, and so they stayed. Yet all of these signs of human settlement here are young when compared with the dignified grave of the young princess.

Some call the upper peninsula the Messapian, for an imported people that first smelted iron here as recently as 1000 BCE or earlier. They traded with Greeks and Minoans and made a robust, wheel-turned pottery colored with blue and pale-brown glazes. They wrote in their own language, Messapic, and in recorded times sided with Carthage against Rome during Hannibal's invasion. It was an unfortunate choice. The Romans dealt severely with them, and their language, either from suppression or disuse, had vanished from Italy by the time of the Caesars. I wonder what it sounded like and if the princess and her maidens sang in southern Italy more than twenty thousand years earlier.

We had found an attractive, somewhat underutilized hotel, the Novecento, a kilometer south of the town of Ostuni proper. It was equipped with a disused and slightly murky swimming pool, but it

was early April and I assumed the pool would surely be cleaned up
before the warm weather set in and the summer guests arrived. The
albergo is surrounded by a park of pine trees. The accommodation
was modern and the restaurant and breakfast room first-rate. We did
have to call their attention to plugged drains in both tub and basin,
even though toilet and bidet worked to perfection. Once informed,
the management hastened to repair these difficulties while we went
downtown to a nice bar which bore the sprightly title The Bloody
Mary. It was soon after this that we began to realize that fish, shellfish,
squid, octopus, *spigole* or *branzino* (bass), *cozze* (as mussels are called
here), and even *pesce spada* (swordfish) have been the mainstays of the
Puglian diet for more than a hundred centuries. Since there were
some carbonized seeds and cereal grains in the burial excavation of
the pregnant princess, her people must have practiced some sort of
agriculture (or at least organized gathering) as well.

The northern part of the heel of Italy's famous *stivale* is a little
less windswept than the Salentine, which is the true stiletto heel of
the boot. It probably supported a larger population in early times
than did the narrow and rocky shore that runs down to San Maria
di Leuca, where a tall, modern lighthouse marks land's end, Italy's
southeastern termination. But whatever those early inhabitants
thought of this land, they left the signs of their burials in caves and
under dolmens, which are marked on the best tourist maps[1]. The
hills are pockmarked with caves, good places to come in out of the

---

[1] A good *Atlante Stradale* (road atlas) scaled 1:250,000 is essential for touring in a car.
It will indicate some of these ancient sites as well as the smallest villages. If you are also
equipped with a good list of hotels and restaurants, such as Quattroruote DeAgostini's
Alberghi & Ristoranti, you will be able to plan travels for both day and night in advance.
We found both volumes more readily available in the book and magazine racks at the
rest stops on the major highways than at city bookstores. Although written in Italian,
DeAgostini is easy to figure out, e.g., DC = *dopia camera* = double room etc.

weather in a time when there were no houses and when tools were being made from carefully chipped pieces of flint. Paleontologists call this sub-era the late Mousterian, after a type site in faraway France. The Princess of Ostuni was of this period.

Modern Ostuni is more charming and a bit more like everybody's hometown. The cathedral was graced with a group of German tourists who were listening to what was to us an incomprehensible lecture from their guide. We moved to one side and listened to the wizened and wiry organist perform on an electronic organ, mostly modern hymn tunes mixed with Neapolitan love songs, until the group left. Then he smiled at us and switched to popular songs of 1950s America. We asked him for J. S. Bach, but either from disinclination or lack of knowledge, he kept to the more contemporary literature. Cathy said that it gave the rather dignified church something of the air of a suburban skating rink.

When we came out of the cathedral, an elderly woman asked Cathy if we were *Inglese*; she replied that we were *Americani*. The woman's reaction was to shake my hand and kiss Cathy on the cheek, saying that they would never forget the Americans because they rid Italy of the rule of Mussolini. Her affectionate embrace stemmed from recalling events that must have come from her childhood, when *Il Duce* was in power more than sixty years before. We wondered what particular experience could have fixed the result of the GIs' arrival so firmly in her memory. Did she react so warmly to every American tourist she met at church? And this took place while America was being criticized for having invaded Iraq.

On another foray into Ostuni proper, we inspected a street of shops offering hardware and other useful things, as well as pretty ceramics and glassware. While strolling the street we noticed a strikingly beautiful girl; tall, quite blonde, and with an intelligent look to her. Later when we had settled into a bar for an *aperitivo*, she appeared again and ordered an *aranciata* at the bar. Now one of the great advantages of being a senior citizen, traveling with spouse, is that a white-haired gentleman can invite such a pretty young creature to join his table without soliciting shock or scandal. This girl turned out to be a graduate student from Germany preparing to take her doctorate in archaeology. Our little Italian matched pretty well with her English. It turned out that her friends had gone shopping and she was without a key to get into the apartment until they returned. Her striking good looks and lack of a key made me think that she was sort of a combination of the princess of Puglia and *Mimi of La Bohème*. She gave us good advice about a restaurant and several ancient sights to visit.

Finding our way back to the Novecento was a challenge. Ostuni is a tangle of one-way streets that always seem to lead one away from home. We were almost as confused as we had been on the prior day when we had made our ritual visit to the cathedral, a pretty, fifteenth-century building which houses rather too much seventeenth-century visual biography of the wretchedness of being martyred. Cathy correctly dismissed most of the interior decoration as being composed mostly of "hideous paintings" and one striking statue of the risen Christ.

But the general effect of Ostuni is delightful, rather like a North African city in its stark white buildings and in the excellence of its seafood. From the eastern edge of the town, high on its protective cliff, you can see the Adriatic ten miles away, dark blue in the distance.

II.

A PILGRIMAGE TO PAESTUM

Almost no one starts an Italian visit with the Greek settlements, but they did come before the Romans. We boarded a train at Roma Termini and were taken swiftly backwards in time, more than twenty-five centuries, to the location of Posidonia in Magna Graecia. Here, a dozen or more cities were settled from Corinth and Athens, long before there was a Rome. The speedy Naples-bound train traveled through the expected jumble of the ages we had seen all over Italy. The Ferrovia dello Stato (or "FS") passed urban alleys, small factories, and junkyards, but suddenly, the ancient form of a Roman aqueduct appeared beside our track. Gaps in the seemingly endless series of great brick-and-stone arches showed that the gigantic construction could not have carried any water for centuries. Still, after nearly two thousand years, it is remarkable that it is standing at all. Our guidebook indicated that it was the Claudian Aqueduct, which at one time supplied more than a million gallons of fresh water to Rome every day.

After the right-of-way parted company from those tremendous arches that spanned the horizon, our train sped quietly on to the south, through green fields of lettuce, spinach, and artichokes (the delightful *carciofini* that please the palate all over Italy). Occasionally there were brilliant yellow fields of rapeseed, and then a miraculous patchwork of pink, fuchsia, and white, where splendid orchards of peaches, cherries, and almonds were in their brief moment of spring blossoming. Along with all its modern and very successful industry, Italy also has a huge agricultural output. Individual householders and apartment dwellers take advantage of any scrap of vacant land to grow their own vegetables.

Now that the Caesars, dictators, and conquering Austrians and French are gone and the popes are no longer a determining political force, Italy seems interested largely in three things: food, the automobile, and prayers of petition. These three preoccupations are very old in Italy. The Roman network of good, all-weather roads was the world's first, and for many centuries, the only transportation system in Europe. The slender Italian peninsula has always been able to raise more food than its own population needed, although they didn't bother to do so at the height of the empire. And over the centuries Italy has seen the construction of more churches, temples, and houses of worship than any other place in the world.

We had already visited Baroque Christian churches and had paid proper homage to Bramante, Michelangelo, and Bernini for their enormous creation of Saint Peter's in Rome. We had looked further back to the Renaissance cathedrals, Gothic baptisteries, and Romanesque basilicas in the north of Italy. We had seen the ruined temples of the Roman forum. We had even looked at the remains of some Etruscan religious objects, most notably a bronze chandelier at Cortona that displays a circle of ecstatic dancing girls being pursued everlastingly around the lighting fixture by a matching set of lascivious satyrs.

Now we had started on another quest back in time, in search of even earlier religious architecture. We had come to Italy and found a travel agency where we purchased railroad tickets that said ROME-PAESTUM. This was obviously a journey through time and history as well as through the Italian countryside, for in Paestum, there are sixth-century BC Greek temples better preserved than almost anything in Greece itself. They stand by the side of the road, forty kilometers south of Salerno, completely accessible to anyone who passes by. Although they rate three stars in the Green Guide ("worth a journey"), only a few travelers go to see them in warm weather, and almost none in the early spring.

Italians call March *Marzo pazzo*—"crazy March"—roughly the equivalent of our proverb that says the first month of spring comes in like a lion and goes out like a lamb. The temperature had dropped on our last day in Rome, and as the train rolled south, we could see a bluish-white snow cover on the Apennines that rose beyond the lush spring fields to the left of our track. Spring was all about us in the narrow coastal plain, but in the mountains that dominate almost all of Italy, winter was still evident. I wondered how the ancients dealt with the cold. Greeks and Romans are always depicted or sculpted in sandals, bare-legged with a sort of kilt worn under their armor. Did they wear socks? Wooly long johns? Hannibal and his African legions came this way twenty-two centuries ago. Riding on an elephant must have been a lot colder than the "EC" (EuroCity) express train that took us to the Piazza Garibaldi station in Naples.

We changed to the local train (misleadingly called an accellerato) that would take us to Salerno and on to Paestum, a total trip of about three and a half hours from Rome. Minutes south of Naples, a conductor looked at our tickets and commented cheerfully in rapid Italian that the train didn't stop in Paestum. We should get off at Battipaglia instead. It would be fairly close to our destination, where we had booked a room at the Pensione delle Rose. The obliging *proprietario* had said that he would come to pick us up at the station in Paestum. What now?

To further complicate the situation, a merry-faced student seated across the aisle leaned toward us conspiratorially and ventured the opinion in carefully pronounced English that the conductor was misled; we should get off at Capaccio, which we would find to be much nearer to Paestum.

Moments later the train plunged into the ten-kilometer tunnel that cuts through the backbone of the Sorrento Peninsula. Exterior darkness distracted us from asking ourselves whose authoritative advice we should follow. Salerno appeared in the daylight in a few minutes, and our friendly student guide jumped up, repeated "Capaccio!", and disappeared.

We moved on through more agricultural wonders. In one field we saw a herd of glistening black water buffalo, source of the finest mozzarella. Battipaglia came and went, and the blue bulk of Mount Eboli rose on our left. In a few more minutes we suddenly stopped at Capaccio, where we descended. The platform was so short we had to climb down a long step to the stone ballast of the track before we could pull out the towing handles of our rolling suitcases and wrestle them over twenty meters of loose ballast to reach the asphalt platform. After watching the train speed away, we looked about for a telephone. The tiny station was equipped with a control panel which displayed a Christmas tree of lighted lines and switches that looked capable of handling the whole national rail system. Two uniformed officials considered our plight. The more elegantly costumed directed us to a bright-orange pay phone, which proved to be inoperable. He then produced a 200-lire piece from his own pocket and commandeered the services of two students who were standing by the station, sending them across the tracks into the village to telephone the *pensione* for us.

Since the boys were waiting for the next train going in the opposite direction (in seven minutes), they set off at a run. They were back in un attimo, and reported that we should wait for our innkeeper at the second crossroads in the part of the village on the opposite side of the tracks. They stoutly refused the fistful of 1,000-lire notes I tried to press on them.

We bumped over the tracks to the hamlet of Stazione Capaccio and took up our stance in front of the drugstore. In about ten minutes a dusty and somewhat rumpled Mercedes of middle age arrived, and a tall, rumpled, and somewhat unshaven man resembling John Cleese burst forth. He seized our bags, bid us a hearty *buon giorno*, and sped us off down the road to Paestum, three kilometers to the south. One of the lovely things about travel in Italy is that although things seldom work as planned ("That's Italy!", the natives mutter), they always turn out well because human kindness compensates for systemic failure.

Approaching the hotel, we could see a rank of Doric columns and a partially ruined pediment among the trees to the west. We inspected the hotel first. It turned out that the Pensione delle Rose was clean, tidy, well-appointed, and absolutely empty. The *proprietario* turned on the heat in our room and showed us where the extra blankets were stored in the wardrobe. (The charge for bed and breakfast for the two of us turned out to be a very reasonable $47.38 when it showed up on the Visa Card bill a month later.) I asked if there was a good restaurant in town. He scratched his stubbled chin for a moment and said that he thought we would eat what he ate for supper that night. Would we be pleased to have spaghetti? He pronounced the name of this most common variety of pasta, lingering over the second syllable as though it were a delicacy. For a second course he proposed prosciutto with bufalo mozzarella and a tomato salad. These seemed to be the items at hand in the family kitchen, and we readily agreed. By this time we were ready to set out to discover Greek temples.

Crossing the highway that fronted the two dozen houses of the village, we bought our 3,000-lire tickets (probably a bit more now in euro) and walked toward the northernmost of the three temples. It sat firmly on the crest of a slight rise in the ground. The path led us through thick, freshly cut grass to this "Temple of Ceres." The guidebook points out that all the temples have traditional names that were assigned in an age that knew little of their actual dedication. But it matters very little if this extraordinary pile of honey-colored marble was raised to honor the goddess of cereal or, more probably, Athena. The columns and architraves glowing in the afternoon sun were a gorgeous tribute to the god or goddess who inspired the stone workers. It seems incredible from our Judeo-Christian,

Temple of Ceres c. 500 B.C.

Muslim, or other monotheistic perspective that such a salad of deities could inspire such active devotion, such large-scale works of public construction, and such elegance of design and balance. All three of the great buildings are of the Doric order, but of differing design because they were built one at a time over the span of more than a century. The northernmost temple's columns, all intact, have a pronounced *entasis*—a tapering in a delicate curve from bottom to top. They present an oddly primitive appearance to our eyes. We were all brought up on the taller and straighter shafts of the Parthenon columns, and these earlier designs, even though in a more perfect condition, appear less intentionally planned than they really are. Should we criticize an early illustration of a Jules Verne spacecraft for not looking like *Apollo XI* or the space shuttle? (Come to think of it, the span of time between the temples of Paestum and those of Periclean Athens is longer than the few years between Verne's imagined rockets and the real ones of the 1970s.)

Walking south through lush fields of more unidentifiable pink, white, and pale-yellow flowers, we traversed the partially excavated foundation walls of the town. The flowers seem to be an almost perpetual adornment of the site, and are even mentioned in some of the guidebooks. Parts of a small theater were visible in the recesses of the meadow, as well as pieces of houses, shops, and other signs of what must have been a busy little town twenty-five hundred years ago, before the river silted in and malaria from the resulting swamp made the area uninhabitable. The houses were knocked down and looted of their cut stone, used for building materials by unknown hands in the Dark Ages. In the eighth century AD, Arabs from Africa and their successors, the Sicilian Normans, also briefly used Paestum as a quarry around a thousand years ago. But none disturbed the three temples. Alone among these ruins they stand almost complete at their original height, entablature and cornices still presenting their elegant, grass-sprouting silhouettes to the sky. The two younger monumental buildings have nearly complete pediments above their hexastyle (six-columned) facades.

We approached the middle temple, named now for Neptune, but built for the worship of the mother goddess, Hera. It presents a huge bulk, an almost complete building from the fifth century BC, glowing on its modern cushion of grass and flowers. To eyes accustomed to looking at classical antiquity in the broken shards of Athens or Rome, it seems totally uncompromised. Beyond it, lacking only its gable pediments, stands the mysterious "Basilica," a complete rectangle of mid-sixth-century Doric columns on an undisturbed foundation, standing amid flowering bushes and small shade trees. No one is quite sure whose temple it was in its heyday; it gets its modern name because, for a while (a millennium or so ago), at least part of it was used as a Christian church. Here the pillars are more sharply tapered at the top and their stone is a paler, ashen gray. Obviously other quarries were opened for the later temples. This oldest of the temples has an odd number of columns across its front, and a single row of columns running down the inside centerline

Paestum
Temple of Neptune

once supported the roof. This unusual pattern has led to speculation by some scholars that it was dedicated to a *pair* of gods, since there is no single nave that could lead the devoted to the image of a single deity. Who these gods might have been remains a mystery.

Each of the three buildings has a different character, as though their design bespoke the personalities of the gods or goddesses they were meant to honor. What reverent awe did they impress upon those who approached them two and a half millennia ago? Could those people have been in terror of their gods? Paestum does not look like a place where worshippers lived in anxiety about the intentions of the divinity. Demeter, Athena, Hera, or Poseidon were the focus of worship here in the years before there was a Rome. But whichever gods belonged to which temple, they must have inspired a great devotion to have been honored by such sanctuaries as these.

We walked slowly back to our starting place along the smooth and round-edged flagging of a street of indeterminate age, perhaps first century AD, Roman in origin, and crossed the busy Campagnian highway to the little Archaeological Museum, thoughtfully kept open for an hour after the field of temples closes for the night. We examined objects and diagrams until the end of the arrow-directed tour. There we found the "Tomb of the Diver," *Il Tuffatore*. He is painted in vivid colors on the inside of the well-plastered lid of his coffin, and is said to be one of only a handful of Greek wall paintings yet discovered. The little man, naked, with genitals in silhouette, appears to be flying through the air, having just plunged from the capital of a sort of Doric column, toward an undefined and uncertain future in what looks to be a pond surrounded by trees. Rendered with a stylized realism, colored a rich red, he soars in a graceful arc with a smile on his face, seeming to approach his destiny with very good spirits.

As my wife and I were admiring this unusual and charming painting, the air shook with the concussion of a loud explosion. The smell of gunpowder filled our nostrils, and a thin puff of smoke came through the museum's windows. Neither the guard nor the half-dozen other visitors paid any attention. With minds full of imagined terrorists, we looked about. All was peaceful, scholarly, and antiquarian. Then another, equally startling detonation shook the building. This too was ignored by all present. We did our best to appear as carefree as the others, but we soon moved outdoors to see what was up.

What was up was the Feast of the Annunciation, the twenty-fifth of March, when the Archangel Gabriel announced her impending maternity to the Virgin Mary. The local church in Paestum is dedicated to Santa Maria dell'Annunciata, and the parishioners were celebrating their own special feast day with appropriate fireworks, discharge of ordnance, and similar explosions. The church was lighted inside by hundreds of candles and still held a few lingering and prayerful people silently murmuring petitions to the Virgin. The aromas of cordite and incense blended in our nostrils.

After a day spent mostly outside in the windy March weather, we were happy to stop at the little bar near the church for an *aperitivo*. As in most Italian coffee shops, there was a bottle of Jack Daniel's on the top shelf of the mirrored dresser behind the bar. We commanded a warming draught and repaired late to the Pensione delle Rose. There we dined amid linen napery and proper stemware in the empty dining room. Since there was no menu to choose from, I entered into the spirit of the occasion by inspecting all of the wines on the sideboard, selecting one of the more choice *Chianti Classici*. The innkeeper's wife did a splendid job on the sauce, the ham was sliced like thin rose petals, and the mozzarella was tangy and fresh enough to be spread with a butter knife. Later, after a *caffè macchiato*,

I walked back down the highway in the darkness and reached the latitude of the youngest temple, the shrine of Hera. Lighted in the total darkness by golden sodium bulbs, it glowed in the void like the treasure that it is, silent witness to the piety and artistry of those who peopled this small town in Italy twenty-five hundred years ago.

"Il Tufatore": Tomb of the Diver

III.

OSTIA AND FIUMICINO:
The Airport on Top of the Old Port

When our plane had descended toward the south-facing runway at Rome's Leonardo da Vinci Airport, we saw little from the windows but the blue of the Tyrrhenian Sea on the starboard side and a nondescript, industrial suburban landscape to port. The thump of landing and swift deceleration told us nothing of what lay beneath us, but we had actually settled down on top of a large portion of a two-thousand-year-old seaport town that had received the commerce of Rome for close to a millennium. I don't know exactly how much of the ancient city of Ostia actually lies under the airport, but quite a lot of it is there, safely sealed away from the wear and tear of our later civilization. Just now, much of the southern part of ancient Ostia and its extension into the Portus has been cleared of the accumulated detritus of the ages, and is exposed to the view of archaeologically minded tourists and scholars. Quite apart from its historical interest, it is a pretty place to stroll in the spring.

We had deplaned at Fiumicino and took the speedy rail connection to the center of Rome. It was almost a month later, returning from the north, that we came to Ostia in a rented car. It would probably have been easier to get there from Rome by taking the train from downtown toward the beach at the small town of Fiumicino, and getting off at the Ostia Antiqua stop. From the almost-deserted parking lot, we walked into the ruined city, amazed at how so central and obviously prosperous a place could come to be so deserted, destroyed, and covered over with soil and vegetation. For though it was the port and principal suburb of the capital at the center of the world for many hundreds of years, when Rome itself was later sacked and damaged several times in the Dark Ages, the parent city was never left as barren and empty as this place. Here are the shells of temples, houses, a large theater, and the mosaic floors of great bath houses. There are warehouses, simple homes, undoubtedly houses of ill fame as well as public buildings small and large, churches, temples, shrines, and law courts. This small city was an entirely middle-class civilization which flourished sixteen miles away from the city it served, and from the courts of the Caesars and the popes. It now seems quite as well preserved as Pompeii and Herculaneum, which are newly rid of their coverings of ash and lava, but Ostia had no volcano to destroy and preserve it, only the hand of man.

Ostia was first built in the middle of the first millennium BC, probably as a town of laborers at the coastal saltworks who were able to supply that essential commodity to the young city inland up the Tiber. During the epoch of the Punic Wars, when Rome and Carthage contested for the rule of the western Mediterranean, the largely agricultural Romans learned the ways of the sea and found they needed a harbor close to home. Their commerce had earlier come ashore at Pozzuoli, just north of Naples, but the overland trip up the Appian Way was several days' journey. In the second and third centuries BCE, Ostia was developed to be the home port of the ships that sailed to Syracuse and Africa itself, whence departed Scipio Africanus and the army that eventually destroyed Carthage. Heeding the grim advice of the honest but bloody-minded old Cato (*Carthago delenda est!*), the Romans left not a stone upon a stone there, and sowed salt in the surrounding fields to prevent its regrowth[2].

Ostia, on the other hand, grew with the prosperity of Rome itself, as the giant capital required more and more commerce to bring in the imported grain needed to feed a growing population that eventually reached a million or more. While the republican city expanded, the harbor town acquired fortifications and dock works. Sulla built a wall around it in the waning days of the republic, the early years of the first century BC. Communication between Cleopatra's Egypt and the Rome of Julius Caesar and Marc Anthony came here by ship. Julius Caesar planned to make a proper seaport of Ostia, but he was assassinated before he could begin the project. Some enlargement of docking facilities was undertaken by Augustus, and the emperor Claudius later decided that a whole new artificial harbor should be built just to the north of the mouth of the Tiber itself, which was silting up to a degree that rendered the original haven too shallow for the larger Roman ships.

Some of these ships were huge. In order to bring back the prize obelisk from Egypt (the one that now stands in the center of the Piazza St. Pietro in the Vatican), an enormous vessel was ordered by the emperor Caligula. The cargo weighed about 1,300 tons. When Pope Sixtus V had it moved to its present location in 1585, it required 800 men, 140 horses, and 40 rollers to accomplish the

---

[2] In the days long after Julius Caesar, two centuries later, the Romans themselves revived Carthage and pensioned off their soldiers with grants of land there. It became the Province of "Africa" in the age of the Severian emperors, and was a very prosperous place. Today it is called Tunisia and preserves some of the finest of all Roman ruins, mostly from the second century AD.

job. Everybody was amazed at their success. Evidently, no one paid much attention to the original task of putting the huge chunk of granite on a barge to bring it down the Nile before loading it on a Roman ship to bring it to Ostia, and thence to Rome itself. The ship that made this Mediterranean voyage seems to have been too large for practical trade purposes after the obelisk was moved. When the new Portus of Claudius needed an offshore beacon to mark its entry from the sea, the great hull was filled with stone and concrete and sunk at the appropriate spot to make an artificial island, on top of which a tall stone lighthouse was constructed. As far as I can tell, this substructure is still there.

Nero, who took credit for completing this project, usually expressed his opinion of himself by striking coins which showed him as the god Apollo or smiling adoringly at his mother, Agrippina. He had such pride in his improvement of the port that he issued a silver *sesterce* with his face on one side and a small fleet of seven or eight different-sized vessels at Ostia on the other. The pretty coin shows remarkable detail in the fine representations of the ships.

Trajan expanded the Portus, and later ordered a canal dug, connecting it to the old waterway of the Tiber itself so that lighters could carry the seaborne commerce upriver to Rome. All of this was of course accomplished without power shovels, bulldozers, or dump trucks.

Roman shipping probably reached its greatest tonnage and then began to decline in the reign of Constantine, when all maritime authority was concentrated at the Portus. Thus Ostia itself was left as a sort of bedroom town for the seaport. But Constantine eventually moved the capital to Constantinople around AD 330, and Rome began the process of degeneration that continued through the fifth century AD, when arrived the invasions of Alaric the Goth, Attila the Hun, Genseric the Vandal, and a variety of warrior Muslims in the Middle Ages.

Even as the empire declined, agriculture upstream allowed a lot of mud to wash into the river, which inevitably silted up still more. The coastline migrated toward the sea until only shallow-draft vessels could venture into the Tiber, and the great harbor of Portus filled in and decayed. Ensuing swamps and marshes probably bred malarial mosquitoes in the early Dark Ages of the sixth and seventh centuries. What was left of the civilized little city received rough treatment from the Saracens in the eighth and ninth centuries, when Rome itself had been reduced to a squalid settlement of probably less than twenty thousand people, digging out a wretched survival amid the broken remains of the imperial marble and brickwork. In the Middle Ages much of the marble at Ostia was burned to make lime for fertilizer or mortar and cement. It seems likely that a lot of classical sculpture went this way in the thousand years between the fifth and fifteenth centuries. The wonderful evidence of the civilization of republican and early imperial Rome that we can see now is a small fraction of what once was here.

Our visit was in late March, traditionally called *Marzo pazzo*, but the day was warm and sunny, and a few blossoming fruit trees studded the ruins. The green growth among the truncated walls is romantic and pleasant to contemplate, but it must drive the archaeologists wild. There is nothing like the vigorous root system of a sapling cherry tree to wedge apart the stones of a thousand-year-old ruin. Vandals aren't nearly as destructive of ancient buildings as are almond trees. Plant life was perhaps even worse than the newly enfranchised Christians, who were bent on exterminating the vestiges of pagan worship of the gods and goddesses who had been given lifelike form as marble statuary. Archaeologists pick up the pieces and prop them up in museums or in the midst of the restored ruins to create a semblance of what once was there. Once, when wandering among the half-ruined brick walls of the city, we suddenly came upon an ancient statue standing quietly in the corner of a courtyard, a presence from another world keeping watch over some sacred spot.

We walked for a considerable distance into the area, enjoying the pleasant sunshine as we followed bilingual signs, but we were unable to locate a bookstall or museum to buy a map of the ruins. We finally found a faded sign that purported to show the way to the libreria. After another fifteen minutes of blind navigation through the maze-like corridors of truncated brick walls, we eventually located a well-appointed museum at the far side of the excavation, where it sits in almost-useless isolation in a site unfrequented by tourists who might want a chart. I suggested to the nice *commessa* that the directions might be better provided nearer the entrance of the site. She agreed heartily but added with a broad smile, "But you know, that's Italy!"

We inspected mosaics of several baths where bold black-and-white tesserae display athletes in performance, as well as sea monsters. Neptune himself is here, cavorting in the deep with a flotilla of Nereids riding dolphins. Some houses have ground floors thirty or more feet square where animals and naked gods disport in multicolored compositions.

The theater at Ostia seats about thirty-five hundred spectators today. It was smaller than this when it was first built in the reign of Augustus, probably 12 BC, but it was enlarged in the time of Septimus Severus, in AD 196. Restorations in this century have put it back in commission again. Dates in Ostia, by the way, are unusually precise, because at one time a record of important public events was inscribed on marble tablets in the forum. The simple farmers of an illiterate civilization in the early Middle Ages saw no use in exhibiting these meaningless characters, and recycled the slabs by placing them facedown in the mud as sidewalks and courtyard pavements. They were rediscovered in the early excavations of the nineteenth century, and have since provided a more accurate dating of civic activity than can be found in Rome itself.

We found the theater populated by several small groups of tourists, including an attractive gaggle of teenaged girls from Germany who sat in the semicircular theatrical *gradinate* (bleachers) while their mentor recited poetry from the grassy stage area to demonstrate the quality of the acoustics. One lissome young beauty then did a series of handsprings and cartwheels across the *proscenium* in what must have been a fair example of the sort of popular spectacle the Ostians would have enjoyed a couple of millennia ago.

Unlike Pompeii, which is famous for its bordello, Ostia is studded with houses of worship. There are temples and shrines to the traditional gods and goddesses of the Greek and Roman pantheon; Jupiter, Juno, and Minerva especially. But Vulcan's presence seems to be even more common here, and archaeologists reason that the lame god of the smithy was the original deity of the primitive settlement. The worship of Vulcan was brightened by his background and later exploits. Son of Juno and Jupiter, he was born with deformed legs, but nevertheless acquired Venus as his wife through his mother's intervention. But Venus, as everyone knows, is the goddess of love, and cannot be counted on to remain faithful for long. She had a famous affair with Mars, the god of war. Their dalliance was a favorite subject with the later Renaissance painters. The cuckold Vulcan took revenge by forging a marvelous net in which he trapped the illicit lovers and then exhibited them to the scorn, derision, and laughter of the Olympian court, still held fast in their guilty embrace.

Another cult, of the Great Mother of the Gods, came from

farther east than Greece, probably from Phrygia in Asia Minor. In 204 BC, a ship came to Ostia bearing the sacred stone of the Mother of the Gods. It went aground in the mouth of the Tiber, and the intervention of a goddess was required to bring it over the bar and up to the port. Thus, centuries before the improvements of Claudius and Nero, the need for better port facilities was obvious. The combination of confronting such practical problems with both human energy and divine assistance seems quite like the contemporary Italian approach to public affairs.

By the early days of the empire, the mix of religious beliefs in Ostia was enriched by soldiers coming home from the East and by the imported cults of the slaves acquired there. Of all of these, the most popular was the worship of the Persian god, Mithras. His sanctuaries were not usually freestanding houses of the gods as were the temples of the Greeks and Romans, but were instead relatively small chambers, often underground, where the faithful gathered to worship. A sculpture of Mithras slaying a sacred bull was a prominent feature of these chapels. There are a half-dozen such chamber sanctuaries in Ostia, and at least one splendid sculpture of Mithras and the bull in the museum. The Roman Christian tradition of building its churches in close proximity to each other seems to have been anticipated in this satellite city.

Ostians were deeply concerned with another, still newer religion. There are a number of Christian symbols in the ruins and traditions from the period of the great persecutions, which give accounts of the martyrdom of some of its early Christian citizens. St. Augustine refers to the town as one of the important bishop's sees close to Rome. Ostia also gives examples of how the ancient and modern Italians are similar people. Their marketplaces and wine shops, their obvious delight in public entertainment, and the profusion of their houses of worship make them seem very much like the people of today. The scale of their community, far removed from the huge remains of the Forum and Coliseum in Rome itself, provide a feeling of daily living that makes life in the time of the empire easier to imagine.

For the first time, I began to feel that the general population of the Roman world did not feel that they were suffering under the despotic or demoniac or sometimes insane oppression of the emperors. In all probability, they lived in some comfort, perhaps even contentment, in this middle-class community of importers, shopkeepers, dockhands, shipfitters, and boatwrights. They probably followed our pattern of work and recreation, going to church on the Lord's Day, and the men probably getting drunk on Saturday night as well. It is the sort of town where you can imagine householders or apartment dwellers buying a Fiat on the installment plan, or a young man preparing to acquire first a Vespa, and later a girl to ride on it with him, both of them wearing medallions around their necks to honor a god or goddess who would protect them.

Today the sea is over a mile from the excavations at Ostia Antiqua. The relentless current of the Tiber has washed lots of the landscape down the river's course and deposited it on the beaches to the east of the original Ostia, and the later Portus. The several mouths of the river are the site of the moving channels of Father Tiber and the canal dug at the order of Hadrian. Farther down the coast to the southeast are the Lidos where modern Romans come to play at the sandy shore in the hot weather. North of the mouth of the river is the Isola Sacra and the beach town of Fiumicino, from which the great Roman airport gets its common if not its official name. Our visit was on the verge of April, a season when beach towns exhibit rather more character than they do in the hot summer months. When the weather is swimmable, all Italian beaches present about the same expanse of well-oiled rumps and brightly colored bikini thongs. When there is something of an edge to the wind and the water breaks in explosions of cold, white foam over the bulkheads and breakwaters offshore, you can tell where you are more surely than when *la spiaggia* is merely a vast cushion for the tanning bodies of the young.

Leaving the ruins hungry, we followed our noses to the west and drove through the close streets of Fiumicino in search of lunch. Eventually we parked alongside an unidentified waterway which seemed too narrow to be the Tiber, but too broad to be Trajan's canal. There was a sizable fleet of professional fishing boats warped up to the bulkhead, painted bright blue and white and festooned with rusty maritime equipment. They bore the names of women, wives, mothers, or saints—Rosalia, Lucia, Cecilia, Maria Stella Maris. Sailors have always dedicated their vessels in this way. They depend on them for livelihood and for salvation from the treachery of the sea. The names are a combination of deserved honor and propitiatory offering for the security they long for when on the bosom of the deep.

Enquiring of a group of children, we learned that although most of the restaurants were not yet open for the season, the Trattoria della Marina functioned year-round. It was on the other side of the waterway, canal, or Tiber, as the case may have been, but there was a marvelous one-armed bascule bridge that we could cross. The view from the bridge in the bright sunlight was unforgettable: fishing boats in pure spectrum colors, pink and yellow stucco buildings, brilliant reflections from the still waters below.

The trattoria was a warm and friendly place which offered lots of the fruits of the sea. I had a bowl of their clam and mussel soup, and we both ordered the antipasto from the ocean: baby mussels, octopus, and squid, with a mixed vegetable salad and crusty fresh bread.

Later we stopped by the beachside to walk for a few minutes on the gray sand. Offshore we could see a pair of large oil tankers anchored in what looked to me like moderately rough seas. The great vessels didn't seem to be rolling at all. There was no close harbor that could accommodate them here. I guess they were to offload their petroleum at some sort of pipe connection out in the Tyrrhenian Sea. The method of getting cargo ashore has changed a little at a time since the era when Julius Caesar planned to improve the river mouth of the Tiber, but the need for Roman seaport facilities is quite the same as it has always been, for the past twenty-five hundred years.

IV.

OVER THE GREAT
MOUNTAIN BARRIER

The uneasy crust of our planet is made up of a number of independent plates that seem to slide about its spherical surface and collide with each other with very slow speed but immensely powerful impact. Some of these huge slabs of rock bury themselves under each other; some ride on top; and some crumple their edges into one another to raise wrinkles on the surface of the earth that now rears many miles in the air. A plate that moves two or three millimeters in a year is doing this sort of thing quite rapidly, and will have traversed twenty or thirty kilometers in twenty million years. Since the great age of the dinosaurs, it would have moved ten times as far, 150 statute miles or more. It seems that the entire boot of Italy has thus been rammed into the European continent quite violently, and the great mountains raised in places to an altitude of four or five miles. In some places it is still growing, while the ice and rain wear it down in others.

The fan-shaped ring of these mountains is a sort of umbrella spread over the north extremity of Italy, sealing it off from the lower plains of Austria, Germany, and France. The whole mountain chain area is called the Alps, a Swiss-German word that means a mountain pastureland among the hills, a place where the edelweiss grows. But the shape of these mountains is in reality far more rugged and threatening than those green fields suggest. The Dolomites, easternmost of the ranges, are amazingly sharp prongs that make the American Rockies look like gentle slopes in comparison.

Once on a *vaporetto* crossing the Venetian lagoon, we were blessed by a very clear day, and suddenly saw the snow-mantled heights of the Dolomite Alps rising in our sights above the towers of Venice itself, although the mountains were seventy-five miles away. It is impossible to enter Italy without either flying over them, sailing around them, or tunneling through them. And yet this formidable barrier has done little to protect Italy from its rapacious neighbors to the north. From the second century BC, when Hannibal broached it with his famous elephants, to the immigration of the barbarian hordes of Goths and Langobards, whole armies have come through the high passes. Even languages have passed this way and mixed tongues like Suisse-Romand have developed on both sides of the hill. Parts of Italy wrested from Germany as the prize of two world wars are still bilingual.

Flying into Milan, Torino, Venice, or even Rome treats air travelers to breathtaking views of range after range of huge blue mountains, which eventually give way to the south-facing slopes that drain the snowpack into the great lakes: Garda, Como, Lugano, Maggiore, and Lago d'Orta. Small rivers flowing from these sparkling reservoirs of meltwater are tributaries of the Po, Italy's greatest river, which is bordered by huge rice fields in the west and bounded by the transverse thrust of the Apennines to the south. In the east the Po is paralleled by the Adige, which also drains the waters of the Alps into the Adriatic south of Venice.

You can never be far from the mountains in Italy. The main branch of the Apennine chain extends south to the toe and heel of the boot, and includes active volcanoes such as Vesuvius. Across the three-mile Strait of Messina, Sicily is equally mountainous, and its eastern shore is ornamented by Etna, Europe's largest volcano. And for all of this expanse of rock and precipitous slope, Italy, a country only a little more than the size of North Carolina, supports a population of 60,000,000 by growing almost everything its people need to eat. Traveling about it, we observed that there is a garden plot behind every house, even in the middle of modern cities. There are water buffalo contentedly chewing their cud in the boggy land of Campania, producing the finest mozzarella cheese in such quantity that it is not only on virtually every table in Italy, but is also shipped fresh all over the world. Durum wheat and maize make pasta and polenta, Arborio rice and many cheeses abound, and there always seems to be enough veal to produce all the vitello al limone and osso bucco you might ever desire.

In Piacenza, in the mountains, surplus donkeys are stewed into *stracatto d'assino* (donkey stew), which is tender and delicious if you are not put off by the name. The peninsula has always fed itself well, except during the decadent years of the later Roman Empire, when wheat was imported from Sicily and Egypt to make the free bread that the Caesars combined with circuses to keep their subjects more or less happy, and at the very least, not rebellious.

The climate doesn't always cooperate in Italy. We have generally visited this wonderful country in the spring, and made sure to come equipped with layered costumes that provided comfort in cold as well as sparse March sunshine. Summer is too hot, as it usually is in New York or Washington. Autumn is ideal. Friends have told us that Venice is grand in December, and peering up at the coffered ceilings of the *piano nobile* of a Venetian palazzo from a gondola in the dark is the best way to see the real essence of the town.

Traveling about Italy is easy whether on the state railroad, the Ferrovia dello Stato (known as the FS), or by car. Large cities are as intimidating to drivers as they are in America, but no more so. Parking is simpler, since Italians who lack a place to leave the *macchina* on the street often create a makeshift parking space on the sidewalk (if there is one). A good paperbound volume of large-scale road maps (an *Atlante Stradale*) is an essential guide, and far better than the accurate Michelin maps which, for all their elegant folding, are a hopeless mess when undone in the front seat of a small car.

"Italy," says Cathy, "is like exploring a box of chocolates." These delicious cities and towns have unique flavors and are wrapped in all sorts of tempting shiny foil and twists of colored paper. It is hard to make a choice about where to begin. But we decided to go ahead, on the assumption that we could hardly go wrong poking about in a country where so many had found so much to enjoy. The urge to explore the South described in *The Wind in the Willows* remained in our adult psyches, ready to be followed when we were, as the Italians say, *in pensionata*.

We began our innocent journeys without the slightest knowledge of Italian, and only a sketchy acquaintance with Italian geography. We knew Rome was in the middle and Milan was up near the top, but not much more. We have since made a number of trips to the towns made famous by the Renaissance, to the Eternal City of the popes and Caesars, and to the sites of "Greater Greece," where Greek civilization flourished before Rome began. This collection of essays on towns of both southern and northern Italy is presented from the perspective of our personal experience, much as it will be revealed to any tourist who puts a finger down on a map of the famous boot and chooses a destination with the sense of anticipation and enjoyment he or she might find in selecting a prettily wrapped confection from a box of *caramelle* or one of the famous *baci* of Perugia.

Americans can enjoy Italy without knowing any Italian, but like most things in life, the richest experiences and the greatest bargains are found when we can understand something of the language of the provider. Even when we were at the linguistic mercy of hotelkeepers and restaurateurs, we found them uniformly kind and helpful. We were never taken advantage of, although a rather aristocratic English con man once unsuccessfully attempted to "borrow" money from us in Rome. Any three-star hotel (*un albergo di tre stelle*) has a desk clerk who speaks English, and will not only recommend good places to eat, but will also make reservations for you in grand style. But learning even a little Italian will increase your enjoyment in this voluble country, and your attempts to make yourself understood will delight the Italians, who will congratulate you quite heartily for having gotten off a successful "Good morning!" or "How goes it?" in their pleasant language. Living with even the simplest language tape or CD running perpetually in your car for some weeks before your trip will pay great rewards.

We suggest you buy a good guidebook[3], and a phrase book like the Berlitz Italian-English dictionary, which includes a selection of useful phrases and a good menu decoder. Airfare in and out of Italy is cheap in the off-season. Make a reservation by fax or telephone for your first couple of nights, and take off!

---

[3] There are many, and you may want to try several. If we had only one to carry, it might be The Lonely Planet: Italy, although Let's Go Italy is great for those on a tight budget, and has good interior maps. The Cadogan Guide Italy has wonderful information about art and history. If you can master the coded symbols and find your way among the different provinces and other political divisions of Italy, the DeAgostini guides will help you find the best hotels and "agriturismo" accommodations at a level of three stars and up. Less-expensive places are listed in Let's Go.

Since all airlines lead to Rome or Milan most directly, you are likely to begin your trip in one of these large and busy cities. Starting in one of these cities may be inevitable, but I urge you to resist the desire to begin with the dessert. Start with a smaller city where you can acquire some skill in navigating Italian habits and customs before you take on the larger ones. Cremona, Torino, Bergamo, and Parma are all a short drive (or train trip) from the Malpensa Airport of Milan, and delightful little Lucca is just minutes from Aeroporto Pisa by train or by car.

Once you get to looking around you in Italy, you will find that, as in all places, you can see much more of what you know about than what you don't. A line of worn standing stones in the center of a traffic circle takes on an awesome dignity when identified as part of the wall built to encircle Rome by its legendary second king, Numa Pompilius, around 700 BC. The king may be a legend, but the stones are real. We can really only see what we know something about. And the more we know, the greater the range of our vision. By providing some history and descriptive archaeology, this book attempts to help you explore beneath the everyday surface of these Italian towns and cities. There are even a few dates included here, since the great span of time recorded in this small country is one of the things that drew us to explore it in the first place.

But in spite of the duration of its history, Italy itself is a young country. It was created out of the fragments of a number of independent cities and kingdoms in the latter half of the nineteenth century. Dukes, popes, doges, emperors, and elected councils governed its pieces for a millennium and a half after the death of Romulus Augustulus in 476. He was the last of the Roman emperors to rule in Italy, and spent almost no time in Rome. Before him the famed Empire lasted a bit more than five hundred years. The Republic dates back a half-millennium earlier. Before that there were kings and legends.

We don't know much about what came before 1000 BC, but there were people in Italy then called the Villanovan culture. Their origins are distant, but their remains are visible in the many museums of this history-conscious people, especially in Perugia, Bologna, and Rome itself. Later came the Umbrians, the Ligurians, the Etruscans, the Latins, and a number of others who mingled together to become the amalgamated peoples of the Roman Empire. Still later, Goths, Lombards, and other Eastern European people settled in Italy and defended their newfound turf.

In spite of this diversity, the language of the Romans gave some sense of unity throughout the Middle Ages, even though the people of Italy thought of themselves as Venetians, Neapolitans, Piedmontese, or Tuscans. Today they proclaim that they are Italians with a great sense of national pride. Even the somewhat separatist Sicilians and Venetians share in this unity, although the most right-wing political parties murmur occasionally about seceding from the South (where the poverty is) and making themselves into a neo-fascist sort of clean and prosperous state that need not worry about the disadvantaged. But for now, at least, the sense of national unity is too great for them to make much headway.

Every town and city has streets named for Cavour, Mazzini, and Garibaldi, the remarkable trio of mutually hostile heroes who created modern Italy in the middle of the nineteenth century. The three are sometimes thought of as the brain, the soul, and the sword which fused into Italy. Along with the music of Giuseppe Verdi, they define the very essence of Italy. The dates of the great national holidays commemorating the end of World War II are themselves used as the names of streets radiating from the piazze in many towns, both north and south. I think there is a Via Roma in every city in Italy. Almost no roads remember the names of the popes or Caesars, with the exception of an occasional designation of a street named for the dear and popular Giuseppe Roncalli, Pope John XXIII. The final unity of the country was achieved over the strenuous objection of Pope Pius IX, and strict limits have been placed on political action by the successors of St. Peter since his time. The Italians are enthusiastic about their church, but they insist on governing their own lives and behavior without much interference from pope or theologian. They take their troubles directly to the Madonna (as they would to their own mother, swearing by *Mamma Mia!*), confident that she is interested in their welfare without being encumbered by philosophy, moral theology, or civil law. (Reviewing Federico Fellini's *Armarcord* might be a good way to get in training for your trip.)

PART II

NORTH AND WEST

V.

MIRANDOLA
AND THE LAKES OF THE NORTH

Italy's necklace of lakes seems to dangle from the breast of the mountains of the Swiss border toward the *padano*, the valley and plain of the Po. It is a sparkling series of freshwater reservoirs fed by the melting snow and glaciers of the Alps. Orta, Maggiore, Como, Lugano, Iseo, great Garda, and little Idro are much favored by Italian and German tourists, but are visited less often by Americans. We determined to give several of them a try and entered Lombardia and the Veneto by renting a French Renault Clio at the Bologna Airport. Traveling through the pleasant spring green of that fertile country for an hour to the west brought us to Mirandola, a thoroughly civilized little city which has an attractive *piazza maggiore*, an excellent hotel of modest price (the Pico), and a number of nice restaurants, most of which we were discouraged to discover are closed on Monday night.

The Picos of Mirandola were one of those powerful and rich aristocratic families that created the intellectual revolution in northern Italy, later designated as the Renaissance. Although less famous than the d'Este, the Gonzaga, the Borromei, or the Medici, the lords of Mirandola were cultivated masters of urban defense and political savvy. Best known of all is Giovanni Pico della Mirandola, who was a

Renaissance man in every sense. He read Greek with ease, which was a skill only recently discovered since the medieval and post-Crusade linguistic isolation of Europe. He became a learned Platonist who set himself the task of reconciling Christian theology and the teaching of the ancient philosophers. In spite of his immense learning, he didn't get very far on the project because the poor chap died at the age of thirty-one with his magnum opus well begun but far from complete. His work on the Hebrew kabbalah merited him a period of condemnation from a conservative pope, but he was eventually forgiven (perhaps through the influence of his admirer, Lorenzo [Medici] the Magnifico). He also earned the admiration of other fifteenth-century intellectuals such as Thomas More, who translated much of his writing from the usual crisp Latin of his day into English. There is an interesting exhibit of pictures of him and some explanation of his work (in Italian!) in the town museum attached to the palazzo pubblico. The young intellectual is much honored in his hometown, often painted in profile, showing a rather soft countenance, a turned-down nose, and an overhanging lower lip.

Mirandola[4] is in an area known for its good food. Parma, Modena, and Reggio are close by, and all of these towns produce the great cheese named for Parma. The *zampone* (stuffed pig's feet) are essential ingredients of the legendary *bollito misto*. Gnocchi and tagliatelle are notable here, and I think the dry, bubbly, red Lambrusco goes wonderfully well with them all, even though Cathy prefers the still Sangiovese.

We dawdled for a couple of days in Mirandola, where we enjoyed the Hotel Pico and made use of their e-mail connection, the fine

---

[4] Another quadrosyllabic name accented on the second—rather than the penultimate—syllable: Mirandola.

spremuta d'arancia at breakfast, and the generous ration of ice with the evening gin and tonic. The staff was kind about our less-than-perfect Italian and recommended good restaurants, as well as the *enoteca-cucina*, which is open on Monday night and served us the best white wine we met in Europe. Unfortunately, we lost the note of its name, but the *enoteca* itself is in the *centro storico* and is the only self-styled *enoteca* (or wine shop) there. Trust their selection of wines.

We took off one day to visit Sabbioneta, thirty kilometers to the west. It is a town described in our reliable Lonely Planet guidebook as "one of those failed Utopias" governed by rich intellectuals of the Italian Renaissance. This one was arranged and largely paid for by Vespasiano Gonzaga, whose family produced a cardinal or two and later on one holy, young saint who died tending the sick during a plague when he was scarcely twenty years old. Vespasiano's city has lovely, rose-brick walls about it that are crumbling gently into the lake and the castle moat. Cathy maintains that they were built to hold off the ravages of the Po rather than warriors from neighboring cities, or French armies attacking from the North. During our visit the town was being held hostage by hordes of charming schoolchildren and their somewhat anxious chaperones, who were explaining both Italian history and art to their young charges. At the stroke of noon they wolfed down sandwiches from their fanny packs and took to playing soccer with a nonregulation soft *pallone* among the lower courses of the arches that support the great gallery of the ducal palace. We observed their exercise from a shaded table in an adjacent outdoor *tavola calda*, where we were served *tortelli con salvia* (ravioli stuffed with sage). With a generous glass of ice-cold Prosecco, it was a treat hard to match in any other country.

There is plenty to see in the duke's ideal city. The great gallery itself is several hundred feet long, decorated with delicate frescoes of what appear to be the heads of Roman emperors. There is a splendid theater designed by Vincenzo Scamozzi, who collaborated with Andrea Palladio on the design of Europe's first indoor theater in Vicenza in the sixteenth century. Above the curved benches for the courtiers there is a loggia with an elegant tier of Corinthian columns supporting statues of the gods of Olympus. The ducal seats are dead center in the first row, where the local sovereign could rise from his place and take part in the denouement of the finale as a sort of deus ex machina who could bring harmony out of the tangled plots of the seventeenth-century dramas.

The Garden Palace is the duke's private dwelling, simple without but elegant within. Among its frescoes is a painting of the trio of lovely nudes known universally as the Three Graces. Here they are standing under a crusty, almost Chinese roof, their arms characteristically intertwined. There are churches, chapels, and other architectural follies here, almost all of them built in the second half of the *seicento*.

One exception to the uniform dating of the town is the 1824 synagogue designed by Carlo Visioli. It is the third such place of worship in a succession that reaches back to the foundation of Sabbioneta itself. The Jewish community here flourished and produced a number of wonderful printed books of both religious and secular content, and set in elegant type of both Roman and Hebrew faces. Here was published a Hebrew Bible in 1488, only a few decades after the very first books were set in metal type by Johannes Gutenberg. But although the Jewish print shop was the pride of Sabbioneta for years, the fascist laws of Mussolini in 1938 resurrected the medieval anti-Semitism that had been on the wane in Europe since the Dreyfus Affair. The community was scattered and many were murdered by the Nazis; their lovely temple of worship decayed, empty, and dusty. Repair and restoration began quite recently and was completed in 1994.

In the entry to the upper room are printed posters that display the history of Jewry from the time of Moses up through David, Solomon, the Maccabees, and the despoiling of the Second Temple by the emperor Titus. The history goes on through the dreadful abuse of the Middle Ages, the burning and slaughter of the Crusades, the forced conversions and the persecutions of the Cossacks, and the "registration" of Jews by the Austrians who governed northern Italy in the nineteenth century. The last picture in the set is of a woman, bent with fatigue and discouragement, walking beside a railroad track and a barbed-wire fence strung on concrete posts. She is leading two ragged children toward an unknown destination. The room is on the third floor and a small fee is charged for visiting it. It is a beautiful place and well worth seeing, despite the inescapable melancholy of being brought face-to-face once again with the horrors of the "Shoah" (the Holocaust).

We drove east again toward Mirandola, seeking the long viaduct and short bridge that would take us back to the south side of the Po. In spite of a few wrong turns among the newly sprung green fields and lilac bushes near the old farmsteads—most of whose inhabitants have been displaced by the more efficient if less picturesque agriculture of the twentieth century—we eventually found our way back to Mirandola. Road signs in Italy are numerous and legible, perhaps more so than in New England.

Mirandola is a town that only a few tourists will visit. Even the agreeable desk clerk asked, as if in wonderment, why we decided to visit it. But like many small Italian cities, it has a gentle charm of its own that we have remembered with fondness ever since. And the people are so nice, *così gentile*.

LAGO DI ISEO

We then set out for the lakes by driving west along the rapid and modern A4 in the direction of Brescia and Bergamo. We left the grand highway between these sizable cities and turned to the north to find little Lago di Iseo, one of the smallest of Italy's Great Lakes and surely one of its prettiest. It also bears the largest island of any of the Italian inland seas, Monte Isola.

Directed by a beguiling description in the Lonely Planet guide, we had telephoned ahead to reserve a "room with a view" at the Ambra Hotel. For five extra euro we got a balcony that looked down on an embarcadero where young mothers pushed baby carriages and old men and boys threw bits of bread to the swans who came in from the lake to participate in the free lunch. Everybody seemed accustomed to getting the best out of the pleasant lakefront. No one seemed in a hurry to do anything. The whole town gave a fine example of the Italian enjoyment of *dolce far niente*—the sweetness of doing nothing at all.

We had lunch at the Leon d'Oro. The "Golden Lion" is the symbol of St. Mark, patron of Venice, who ruled this territory for some centuries when the *Serenissima* decided that the lagoon was not protection enough from the other powers of Europe. Her water barrier kept her safe from attack, but she needed terra firma to provide her with food in times of attack and siege.

Besides food, one of the more modern necessities of travel is the matter of laundry. Iseo provided us with a fine *lavasecco*, which translates neatly as "wash-dry," a promise that was promptly fulfilled by the cheerful, handsome, and robust woman who seemed to be both proprietor and sole employee. It turned out that her agreeable knowledge of the town was to be useful to us a few days later.

Walking out of the Ambra on the following morning plunged

us into the confusion and delight of a typical Italian movable market, which opened on this day once a week. The movable market is a tradition that probably reaches back to early medieval times. It is hard to catalog what is to be found at these traditional street fairs in Italy. Iseo featured four or five shiny, white-and-stainless-steel refrigerated trucks, one side of which opened up as a shop counter to display meat, cheese, fish, or other fresh food. Butchers prepared special cuts at the demand of the housewives. Vegetables were provided at other stations. There were books and magazines, hats, scarves, shoes, and lingerie. I managed to buy an acceptable shirt for seven euro. There were tables that displayed dozens of brightly colored Italian ladies' shoes of the sort that young women all over Europe and America would die for. As a final tribute to Italian *cucina*, we purchased a neat, modern kitchen scale denominated in grams, a necessity for following Italian recipes when we returned to the U.S.

Standing solemnly above the color and confusion of the market, on a column mantled with green moss, stood a likeness of Garibaldi, complete with sword and high-topped boots. Our guidebook maintained that this was the earliest effigy of the great liberator and unifier of Italy. He looks only mildly heroic in the square at Iseo, but there is no doubt that this northern town acknowledges the primacy of the brave and idealistic swashbuckler who routed the Bourbon troops in Sicily (despite being outnumbered at least five to one), and then crossed the Strait of Messina after having set in motion the first land reform that the island had experienced in better than six hundred years. He rolled up the south and was greeted as a liberator in Naples. He then braved the benisons of the pope, Pius IX, who tried to protect himself behind a small army of French mercenaries who all left town at the first close encounter with Garibaldi's Red Shirts. Pius then declared himself a prisoner in the Vatican and Garibaldi a heretic.

Pio Nono (as he is known in Italy) followed up on this course by determining that anyone who voted in an election in the "Papal States" was in a state of Mortal Sin, and would presumably be damned for eternity if he died unshriven after the conflict. Garibaldi and his army of mostly devout Catholics all suffered in silence, and their leader took Rome and then symbolically presented his sword to Victor Emmanuel II, the sovereign of Piemonte, the only constitutional monarchy among the patchwork of Italian states in the mid-nineteenth century. The result was the creation of the nation of Italy, unified for the first time since the days of the Roman emperors.

We were told that a drive around Lake Iseo would take about an hour and half. We set forth and enjoyed the pretty shoreline until we came to a branching of the way and took the lower, waterside route. The road grew alarmingly narrower as we progressed and found ourselves traveling between large concrete pillars; eventually, we had to thread between these examples of some modern Stonehenge. Finally, I rashly assumed that there must be a way through the rocky grove of trilithons, and managed to scrape the right front fender of the little Clio on the way through, and the left fender in my attempt to disengage us. Peering ahead we saw an authority figure approaching. He turned out to be the engineer in charge of building the elevated highway above us. Our chosen path, although not marked as such, was designed to provide a bicycle path and was not meant for cars. He agreeably took the wheel of our car and turned it around to send us back three or four kilometers to find a more suitable route.

Rounding the north end of the lake, we came at length to a small lakeside park where we enjoyed a lunch of packaged pumpernickel bread and cheese we had gleaned from the generous, German-leaning breakfast buffet at the Ambra. The park provided a drinking fountain to refill our water bottle, a comfortable bench, shade trees in profusion, and a view of a yacht harbor in front of us opposite an industrial development behind.

The rental of the car included all sorts of insurance for damage repair, but a certain sense of shame overcame me, and when we got back to Iseo I sought counsel from the lavasecco lady as to where I could find someone to make the car more presentable. She directed me to a heavy-duty car wash a few blocks from her shop. The proprietor, Giovanni, said that the scratches were too deep for his shop to even camouflage, and directed me to a body shop. His directions were too complex for me and I had some difficulty even getting back to my starting point. I explained to Giovanni that like any sinner, I had been lost, and now was found again at his car laundry. With the characteristic and ready sympathy that is so common in Italy, he sent his wife to lead me. She was on her way to collect the children from school but took what must have been a considerable detour to set me right.

The body shop was also under the governance of a woman. She summoned one of a number of her workers who shook his head sadly and said little could be done. She didn't seem discouraged but faced the gloomy interior of the *officina* and gave voice in a volume that must have waked the neighborhood: "BOOGA!" she cried; and "BOOGA!" again.

Presently a pleasant young man emerged from the dark depths and came to inspect the Clio. He anointed both fenders with some unknown solvent and reduced the damage by at least half. He then looked up the paint code on a label inside the front door and returned to the interior of the garage only to emerge again with a plastic cup full of dark-blue paint which he was stirring thoughtfully with an artist's brush. We talked, in English, while he painted over the offending marks. He confessed to being a Croat who was a recent immigrant to Italy. He spoke three languages well—Serbo-Croat, Italian, and English—and several more limpingly. The whole repair took less than fifteen minutes. When I returned the car in Verona ten days later, the clerk in the Auto Europe office seemed pleased with the effect. I hope Booga finds further opportunity in his new country. I tipped him well and wished him the best.

A celebration of unknown origin was under way in busy downtown Iseo when I returned to the Ambra. A marching band dressed in dark-blue blazers and gray trousers or skirts was drawn up in the square that had housed the market the day before. They played with a brisk and yet mellow style for a matter of twenty minutes, and then moved on to some other venue.

We searched out an outdoor bar and observed the conclusion of a wedding emerging from an attractive eighteenth-century church across the square. The organist struck up Handel's "Ombra mai fu," suggesting that there never would be shadows where e'er the lady would walk. The bride, a lady of a certain age, came out to a shower of rice and embraced and bussed virtually everyone in the square save us, but we had retreated to the covered outdoor bar and were a bit out of her direct line of fire.

We set forth on the following day to visit Monte Isola by boat. The vessel was rather grandly named the *Città di Brescia*. It was a sturdy little ferry and accorded us good views of the island as we approached its several towns. We disembarked at Pescheria and found it to be a rather charming fishing village as its name suggested. A shoreside walk of a half-hour brought us to Sensole, where there were restaurants and tourist accommodations. Neither village presents much more than views of the water and a scattering of olive trees, old, twisted, and picturesque as they always are. The island is the sort of place a writer might choose to settle in to bang out a few chapters.

Despite its isolation, there seems to be adequate electricity to power a word processor.

A glowering dark sky made the trip back on the *Città di Brescia* both beautiful and exciting. We hurried from the dock to a *pizzeria-ristorante* where we took cover in the nick of time. The thunder rolled among the hills and lightning bolts lit up the sky. The effect suggested that Jupiter Pluvius was up there someplace settling scores of long ago in this classical country.

We enjoyed Iseo greatly, even the ritual of paying the bill at the Ambra where the elderly *proprietessa* gave one more example of her insistence that accuracy should be valued over convenience. She totaled up our charge on the computer, and then checked the machine by adding it up a second time by hand with a fine fountain pen and a sheet of stiff writing paper. We left with some reluctance to travel back east and visit Lake Garda.

LAGO DI GARDA

Garda is the longest and largest of the Italian lakes, stretching from the lowlands near Brescia to the mountains around Trento, fifty or more kilometers to the north. There are many towns along its shores, some of them historic.

We chose Sirmione, perhaps the oldest and most classical site on the lake. Vacationers such as the lyric poet Catullus came here just before the time of the great expansion of the Roman Republic when Caesar, Pompey, and eventually Augustus pressed the northern borders of Roman Italy beyond the Alps. Some very rich man built a villa of palatial dimension at the north tip of the Sirmione peninsula. Local pride suggests that it was Gaius Valerius Catullus (or at least his family), because his graceful lyric poems proclaim his devotion to the attractions of the lake-girt place. The whole northern end of the peninsula is occupied by a wonderful ruin of magnificent dimensions from which you may look out in three directions to the lake. It is a huge site and suggests the location of an emperor's summer home. But if it was such, it could not have been connected with the Catullus family, since the great poet died in 54 BC, before there were emperors in Rome. It always stirs me to visit and walk upon the remnants of great constructions that for all our history and archaeology are still in our day of uncertain origin. Who built this palace by the lake? He is really as unknown now as Shelley's Ozymandias, who says to us, "Look on my works, ye mighty, and despair!"

Italians celebrate Italy's termination of World War II as a national holiday on the twenty-fifth of April (as well as the weekend that follows). We were lucky to have reserved at the Hotel Oliandre a week in advance, even though the Lonely Planet guidebook tells us that the slender spike of land jutting into the lake actually boasts around eighty hotels and guesthouses. Such a crowding is somewhat relieved by restriction of automobile traffic: cars are admitted to the old center only before 9:00 A.M. (or to drop off luggage), and then must be removed to a municipal parking lot a kilometer or more outside the walls to the south. But getting into the center to deposit baggage takes skill and a certain amount of daring. The day we arrived, crowds of pedestrians ambled gently through the medieval gateways and almost had to be pushed to one side by a mild shoving of the car. Having successfully arrived, I was much discouraged at having to push my way out again to park. The kindly father of the young lady of the house sensed my plight and took the car in hand and disappeared with it. We were revived by an *insalata nicoise* under an umbrella where we studied the extraordinary consumption of gelato by the vacationing tourists.

We decided that Garda was too long to drive around and settled for a cruise across the lake to visit one of the forty or more towns and villages that encircle the lake. We chose to go to Salo, a fairly sizable town which had a considerable promenade facing the east side of the lake. There was a profusion of private motorboats tied up to the municipal dock and a good scattering of sailboats as well. Crossing back to Sirmione, we encountered a pair of three-meter sloops splitting tacks in an informal race. If you need to be convinced of the success of the Italian "economic miracle" of the past half-century, you need only examine the yachts in these northern lakes. Judging by the standards of the boats in Long Island Sound, I would venture a guess that there are several hundred million dollars' worth of private boats moored along the banks of Lake Garda alone. And these expensive toys lie alongside the elegant *palazzi* built over the past three or four centuries by the aristocracy of pre-unification Italy. It seems to me that the number of underutilized yachts is an index of unproductive wealth in any country. Almost no one spends as much as 2 percent of their time in those pretty boats. For the rest of their days they serve as ornaments for the harborside, where they give scale to the majestic mountains that rise behind them.

Looking from the town of Sirmione, the gradually narrowing, long, lakeside hills seem to grow higher in the distance. Their color changes from a strong blue-green at the base to a pale cerulean, topped by a crust of white where the last of the April snow clings to their peaks. The lead- and silver-tinged water stretches almost thirty-five miles to the north. The fringe of houses and palaces along the shore gradually shrink to matchbox size, until they merge into invisibility in the distance. The late-afternoon sun paints the summits orange and pink. Small wonder that the fortunate, since the time of Catullus two thousand years ago, have cherished the time spent among these lakes.

VI.

TRENTO:
On the Verge of Austria

Trento is surely one of the most overlooked towns in Italy. Skiers visit in the winter and hordes pass through its narrow valley, but we felt we were doing something rare and choice when we came to visit it as tourists of art and history. High up in an ancient Alpine valley, Trento is the capital and namesake of its province, Trentino. It is also the next-to-last significant stop on the rail line that connects Italy and Germany through the Brenner Pass, where Mussolini and Hitler met to discuss the New Order that they planned to impose upon Europe, along with the "thousand-year Reich."

But the savages of World War II were mere parvenus of this famous corridor. The road to Brennero is the only thing close to an all-weather passage through the great barrier of the mountains, and it has served the bloody-minded and the rapacious as a route of conquest since before the time of the Romans. Men clad in skin garments came this way ten thousand years ago. More recently the various Holy Roman emperors descended from Germany to the north Italian plain when they squared off against their inevitable adversaries, the popes.

Trento is a part of the somewhat autonomous region of Alto

Adige, which takes its name from the headwaters of the River Adige, second only to the mighty Po among the rivers that take the great snowmelt from the south side of the Alps and distribute it over the fertile fields of all of north Italy, from whence it eventually debouches into the Adriatic. The river starts near the Brenner Pass itself, the dividing watershed where the sources of the Rhine and Danube lie on one side of the hill and the irrigation of most of Italy lies on the other. The valley it has carved for itself through the ages of prehuman time is narrow, and now quite crowded with man's necessities of communication. We took the train from Verona and traveled almost directly north toward the mountains that we could not yet see from the train windows as we approached them. White tops appeared as distant glimpses here and there, but the snow pyramids are farther up the valley in spring. Glaciers do not seem to be present in this area of the Dolomite Alps, although there are a number on the other side of the border in Austria. These mountains are not quite as high as those to the west, but they are shaped in spikes and rearing towers that would challenge any rock climber.

Beside the sparkling water of the Adige runs a second railroad track, a broad and well-metaled local road, a four-lane Autostrada, a farmers' dirt lane, and several ranks of electrical line pylons and telephone wires. Fitting all of this into a worn cleft in the mountains less than three hundred yards wide leaves only narrow strips of ground between the modern channels of communication. But the alluvial soil is perfect for grapes, and there are orderly rows of vines between the highways and rail lines. For this is the area that produces some of the best of the Pinot Grigio grapes that are made into the delicate, dry white wines that have become hugely popular in America in the last decade. They also produce the Prosecco grape that north Italy processes into a dry and sparkling *aperitivo* or dessert wine that is fashionable in Italy but only recently known in America. The vines we saw in the spring were just beginning to sprout, but all of them looked carefully tended and pruned. This care seemed to be provided by cottagers whose houses are perched on the steep shoulders of the mountains on either side.

Trentino is a completely Italian province, unlike the German-speaking city of Bolzano and the area formerly known as the South Tyrol immediately to the north. But although this is the northernmost Italian area, the mountain-perched houses suggest Tyrolean architecture. The Val d'Adige is very narrow between Verona and Trento, but appears to be very prosperous. I wonder what sort of neighborhood it was when the Sicilian Frederick II Hohenstaufen went north to claim his empire at the beginning of the thirteenth century. It was probably not very different then from its state when Charlemagne came south four hundred years earlier. Four hundred years of such social and technological stability in the very heart of Europe seems strange when you consider that the whole English-speaking culture of North America with all its change is only a little more than four centuries old.

We had booked a room at the Albermonaco, which turned out to be listed as the Hotel Monaco in English on their fax stationery. At just under $96 a night, this was at the top end of our range for an Italian three-star hotel. There may be perfectly satisfactory lodgings in town for less, and the Venezia rates two stars and may be a good bargain. Often a hotel with a lobby on the *primo piano* (Americans read second floor) rates only two stars, but is otherwise the equal of the more-expensive three-star standard. On the other hand, the Albermonaco had a nice little bar, a comfortable breakfast room, and an almost splash-proof shower along with the usual color television, a swift modern elevator, and a broad balcony commanding a fine view over the city toward the low mountains to the south. The ancient tower of the Castello del Buonconsiglio rose over my left shoulder as I was searching the horizon from the balcony. I am sure that no prince-bishop had a better site from which to survey his demesne.

Trent was one of those unusual political-ecclesiastical entities that used to stud the lands of the Holy Roman emperors, a city-state under the absolute rule and authority of a prince-bishop. There is only one such left in the world—the pope, who is the sovereign of the Vatican. Trent was granted such an independent status in the tenth century by Emperor Conrad the Salic, and maintained the mix of episcopal and civil government until 1796, when the last ecclesiastical ruler fled shortly before the pursuing forces of the revolutionary French arrived. Perhaps he had heard of the Jacobin desire to "see the last king strangled with the entrails of the last priest," and hastened to get out of town.

Instructed by the helpful desk man at the Albermonaco, we sought out the Cantinoto for dinner, a cellar restaurant of some style in spite of its subterranean locale. Here I ate my first stewed goat. It was delicious.

In the center of Trent, the Piazza Duomo is still the focus of the old city. The central post office, the *questura* (police station), the Chamber of Commerce, and similar accoutrements of a modern city are all within a block of it. Tourist vending merchants have stands selling T-shirts, postcards, balloons, and disposable 35mm cameras. But unlike towns in other parts of the world, this public square features (besides its cathedral) a very large-scale eighteenth-century fountain surmounted by a bronze Neptune perched upon a wave and dolphin, holding his trident. Now the Latin name of Trento is *Tridentum*, and it may have some ancient connection with the three-pronged goad with which the god of the sea stirs the waters. I would prefer, however, to think that it recalls the charge given Odysseus in the underworld by the blind prophet Tiresius: that he should take an oar upon his shoulder and walk inland until some landsman should happen upon him and ask why he carried a winnowing fan. Here, where the inhabitants were thus innocent of the sea and its ways, the wanderer of the ancient wars should offer sacrifice to Poseidon, the god of the sea. Now Neptune and Poseidon are one. Is this inland hollow in the mountains thus a distant site acknowledging the lordship of the ocean god? Will world wanderers who do obeisance here be allowed to return to their own Ithacas with fair winds and escape the enmity of the other gods? Is it even possible that Tennyson's elderly Ulysses set out with his companions and came to this distant place in the mountains in their final adventure?

The cathedral itself was designed by Adamo d'Arogno, and was started around the end of the twelfth century and finished three centuries after his death. When a building requires such a length of time for completion, subsequent architects have always had a hand in it. Bramante's plan for Saint Peter's was improved by Michelangelo and expanded by Bernini. But here the original marble building seems a wonderfully unified design. Its basic shape is that of a simple Romanesque building with massive square towers, surmounted by green copper, octagonal onion domes, almost surely added by another designer. But the delicacy of the colonnades that trim the nave and circle the octagon of the dome over the crossing are quite probably part of the original. The building has the dignity of simple architecture and the characteristic strength of pre-Gothic designs. Beneath it is the Paleo-Christian basilica of San Virgilio, which must date from the time that the Langobards quieted down in the eighth or ninth century. The excavation of this church, which has only been reexposed since World War II, looks to have been a miraculous replacement of most of the foundation of the thirteenth-century church, with poured concrete trusses that now support the greater part of the edifice.

The most startling thing in the cathedral is a pair of long, steep stairways that rise on either side of the nave, built flat against the wall, giving access to a choir gallery high up in the west end of the building. The stairs consist of marble blocks let into the side walls. They are narrow, require a high step to mount, and are entirely without railings or handholds. Climbing must have been a dizzying experience when it was allowed; they are now closed off by gates.

There are many treasures here that were collected by the prince-bishops over the years. Some frescoes may well be the work of Tomaso da Modena, and the crucifix over the high altar was done by Sixtus Frei of Nuremberg. I know of no other church with such a happy blend of German and Italian creations. We were especially taken by an Expulsion from Paradise scene that looked paradoxically very medieval, while at the same time reminding us of Jacopo della Quercia's great version of the same scene on the border of the main door of the Basilica of St. Petronius in Bologna. Although a bit dark and gloomy, the cathedral itself is worth a lingering visit. And it was in this rather uncompromising place that Trento's most famous moment took place—the proclamation of the decrees of the Council of Trent.

The Council was a mixture of the sort of good news and bad that comes when men of goodwill try to fix things by taking care of all that has gone wrong in the past and might yet go astray in the future. Martin Luther's propositions were not really taken seriously by the Roman Church until it became obvious that he and the other Protestant reformers were taking better than half of Europe with them. The seriousness of this defection became still more obvious when a horde of Germans, Burgundians, Swiss, and even some French Protestants marched successfully through northern Italy and sacked Rome itself in 1527, with great bloodshed and rapine. The looters stole altar vessels and reliquaries from the churches of Rome while the pope, Clement VII, cowered in the Castel Sant'Angelo and hurled excommunications at the heedless northerners. They wore embroidered vestments looted from the churches while they went about torturing and raping in the process of discovering hidden treasures in the homes of the wealthy Roman families.

But although Pope Clement failed to check the German Protestant explosion, his successor did make a stab at it. Pope Paul III Farnese was really interested in the welfare of his own family rather than the niceties of church discipline. After all, Titian's startling portrait of the old ecclesiastic with his two sons shows the family group well enough for us to draw conclusions about personalities and motives. He obviously doted on the oily young men, but Paul III also appointed cardinals of ability and learning and established a commission to reform the church. This unfortunately resulted in the formation of the Universal Inquisition, but also eventually led to his summoning a church council which was to meet in the Italian city closest to Germany, from whence all the trouble seemed to originate. This was, of course, the Council of Trent, which first sat in 1545 in the Church of Santa Maria Maggiore and concluded four papacies later with the proclamation of its decrees from the cathedral itself in 1564. The decrees did much to clean up the Catholic Church over the course of time, and (on the downside) also helped close off the free intellectual speculation of the Renaissance years. Thence came a certain amount of torture, the Spanish auto-da-fé, the difficulty with Galileo, and the general mindset of the Counter-Reformation. The Catholic Church stuck by these decrees in spirit and in minute detail until the Second Vatican Council, which was called by Pope John XXIII in the 1950s. Some have always felt that the Tridentine pronouncements put too great a stricture on the life of the church, but others have found such a security in the definite rules that they have broken away from the modern church and established renegade parishes in many countries. There has been at least one loose canon bishop in France who savors the Latin Liturgy.

Across the neighboring side of the cathedral square is the Museo Diocesano Tridentino, an excellent modern museum fashioned out of the old Palazzo Pretoria where the prince-bishops held forth before the great castle was reconstructed in the Renaissance. The museum has several paintings of the council in session, looking quite orderly and modern in the nave of the Chiesa Maria Maggiore. The attendant bishops are all in white albs with black rochets, save for the cardinals who sport their characteristic scarlet. One detailed painting also shows a battery of clerks and recorders at desks in the center of the horseshoe seating of the deliberating prelates. It is faintly reminiscent of a meeting of the Security Council at the United Nations.

The best of the works of art from around the town have been gathered into the Museo Diocesano for safety and proper conservation. It must be distressing to have the Madonna of one's favorite shrine removed to the city museum and replaced with a replica, but these remarkable examples of German wood carving and Italian painting were deteriorating in situ and had to be placed in a museum environment.

Turning from the historic and artistic to the modern and the natural, we spent the afternoon walking down to the river and mounting the funicular for the trip up the midsize hill across the valley to Sardagna, a village up in the mountains that can be reached by road via a long detour, or in a few minutes on the high-flying cables that lifted us over the river and about a thousand feet in the air to the mountain cliffs above. The distant views to the east revealed lots of snow-topped Dolomites. We descended on the next car which seemed to run largely for commuters going both ways from Sardagna and Trento itself. Walking back to the Albermonaco, we traversed the green Piazza Dante where we paused to admire an excellent statue of the great poet standing on a sizable pedestal at the edge of the park.

After a full day of it, we were a little *ubriaco* from the richness of the Baroque and ready for plain fare for dinner. Goat is not to be essayed more than once a week.

On the following morning we set out to do the gem of Trento, the great Castello del Buonconsiglio, which was the residence and governmental seat of the prince-bishops for more than seven hundred years. Its round tower and crenellated roofline suggest an even earlier origin, but it also displays a handsome set of Venetian Gothic openings across its southwest facade. This loggia was let into the Castelvecchio wall in 1475 by Prince-Bishop Johannes Hinderbach, to open up a luxurious space across from the two-story porticoes he had built in the internal courtyards. I have no idea how many ecclesiastical princes ruled the town, but the ones who reigned in the greatest luxury are the best known because of the paintings they commissioned and the architecture they paid for.

Among the best of these is the decoration of the Eagle Tower that Bishop George of Liechtenstein created at the far southeastern end of the complex building. It requires a guide to enter it, presumably to keep the grubby hands of tourists off the priceless walls. We waited for about ten minutes for a guide to show up, and were then led along a distant, windowed passage on the crest of the castle walls to a destination well beyond the central bulk of the buildings. Here there was a noisy unlocking process before we were ushered into a room that measured at most twenty-five feet square. The lights were turned on and there appeared a throng of medieval peasants, horses, winepress operators, girls in low-cut dresses being wooed by dignified suitors, cats, goshawks, falcons, sowers and reapers, walled cities, wagons coming in from the harvest, and jousting knights and ladies romping in the snow, throwing snowballs at their boyfriends. The frescoes are arranged to show the months of the year and are a stunning representation of late medieval life. They were painted around the very end of the thirteenth century by an unknown Flemish artist. Although the paintings concern the age of chivalry and show not a trace of classical style in their execution, they are an opening to the Renaissance in their rich and boisterous depiction of the sweat, plenty, humor, and conflict of the time. The snow scenes are thought to be the earliest paintings of people in winter yet to be found in Europe. The room itself merits a couple of stars in any guidebook.

The guide was patient, but there was so much to be seen in the little room that we had to be asked to leave at the last in order to make room for another group of visitors. The Eagle Tower is not pushed on you as you tour the Castello del Buonconsiglio; you have to ask for it. By all means, do so, as it is a stunning room.

Greatest of the prince-bishops was Bernardo Clesio, who ruled Trentino in the first half of the sixteenth century. I believe he was the home-court host cardinal at the sittings of the Council. To create a magnificent Renaissance palace inside the shell of the old castle, he hired the best painters of the time, including both Dosso Dossi and Battista Dossi to decorate his palace. Being a cardinal, his portrait in the castle proper shows him in his scarlet robes, heavy of cheek and jowl, pleased with himself and the improvements he has wrought on the old place. All around are Dossi paintings of Greek goddesses, fauns, and a tousle-haired maiden with a unicorn resting in her lap, its horn projecting beyond her head. I know nothing of Clesio's private life, but the lush and sexy paintings he commissioned suggest a more than scholarly interest in the flesh of the mythic creatures that decorate his house. Even in the age of the Tridentine reforms of the church, the severe celibacy expected of the clergy doesn't seem to have sunk in instantly.

Later we visited the church of Maria Maggiore, where most of the councilor sessions were held. It has, in Cathy's judgment, been considerably "baroqued," and is not very attractive inside, despite the presence of a handsome carved crucifix. A group of children were rehearsing a pretty song under the severe rhythmic direction of a teacher. We pressed on and investigated the Ristorante Spada, but eventually passed it by in favor of the Due Mori. We were early but welcomed and dined on tagliatelle with lobster sauce, veal scallopini, and white asparagus. We finished off the evening with fresh strawberries. The Due Mori is a pleasant place with pink tablecloths and fresh flowers on the tables. A memorable dinner for two with a good exemplar of the local white wine came to less than $45.

The next morning we boarded a train to slide quickly south again to Verona, which seemed a much more contemporary place. In that railroad station we were even able to find an e-mail connection and took the opportunity to get back into communication with children and grandchildren. It felt as though we had left the era of the Inquisition and reentered our own time again.

VII.

TREVISO:
A Painted City

Traveling across the broad top of the boot of Italy, going east from Reggio and then north toward Verona, we joined a high-speed stream of traffic, both private and commercial. This route goes on to the Brenner Pass and connects Italy and Germany both commercially and historically. Just south of Verona we turned to the east in company with huge trucks by Mercedes and some of unknown East European manufacture. These double-jointed tractor trailers trade the busy commerce of the European Union to its members and to other countries beyond. Vegetables from Poland and Italy were being transported in opposite directions. We chatted with English lorry drivers with cockney accents while standing in line at an Autogrille. They were on their way back north with a cargo bound for the Channel Tunnel. Fuel and food stops on the Autostrada are not unlike the service areas on the interstates of America, but the food is vastly better. We joined the truck drivers and had a steaming bowl of minestrone (or *zuppa di verdure*) and a glass of red wine, followed by that wonderful *caffè espresso* to ward off collapsing into dreamland while on the road.

And the sights along the way are so different. American

Eisenhower freeways pass well outside the outer limits of most of the American cities[5] they connect, often passing through woods or vast acres of cultivated cropland. In northern Italy there are few places where you can be out of sight of a village, either close at hand or on the top of some neighboring hill. We drove by little towns and their circumambient villas, some of them large enough to remind us of Andrea Palladio's perfect farmsteads. They might have been such, as the Vicenza area where Palladio flourished was just north of our route.

We were heading for Treviso, north of Venice by about twenty miles, a small city of less than 100,000 built astride the braided branches of two rivers, the Sile and the Cagnan. The amount of water running in orderly channels beside and beneath the streets is said to make this town reminiscent of Venice, but it did not appear so to me, perhaps because Venice is quite flat and has lots of boats in its canals while Treviso lacks water taxis and its streets run up and down small, lumpy hills. But the town was reputed to be pretty, with a number of churches that feature fine early frescoes of the *trecento*. We put it on our list because we had developed a taste for the smaller, lesser-known Italian cities.

We left the A4 at Mestre with the Venetian campanile in the Piazza San Marco just visible on the horizon to the south. There was another Autostrada heading north, the A27, but I managed to miss the exit and we wound up on the older road, tree-lined and green with a border of the vegetables that the mainland has been raising for the markets of Venice for more than twelve hundred years. Before that the Venetians harvested that bounty from small fields of the islands in the lagoon and lived mainly on fish. The road was also punctuated with

---

[5] Except where they have carved into pieces the oldest cities of the Northeast, as in Boston and Hartford.

guesthouses and small hotels, accommodation for thrifty visitors who would use local buses to get themselves to the great tourist capital to their south, or perhaps even to the beaches of the Lido.

We had telephoned ahead to make a *prenotazione* at the Hotel Campeol and had a street address (Piazza Ancilotto 4), but no map of the city. We drove through a number of one-way streets toward what we presumed to be the center of the town and stopped to ask directions. An accommodating Italian housewife who was loading a bag of groceries into her car listened for a moment and then suggested that since the directions would be confusing, we should follow her. Routing modern cars, even small ones, through medieval streets is a challenge to which the city fathers have responded with a maze of one-way (*senso unico*) streets that circle in directions that I cannot fathom, propelled perhaps by the Coriolis force. The kindly lady led us through a labyrinth that left us still separated from our destination by fifty meters through a wrong-way street. Smiling gratefully to our guide, we plunged on and made a 360-degree reversal, backed into the little Piazza Ancilotto, and arrived at the very door of #4. It was locked and there seemed no one in attendance. Questions asked at the Antico Ristorante Beccherie across the tiny square revealed the hotel desk, keys, and our reservation. It seems rooms are reserved by the same cameriere who reserves your table at what turned out to be an excellent restaurant. A chambermaid was dispatched to carry our bags (two at a time) to our room. For $70 a night it was a pleasant accommodation, even though we did have to climb a couple of flights to get to the room. Treviso is not one of the bargain towns of northern Italy. This is, after all, where Luciano Benetton started his empire of United Colors. His factories are all around the city outside the walls.

We set forth to find the tourist office and a map. Both were

forthcoming in the Piazzetta Monte di Pietà, just off the Piazza dei
Signori. We began an exploration of the cathedral which connects
with the Museo Diocesano d'Arte Sacra. Here we discovered a pair
of frescoes of St. Thomas à Becket. This demonstration of the English-
Italian connection crops up in many parts of Italy and underlies the
idea that Christendom was a seamless garment in the early Middle
Ages. The Diocesan Museum is a gem of a small collection, well
displayed in an interesting, oft-remodeled building. In both museums
and churches of Treviso we kept running across the work of Tomaso
da Modena, who evidently spent years in this prosperous place. His
frescoes are worth seeking out.

The Museo Civico is off in the northwest quarter of the walled
city on the Borgo Cavour, a ten-minute walk from the Piazza Duomo.
The Italians say it is *due passi* (two steps, that is) for any distance,
from just around the corner to the other side of town. The Museo
is worth the walk. There is an interesting collection that includes
one or more works by the Bellinis, Tiepolo, Titian, Pietro Longhi,
Francesco Guardi, and lots of others. It also gave us the opportunity to
get close-range experience with some of that vast number of Italian
painters of the fifteenth and sixteenth centuries that are often left
out of art survey courses in American universities: Salvatore Rosa,
Pietro Lombardo, Cima da Conegliano, Paris Bordone, and a host of
others. Someplace I read that 50 percent of all the paintings in the
world are in Italy. Probably untrue, but it seems that way after a day
spent touring museums and churches in midsize Italian towns.

To us the most interesting church in Treviso was San Nicolò, a
simple but bulky, massive, rosy brick structure that we visited while
it was admirably lighted by slanting afternoon sun, which picked out
frescoed columns done in the late thirteenth and early fourteenth
centuries by Tomaso da Modena and several others. On the south

side there is a faded but legible representation of Saint Christopher that gives character to the whole building. According to legend, Christopher was a giant and thus able to carry the young Christ across a deep river by perching his savior on his shoulder. With the poetic literalism of a medieval artist, Christopher is depicted here as about thirty feet tall, truly a giant in whom any traveler could place their confidence for any journey. The fresco artist is said to have been Antonio da Treviso, an attribution that demonstrates the possibilities for confusion among historical personalities in an age without surnames.

Even if Treviso does not resemble Venice, it is a gracious and, along some of the waterways, an almost elegant town. The many bridges are low-arched spans, sections of perhaps one-third of a semicircle. There are delicate, iron-railed balconies where you can pause and watch the steady flow of the multi-armed rivers. During our visit, pink and dark-red flowers grew in patches along the stone and brick walls that confine the watercourses. In one spot a slowly turning waterwheel decorated what must have been at one time a mill building. I suspect that the wheel was merely ornamental now that all of Italy is lavishly electrified. But the old mill building is stuccoed in a dusty orange and is obviously worth keeping, if only for its appearance. Not far away, where the river Cagnan divides and then rejoins itself, a resulting block-long island has for centuries been the town fish market. Treviso was at one time called the *città dipinto* for the outdoor as well as indoor painting of the buildings. Perhaps because painting cornices and swags was cheaper than having them carved in stone, sixteenth- and seventeenth-century Trevisiani decorated their homes in colored stucco. The medium is not, however, truly weatherproof, and the remains of the outdoor decorations are really only visible high up under the broad eaves that have protected them from the rain. But catching a glimpse of one around a corner or in a sunny piazza is a delightful surprise.

Since the Antico Ristorante Beccherie was under the corporate umbrella of our hotel, we reserved a table and arrived early to essay the fare. It proved to be a fortunate choice. *Carciofi al tegame* were splendid, and they were followed by scallops on the half shell, *tortellone di zucca*, and a bottle of bubbly Prosecco (which seemed to be the house wine). We wound up with the best tiramisu we have yet found in Italy. This mascarpone and whipped-cream chocolate dessert seems in most other parts of Italy to be strictly a tourist's dish, but everyone revels in it in Treviso, possibly because they do it so much better here.

Just down the slope to the north of the Campeol there is a *pasticceria*, which supports a midsize tearoom where we took to seeking breakfast. The commercial bakery and coffee bar also functions as a cocktail lounge. This pleasant merging of gastronomic functions is here, as all over Italy, an agreeable experience and quite different from anything a tourist could find in America.

Our final destination in Treviso was the Tempio di San Francesco, just north of the fish market. It is one of the best-kept churches in town and is actively in use for worship in spite of the art treasures inside. It was built originally in the early thirteenth century, quite soon after Francis welcomed Sister Death and went peacefully into the other world he yearned for. It is amazing that this gentle friar had such an immediate and lasting impact on the people of his own time and the century immediately following. Thousands became secret Franciscans of the Third Order so that they could be buried in the simple habit when they died. Churches in his honor were built all over Italy, and soon all over Europe and the rest of the world.

Although the Temple has seen a lot of remodeling and repair, it preserves a peaceful purity that is not at all disturbed by a modern statue at the entryway. Tomaso da Modena also painted here; two frescoed versions of the Madonna Enthroned are here, done by the prolific follower of Giotto who was painting less than a century after the death of Francis himself. The people of this town quite obviously have held the church in reverence for centuries and still do so today. Buried here is Dante's son, Pietro Alighieri, who died in 1364. His tomb is high on the wall of the north transept. There is also a simple slab in the floor to mark the burial of a girl of famous ancestry who did not survive childbirth. It reads:

A FRANCESCA MORTA DI PARTO
FIGLIA DI FRANCESCO PETRARCA POETA
IL MARITO FRANCESCOLO DA BROSSANO MILANESE
AUGUST 1384

"To Francesca, dead in childbirth, daughter of Francesco Petrarca, poet; the husband of Francescolo da Brossano of Milan; August 1384." The entire inscription says that Francesca was Tuscan by paternal blood, and became Ligurian by happy marriage. She is proclaimed to be the mother of a noble and copious issue. No one was more faithful to husband, more subject to father; no one, he states, made him more a stranger to joy by her death. Francesca, he says, was my chaste passion, my simple dowry of spotless modesty. Mother of the family, in the flower of her years she was carried away from the earth and returned to the heavens.

Francescolo's expression of grief would seem to be worthy of his father-in-law's gift of poetic expression. Many women may have been bartered in political marriages in the fourteenth century, but there were obviously also deep bonds of affection between a number of husbands and wives.

VIII.

PADUA:
A Return to a Favorite City

Padua is an easy stop on the main northern line of the FS (the Ferrovia dello Stato), the swift, clean, and efficient state railroad of Italy. We arrived on our most recent trip in intermittent rain, encumbered by a rented Fiat Uno. Because we had been there before by train, we assumed that finding our way into the little central city by car would be easy. A mistake. Padova is really quite a sprawling town of close to a quarter million people, and the routes in through the suburbs require imaginative and expert navigation. When you reach the station where the rental car returns are located, you have penetrated to the very verge of the old walled town which is really quite compact. We exchanged the car for an obliging taxi that took us down the multi-named main drag that runs straight through the center of the town under the successive titles of Corso del Popolo, Corso Garibaldi, Via VIII Febbraio, and Via Roma. The lavish distribution of names among fragments of a limited number of streets makes it possible to commemorate lots of people and events in the center of a town without eliminating the heroes of the last century to make space for the new ones. It also results in long avenues being named in manageable chunks so that any address can be located within a few blocks without reference to cross streets, which are in any case irregular and variously spaced in cities of ancient origin.

On our earlier trips to Padua we had put up at the Albergo Sant'Antonio in the north end of the old city. It was no distance from the fashionable shops of the Via Dante, but at the opposite end of town from the famous basilica of Il Santo. It was a bargain and perfectly adequate. But on a later and longer stay, we settled at a far more interesting place, a B&B under the protective listing of the Caffelletto company (www.caffelletto.it), one of the few in their brochure that was actually located in the center of a major city. Our hostess, Signora Maria Piccolomini, is a distinguished lady whose husband's family is descended from the intellectual humanist, Enea Silvio Piccolomini, best remembered for his later career as Pope Pius II. Having become familiar with his life from the great Pinturicchio murals in the library at the cathedral in Siena, we were more than delighted to meet the rest of the family in Padova.

The cab driver left us at a formidable *portone* where we rang for some time until we were admitted by a tall, dark-haired lady of distinguished bearing who greeted us in English, and then explained that she didn't speak it well and preferred to use Italian. Her English had been perfected when she was a girl and spent some time in England. It was obviously far better than our Italian. We compromised and spoke a sort of animated pidgin of both languages. Her rusty English got better with every day we passed in Padua.

The house was a palazzo shared by five or six families. The Piccolomini domain turned out to be the rental of a large, ground-floor apartment (their own home is in Siena), arranged around one corner of a sunny courtyard full of flowers, a green lawn, several trees, three cars, a motorcycle, several well-domesticated dogs and cats, and ample space around the corner to hang the laundry up to dry. We were allocated a large bedroom with lots of comfortable furniture, a fair-sized library of architectural books, and an attached bathroom of noble proportions equipped with elegant cosmetics, rare soaps, shampoos, and a tub at least two meters long. As befits a first-rate B&B, the *prima collazione* was of similar high quality. Signora Piccolomini provided cereals, fruits, toast, homemade *marmellata*, and often her own freshly baked cakes and muffins. Beyond this she was a voluble source of what was best to visit in Padua and how to find it. Our stay of six days with this pleasant and gracious lady remains one of the high points of our many visits to Italy.

To acquire proper maps and tourist literature, we set out for the city tourist bureau by taking the bus up the Riviera Tito Livio[6], a street parallel to the *senso unico corso* we had descended the day before. At the south end of these streets is the Basilica of the Saint, Anthony of Padua. At the north wall of the city is a chapel on the site of the old Roman arena, known as the Cappella degli Scrovegni. This wonderful little building is by itself sufficient reason to come to Padua, or perhaps even to Italy itself. After our visit to the nearby tourist information office, we happily made another visit to the chapel.

Enrico Scrovegni was the son of a usurer who needed someone's dedicated good works to bail him out of purgatory. Dante assigned him a location several circles down in the Inferno. His son (or perhaps his nephew) built the chapel and hired a radical young artist to decorate it

---

[6] Some fortunate American schoolboys (and girls) know Tito Livio as Livy, the Roman historian to whom we are indebted for most of our information about republican Rome and its mythological antecedents. He wrote 142 books of Roman history of which some 35 have survived. He surely merits having a street named for him and was, as you might guess, a hometown boy, born and brought up in Padua. It is from Titus Livius that we get the detailed story we have of the Punic Wars with Carthage as well as the great stories of the founding of Rome, the quarrel between Romulus and Remus, and the somewhat romantic rape of the Sabine girls.

with murals that cover every square inch of its interior. The artist was Giotto di Bondone, and his paintings changed the style of European painting forever after. Here for the first time Christ and His Mother appeared as modern human beings, along with the saints and villains of the New Testament. Perhaps the Italian confidence that the Madonna or the patron saint of the local town has a very tender heart and thus a very personal interest in the welfare of every single peasant, housewife, or child has part of its foundation in these very human representations of the denizens of heaven. Perhaps it is the other way around, and Giotto was representing what he felt at heart about his own situation in the care of the Madonna and Santa Anna. Whichever way the influence was felt, it is quite certain that these representations of saints and angels profoundly influenced the painters that saw them, and ushered in the great era of Italian art in the two centuries that followed. The frescoes represent a hinge point of painting, between the medieval and the Renaissance. Giotto's representations of Santa Anna, the Madonna, and even the angels are more modern, reaching ahead to the promise that was fulfilled by the great masters of the *quattrocento* (the very beginning of the fifteenth century).

However long the elder Scrovegni was sentenced to burn for his usury, the little building built to propitiate for his sins did not take long to build; it is only about 65 feet long and 25 feet wide, but slim and tall, almost 40 feet high. There are few windows, just eight narrow lancets on each side and three over the doorway. Most of the 4,000 square feet of wall space was designed to be covered with pictures. When he was given the commission at the age of thirty-three, Giotto was at the very beginning of a spectacular career. He worked in fresco, the technique of brushing pigment into fresh, wet plaster so that the color becomes part of the wall itself.

And Giotto's paintings are still as fresh as the plaster he painted them in. His illustrations are of the people of the thirteenth century, not icons of an imagined time. Even his angels are quite human and seem to understand human rejoicing and sorrow. Joachim and Ann, parents of the Virgin, embrace tenderly at the Golden Gate of Jerusalem where an angel told them to meet. And there is a mysterious figure in black looking on. While critics debate her identity, no one knows just who she is. Then the child Mary is born and is presented to the High Priest (a kindly old Jewish fellow) at the head of the steps leading up to the temple. It is a scene full of light and color. One of the admiring onlookers would seem to be a youthful Joseph, her future husband. There are scenes of other suitors competing for her hand, and finally a formal wedding scene. And high up on either side of the chancel arch are the separated figures of Gabriel on the left and Mary on the right, in the moment of the great announcement, the annunciation of the incarnation, the expected birth of Christ.

The cycle goes on, showing the elderly Elizabeth, awed at the miracle of her own pregnancy. There is a nativity scene with the first realistic shepherds, simple men, heavy-footed and amazed at the message of the angels. There are kingly Magi, young, middle-aged, and old, all paying homage to the child. And there is a terrifying troop of Herod's soldiers in a city square, murdering a host of little boys as their mothers cry out in horror and anguish. In another scene, Jesus confounds the doctors in the temple. All of the New Testament scenes are presented in strong colors of red, blue, buff, umber, and pale green. Judas is all too believable, clutching his little bag of silver pieces. He negotiates the price of the betrayal while a lean, black devil stands behind him with a clawlike hand on his arm. In one of the most famous scenes, Judas, in a golden cloak, almost wraps himself around Jesus, embracing the one he betrays. A great crowd follows them, soldiers and passersby with flaming torches and staves, blowing on the ram's horn. Calvary follows in brilliant color, and then we see the deposition and the resurrection. Mary Magdalene in her crimson dress holds out her hands to the Lord she has just recognized in the garden near the tomb.

But as we turn to leave and face the western wall, we are confronted with a medieval scene of Christ at the end of time, judging the quick and the dead, surrounded by the choirs of angels, his apostles seated on golden thrones on either side of him. The blessed rise up at his right hand, but down below, to his left, are the souls in hell. Some are hanged by the neck, naked and bound hand and foot. One is partially disemboweled. A hideous blue-green Satan squats gigantic in the midst of the damned, chewing the head off one sinner while he clutches the next victim in his free hand.

The small boundaries of the little chapel seem to contain all of creation. It had a startling effect on the painters of the next two centuries. Giotto and his followers went on to do the great fresco cycles at Assisi. He then designed the lovely, slender bell tower, the campanile, next to the great cathedral of Florence. The huge outburst of creativity that we call the Italian Renaissance was by then well under way.

Although Scrovegni the younger was a generous patron, Giotto cut a few corners in his work. Instead of expensive ground lapis lazuli usually used only for the mantle of the Virgin or a donor alone, he did his blue skies in tempera "Giotto Blue," which has over time flaked off in many parts of the murals. He also seems to have done the halos in real gold leaf for Christ, Mary and the most important figures. Apostles were haloed in bronze powder tempera "Radiator Paint," which has turned black over the ages. Our wonderful young docent said there is some evidence he charged his patron for real gold throughout.

Next door to the Arena Chapel is the Musei Civici Eremitani, an amalgam of several museums built into the cloisters and bomb-damaged buildings of the Church of the Eremitani (the hermits). Only a few small fragments of Montegna's frescoed apse remain from the explosion caused by the unthinking bomb dropped by an American plane in World War II. When you consider that the frescoed walls of churches cannot be easily taken down and hidden in the cellar when there is danger of aerial attack (as was done successfully with oil paintings, books, and sculpture), we should probably be thankful for the survival of so much of the great Renaissance painting that we can see today in Italy and the rest of Europe. This museum contains Roman and Egyptian antiquities as well as items from the prehistory of Padua, including a crucifix by Giotto and paintings by the Bellinis, Tintoretto, Paolo Veronese, Titian, and many more. Two miniature paintings of figures in landscapes by Giorgione are quite rare if unspectacular. Today, entrance to the chapel is rationed by ticket and time. You are almost required to visit the museum while waiting your turn, not a bad use of your time. The museum is a place to allow enough time for a leisurely prowl through the riches of an ancient city that conserves its treasures well.

The greater part of a day can be spent in the *quattrocento*, but in the evening we sampled the food of contemporary Padua at the Ristorante Cavalca on Via D. Manin, just south of the great piazze of the town. A sumptuous dinner with wine and *dolce* for the two of us came to around $50 in the era of the collapsing dollar; still, it was less expensive than would be obtainable at a comparable Italian restaurant at home.

The real center of Padua is the Palazzo della Ragione, which was built in the mid-thirteenth century. It is a large building, perhaps sixty meters long, in plan a somewhat irregular parallelogram. Its two-storied construction rises higher than the four- and five-story buildings nearby. The roof, a work of extraordinary engineering, is supported on curved rafters fitted to an overhead keel like the ribs of an upside-down ship. The upper level is thus a vast hall uninterrupted by post or girder. It is known as Il Salone and was the seat of the courts half a millennium ago. Today the chamber is used for art exhibitions, and it was for one of these that we were drawn to climb the lengthy ceremonial stair that leads up the outside of the building to the arcaded porticoes on either side.

You cannot be sure what you will find in this grand exhibition space when you visit Padua, but you can count on it being of interest, beauty, and rarity. During our last visit we found a most marvelous collection of miniatures and illuminations from manuscript collections all over the world. Besides exquisite capital letters and illustrations of the gospels from Austria, Germany, Spain, and England, there were several of the most choice from the Metropolitan Museum in New York, the Cloisters, and the National Gallery in Washington, as well as from the Vatican Library and all parts of Italy. We were surprised to note the degree to which hand illumination continued into the age of printing. Johannes Gutenberg's printers must have spent more time hand-painting capital letters than they did in setting the type for the famous Forty-two-Line Bible. The letters of the work of the father of printing are the black-letter gothic of the German typographers, and thus beyond my ability to decipher the Latin. But beautiful books are uplifting to look at even when you can't understand a word of what is on the page.

All around the Salone are hundreds of frescoed astrological and religious images that are early-fifteenth-century restorations of designs originally by Giotto, which were either destroyed or badly damaged by a fire when they were young in 1420. While they are interesting, they seem to lack the almost unconfined passion of the painting of the Arena Chapel. Perhaps the best permanent exhibition here is a gigantic wooden horse, almost large enough to enclose a small Greek army besieging Troy. It seems to have been made as a party decoration in the fifteenth century and is actually a sort of reproduction in large scale of Donatello's great equestrian statue in the square in front of the Basilica of Il Santo.

On the ground floor of the Palazzo della Ragione is a double row of meat, cheese, and fish markets, perhaps thirty or forty in all. The contents of these stores would amaze most Americans. There are hare (already skinned), as well as boar's heads, luxuriant coils of purple octopus, eels, pretty fish such as dorado and bream, and startlingly ugly ones that I could not classify. The Adriatic Sea is a scant thirty miles away, and the crustaceans and shellfish from that seemingly inexhaustible larder are also here: pink and white clams, blue mussels, and delicate shrimp with antennae twice the length of their bodies. The cheese shops display a half-dozen different kinds of blue-veined cheese alone, and there are huge wheels of Parmigiano-Reggiano used rather like tables to display the more delicate cheeses from farther north. Round balls of fresh buffalo mozzarella sit glistening in their pans of whey. They are served up to customers in modern plastic cups with transparent tops.

On either side of the building are the outdoor markets of the Piazza della Frutta and the Piazza dell'Erbe, commodious squares filled with the white umbrellas that shield all Italian markets from the morning sun. Under them are racks and frames filled with the amazing bounty of the Italian gardens in the spring—a brilliant array of red and yellow peppers, deep purple eggplant, squashes of all colors and varieties, brilliant green lettuce and scallions, onions both red and yellow, golden parsnips, broccoli, fennel, and great bunches of parsley. There are flower stands bursting with color, and very few of the vegetable consumers seem able to resist bringing home a bunch of daffodils or lilies along with the makings of supper. All Paduans living in the centro storico, inside the walls, do their daily shopping here. Most of the shoppers are women, more likely older than younger, but middle-aged businessmen seem to be among the customers of the flower stands.

In the area around the two wonderful piazze of good things to eat, we were not surprised to find a wealth of good restaurants, none of them expensive. We dined twice at the Ristorante Cavalca on the Via D. Manin, just around the corner from the Piazza dell'Erbe. I took the opportunity of being in the Veneto to order the classic dish, *fegato alla veneziana*—calves' liver and onions sautéed in the fashion that has been famous here for many centuries. It was truly superb and unlike anything I have ever had in America. With the excellent red wine of the house and an unremembered but undoubtedly delicious *dolce* (tiramisu or pastry?), which we divided sensibly between the two of us, the check came to 68,500 lire—around $40 at that time.

The Piazza Duomo, which we had explored on a previous trip, was in restauro, its square full of excavation equipment, red plastic netting, and other signs of civic improvement. But the baptistery, under repair during our last visit, was open this time, and resplendent. The idea of the freestanding baptistery was carried on in northern Italy long after it had fallen into desuetude in the rest of Christendom. These richly decorated places are often the site of the oldest artwork

---

[7] The oldest paintings in Italy are not always the greatest, but neither are the most recent. Somehow there seems to have come a moment in the fifteenth and early sixteenth centuries where the improvement in perspective drawing freed artists to do things they had never been able to attempt before. Yet, at the same time the new facility in draftsmanship had not yet led to the excesses of Baroque art or the sentimentality that followed it.

in town, sometimes of the best[7]. In Padua the interior of the octagonal building is richly decorated with the works of a follower of Giotto, Giusto de Menabuoi. The building dates from the end of the twelfth century and the frescoes from 1378, although he must have spent a number of years completing the various cycles in the dome. Genesis and Noah's flood are here, as are scenes from the life of John the Baptist and the New Testament. Perhaps most wonderful are things from the Apocalypse, such as several seven-headed monsters, camelopards, and dragons. In one of these scenes the seven heads are supported by long, writhing serpentine necks and seem to be nuzzling up to nine or ten bishop's miters which are floating in the sky above the fearsome hydra emerging from the sea. I have so far been unable to fathom the meaning of the symbolism, but it may have something to do with heresy.

Another painting of the *Strage degli Innocenti* is easier to interpret: Herod's men are dispatching the little boys with daggers and swords by thrusts to neck and belly without any visible spattering of blood. Both the mothers and the murderers seem to be taking the whole thing rather calmly, and none of the ladies have a hair out of place in their rather modish coiffures. Even so, the sheer scale of the infanticide going on is sufficient to inspire horror.

Great though the religious art of Padua is, the town relates to the modern world in political and scientific terms perhaps more than any other Italian city. The university is the second oldest in Italy and famous for its early studies in anatomy. This is partly because this province, the Veneto, was less under papal control, and the prohibition against dissecting cadavers was less successfully enforced here. In fact, the university here arranged to have felons hanged rather than beheaded in order to keep the body parts together for anatomical study. Medical students came here from all over Europe. William Harvey arrived in the early seventeenth century and learned from the dissection of the one-way valves in human veins that the blood circulated out through the arteries and came back through the veins, as fundamental a discovery about the working of the human body as can be imagined. The multi-galleried chamber where Harvey learned anatomy is still in good repair and can be visited. And of course, the greatest scientist before the modern world, Galileo, was a member of the faculty of Padua for all the years in which he did his greatest work. Here the liberal intellectual attitude of the Venetians protected him from the narrow Aristotleanism of the schools more closely under the thumb of the Counter-Reformation popes and their curias.

At the south end of town there is another scientific wonder, the Orto Botanico of the university. Here the tradition of the medieval monastic herb garden was expanded into a place of study of all sorts of plants for the first time in any university in the world. Starting in the early sixteenth century, horticulturists planted and nurtured trees, shrubs, and herbs that were brought to Padua from all over the then-shrinking world. Being unable to find a mass with music in this rationalistic town on Sunday morning, we decided to give thanks to the creator of the trees and bushes. There must be thousands of specimens in the circular central garden and the arboretum that surrounds it. Everything is labeled, many specimens are dated, and all are obviously very well cared for. We found the ancient palm tree that Goethe marveled at. The tree is over four hundred years old, now flanked by an octagonal greenhouse. There is also a ginkgo nearby that was set out in the garden in 1750. The brochure (helpfully in English as well as Italian) informed us that ginkgo are generally sexually differentiated, but that this ancient male had a female branch grafted onto it some centuries ago and it now provides all that is needed to flower and reproduce. Because our North Carolina home is in the area where the insect-eating plants are found, we asked if they had samples of the Venus fly trap, the sundew, and the pitcher plant. The attendant at the gatehouse directed us to the large hothouse where some of these delicate species must be kept in the winter. There are orangeries, orchid collections, cactus, and water lilies. We discovered examples of trees from Japan and Africa, Brazil, and even the American elm which is so rare a survivor at home. For a visiting scientist, the Orto Botanico is worth the journey to Padua. For the rest of us, it is a wonderful place to visit on a sunny morning, full of growth and beauty.

Perhaps the most unusual place of refreshment in northern Italy is Padua's Caffè Pedrocchio. We were used to seeing Romanesque buildings, Renaissance palazzos, Baroque churches, and even the smooth brutalism of the fascist-era post offices. But here, in a delightful open piazza in the center of the town, stand a pair of Doric loggias with the attendant ruddy granite lions in front and a sizable building of creamy stone connecting them. The Greek revival of the architectural style of the early nineteenth century has put such a stamp on American design that we hardly notice it. But in Italy it is extremely rare, and even more so in a case like this, where the building has a historical significance. In spite of the classical columns and capitals, this architectural fashion looks and actually is relatively modern.

Antonio Pedrocchio favored the unification as well as the liberation of Italy. He hoped to see it become a democracy on the model of the ancient Greek polis. His coffeehouse was established as a place to talk and dream. The doors of the loggias were open twenty-four hours a day, and any student who came in was given a copy of the daily newspaper and a glass of water, gratis. Such innocent largesse was not forbidden by the Austrian authorities who governed Padua at that time, but Pedrocchio's rapidly became *the* gathering place for young radicals from the neighboring university, who helped plan and encourage what eventually became the Risorgimento—the rising up of the Italian people in unity. The caffè flourished through three generations of the Pedrocchio family, until the last of the line, a childless lady, gave it to the commune of Padua. It has recently been restored to its beautiful and pristine state. The elaborately redecorated upper rooms (one of them is done in Turkish style) are used for wedding receptions. We came in for a drink and returned for supper in the splendid interior, imagining the ardent young Italians singing Verdi's "Slave Chorus" from *Nabucco*, which eventually became the Italian national hymn. Pedrocchio's is marginally more expensive than neighboring places, but the ambience and history *valgono la pena*. Still, we had a very pleasant lunch with Prosecco and coffee for 49,000 lire, about $27 in the days before the euro.

But the most famous site in Padua, far older than the Arena Chapel, is the Basilica of San Antonio, known to the natives as Il Santo. Anthony was born in 1195 and only lived to be thirty-six years old. He was one of the earliest followers of Saint Francis, and was assigned by him to lead the new Order of Friars Minor in France. Eventually he returned to Italy and settled in Padua. Evidently he was a wonderful preacher, and for some reason I am unable to discover, became the patron of those trying to recover lost objects. Sixty years ago and more, I was taught by a Franciscan nun to print SAG (Saint Anthony guide!) in the upper-right corner of the envelope I was mailing. Covered with the stamp, it gave an absolute assurance that the U.S. Postal Service would not lose my letter. When in college I used to commend care of wayward golf balls to the good saint. His average in recovering them from the deep rough was fair, surely better than random probability.

The architecture of Anthony's basilica is sprung from the same tradition as San Marco in Venice. There are at least eight bulbous domes seemingly scattered about the upper part of the building in defiance of the symmetry of the design. The principal nave leads to a modest sanctuary, ornamented by Donatello's bronze crucifix. But the space in the nave is dominated by a transverse crossing that contains the tomb of the saint. Determined to get the full Padovan treatment, we followed the crowds of pilgrims standing in line to pray that the saint restore their loss to them. We found rather grisly pieces of his body: his jawbone in one reliquary, his tongue, looking like a blackened fig, in another. Inspecting the high altar, we were rather more moved by Donatello's bronze sculptures. Outside, in the piazza, stands one of Donatello's great secular works, the huge statue of Gattamelata (the fierce *commendatore* named for a calico cat). Equestrian statues were rare in the fifteenth century, and even Donatello hadn't worked out the physics of making such a big piece of bronze stand on less than four legs. He gave the splendid horse a lifelike posture by adding a ball under the raised right front hoof. The powerful stature of the fierce warrior is accentuated by the spurs that extend from his armored footwear; they are nearly a foot long. Inside the basilica the ferocious warrior has a handsome tomb not far from the final resting place of Pietro Bembo, the humanist scholar who seems today to have been the very epitome of the Renaissance man[8].

    Toward the end of our stay in Padua we decided to sample the

---

[8] Pietro Bembo wrote the first real grammar of the Italian language and held out strongly for it being the equal of Latin for both poetry and prose composition. He had a mistress, Morosina, who bore him three children. But after her death he became a priest, a bishop, and, eventually, a cardinal. He is one of the principal characters in Baldassare Castiglione's Book of the Courtier, in which he plays the role of one of the intellectuals at the court of Elisabetta Gonzaga, Duchess of Urbino. The great fifteenth-century printer, Aldus Manutius, named one of his most elegant fonts of type "Bembo" in his honor. Bembo is the typeface you are reading on this page.

Italian version of a fast-food joint. Brek restaurants are up and running in a number of north Italian cities. They presented us with a different methodology than we were used to. The pasta which comprises the principal substance of any Italian dinner was cooked to order in a little wire basket submerged in boiling water, right in front of our eyes. Two or three sauces to choose from were on hand, or were put together at our request by a pretty young lady *cuoca*. The tagliatelle were *al dente* and the Bolognese first-rate. A fine salad was provided, and there was a tap that provided a perfectly acceptable *vino della casa*, either red or white. At any rate, it is a substantial cut above McDonald's, which is now also represented in many Italian cities.

A final adventure in Padua overtook me while walking toward the Caffè Pedrocchio from the Piazza Duomo. The morning newspaper had warned of an impending Communist demonstration protesting the bombing of Kosovo Serb targets which was going on at the time. Until this event no one seemed to be paying very much attention to the war in the Balkans. Late on this Sunday afternoon, the Piazza della Frutta was in its best noncommercial mood, full of children and parents, baby carriages, and balloons. On the steps of the church there was a fourfold rank of spectators bearing a banner denouncing NATO. I had not been concerned about the conditions in the streets around the protest. Asking a member of the *polizia urbana* produced the information that I should perhaps keep my distance from the ranks of marchers who were beginning to assemble. It didn't look like much of a source of violence to me, and there were plenty of *polizia* in evidence, so I relied on the camouflage of my recently acquired Italian jacket for protection and resolved to inspect the event at close range. In about a half-hour the group of protesters had swelled to an enthusiastic fifty. They had arranged themselves in a street-wide phalanx, chanting "*Abassa NATO!*" or something to that effect as they started to march toward a matching squadron of uniformed police carrying transparent plastic riot shields and long, stout batons.

As the officers slowly backed up and the Communists made their leisurely advance, a further rank of *carabinieri*, the cream of law enforcement, appeared to bring up the rear of the parade. The *carabinieri* are actually a division of the army and are uniformed (or perhaps costumed) in brilliant red and black, with immaculate white belts and piping. They really look rather like young and fierce members of the Knights of Columbus. The whole formation moved slowly up the Via Boccalerie, accompanied by the parents with baby carriages and the children with balloons. The gelato shop was doing a brisk business. It seemed a particularly Italian sort of Communist demonstration. The whole thing broke up in another twenty minutes, the municipal street sweepers brushed up the candy wrappers, and we all continued about our business or our pleasure. Cathy and I moved down the Via Manin to the Piazza Duomo, located a table in the square, and ordered a gin and tonic.

IX.

TORINO:
Baroque and Modern

When we came to Torino[9] by air, the city seemed centered in a half bowl of the southern Alps, ringed all about its northern perimeter by snow-topped mountains that lead up to Europe's highest, Monte Bianco, of which the French own the western half and designate as Mont Blanc. Up there it is possible to travel from one country to the other and back again on dizzying journeys by interconnecting funicular gondolas, swinging from cables that go up almost to the very summit of the mountains before crossing a saddle or shoulder and starting down on the other side. From an airplane it looks like an exciting trip, but considering the temperature at the top of the mountains, we decided to defer it until some future summer crossing.

---

[9] Major Italian cities get their own special spellings in English either because of their antiquity (like Syracuse and Rome), or because of their importance to the Anglo Saxon visitors like Florence, or Leghorn for Livorno, which title is sprung from heaven knows what linguistic misunderstanding. Pisa, Parma, Perugia, Urbino, Modena, Volterra, and almost all of the other cities have managed to keep their Italian spelling and more or less its pronunciation through the ages. Torino has an obvious connection with Albion, since it is known as Turin to telephone operators and computer-spelling programs worldwide.

Airport ground transportation is connected with the Stazione di Porta Susa, the northern of the two railroad stations in Torino. Here we missed a bus to the center of the city and had to wait for another one scheduled to make the trip a half-hour later. The delay allowed us to enter into conversation with an informative young man who told us a number of things about Torino, including the identity of an extraordinary church which we could see perched on a hillside above the eastern end of the city. It turned out to be the Basilica di Superga, a liturgical wonder built in the early eighteenth century in redemption of a vow made as a bargain with the Mother of God. There is a long tradition of such bets with the Almighty or the Madonna in Italy, going back at least to the pledge of King Roger of Sicily that resulted in the erection of the great church at Cefalù after he was saved from drowning by the intercession of the Madonna in 1180 or thereabouts. Here in Torino it was not the force of nature that threatened the local monarch, but the armies of Louis XIV, the elegant and self-absorbed bully that the French called the "Sun King."

King Vittorio Amedeo II wagered a huge basilica with the Virgin Mary, and the siege of Torino in 1706 was thwarted by her intercession and perhaps also by Pietro Micca, the heroic sapper who built tunnels for explosive defenses under the French positions and caused much devastation among the attackers. Unfortunately, in the process he was also hoist by his own petard, and is now one of the national heroes commemorated at the basilica. Along with him lie the remains of most of the kings of Savoy between the time of the frustration of Louis and the establishment of the Kingdom of Italy in the latter half of the nineteenth century. The building was designed by Filippo Juvarra, the most prolific and renowned of the Torinese architects of the Baroque era. We saw lots more of his work during the time we spent exploring the churches and an amazing number of highly ornamented royal residences in the town.

The kingdoms of Piemonte and neighboring Savoia made out well in the power shuffling of the War of the Spanish Succession, the War of the Austrian Succession, the War of the Polish Succession, and various other dynastic scuffles that followed the Napoleonic adventurism of the post-revolutionary French. Through a long span of the nineteenth century, it evolved into a constitutional monarchy under King Vittorio Emanuele, with the extraordinary Count Camillo Cavour as the king's *primo ministro*. It became the most effective center of the Italian nationalistic spirit, which was kindled by the inflaming intellectual passion of the exiled Giuseppe Mazzini and given physical reality by the huge bravery and military genius of Giuseppe Garibaldi.

The three did not get along at all well, but are still gratefully remembered by modern Italians as the brain, the soul, and the sword of the modern nation that the newly unified Italy became in the 1860s when the French, Austrians, and Spanish were expelled, the temporal power of the Pope broken, and Italians first began to think of themselves as Italians.[10]

From a published list the size of a telephone book of all the lodgings in each province of Italy, we had found a reasonably priced hotel in the Piemonte chapter before we took the plane from Sicily

---

[10] Along the way to unifying Italy, Cavour swapped Savoy to France in exchange for Louis Napoleon III's military help in ejecting Austria from the rest of Italy. This was the sort of high-level exchanging of countries and nationalities that was common in the way internationally minded leaders dealt with native populations in Europe and Africa. In this particular case it almost made Garibaldi leave the Risorgimento because his own hometown, Nizza, had been bargained away to France and was thenceforth called Nice. Evidently much of the population of the famous French resort still speaks Italian, although the switch was confirmed by a plebiscite in the latter part of the nineteenth century.

to Torino. The symbols in these helpful books are not too mystical after a little research, and we located what looked like a good *albergo* bearing the sign for the center of town: a dot in a circle in a square. This, and a relatively modest tariff for a rating of three stars, moved us to telephone ahead to the Hotel Roma e Rocca Cavour on the Piazza Carlo Felice. Although I was not acquainted with Charles the Happy (and have so far been unable to figure out precisely what he was so happy about), we decided it sounded like a cheerful place to settle and we went for it.

We were not disappointed. The hotel, although short of magnificent, has an elegant lobby and bedrooms of generous dimension. Ours, painted a pretty peach color, faced a large park (that of Happy Charlie), and was equipped with a balcony that gave survey of a large green area with a fountain jet spraying forty feet in the air and the great Porto Nuovo railroad station on our right hand. That splendid terminal was obviously designed in the late Victorian era when such a building stood as a symbol for all that was progressive and modern about the city and its proper place in a new and optimistic steam-powered world.

We stowed our gear and repaired to the lobby bar for a drink. There was a cocktail pianist and a handful of other patrons in attendance. Even the furniture had some style to it—fruitwood chairs with velvet-cord cushions. As usual, we engaged our neighbor in conversation. She was a pretty, pregnant, sari-clad Indian woman with a nine-year-old son who had come to Torino as she evidently did at least once a year, "to shop." The identity of Torino as a place for the well-to-do of the romantic East to spend their money may be recent, but the style and content of the shops in the center of this sophisticated town reach back at least a century and a half.

Torino was a modern city in each of the last three centuries, although many of its landmarks are of the splendid and luxurious baroque style of the seventeenth and eighteenth centuries. Other styles succeeded, always of the latest fashion and often unique. The most prominent of later buildings is the extraordinary spike of the Mole Antonelliana. *Mole* means a massive structure, and this one is the work of Alessandro Antonelli, who was commissioned to design it as a synagogue. Some decided the architect was mad. Almost forty years later the building had grown out of all bounds and the congregation washed their hands of responsibility for it. Somehow Antonelli continued building as the mole rose to a height of almost 550 feet, and the elderly eccentric architect had to be hoisted in an armchair to a dizzying height in order to supervise construction.

It ended up as a monument to Italian unity when it was finally finished in 1897, and is now being reworked to serve as a museum of the cinema. As the tiers of brick, stone, and gilded roofing tiles succeed each other, they are punctuated by rings of columns with classical capitals whose details are

barely visible at such a height. Antonelli is entombed in the huge
edifice of stone engineering under this lofty spire that rises above
the east side of Torino. There is a terrace with a good view up there
somewhere, but the tower was closed *in restauro* during our visit.
The top of the spire today is metal, the original stone one having
blown off in a severe storm a half-century ago. The building is the
symbol of the city and a matter of justifiable pride, as well as the
useful location of the television broadcast antennae for the entire
province.

Torino originated, as did many Italian cities, as a permanent
Roman military camp, rigidly square in layout and entered by four
gates centered in the exterior walls, but here oriented to the course
of the River Po rather than to the points of the compass. It acquired
a star-shaped castle attached to one corner of the rudimentary city
in the Middle Ages. Later, suburbs and enlarged walls were added
during the Renaissance, and the incursion of the railroad to the
center of town came, as it did everywhere, in the nineteenth century.
Despite serious Allied bombing of its industrial works in World War
II, Torino recovered quickly, and in the 1950s was one of the principal
engines of the "economic miracle" that lifted Italy to become the
sixth-largest industrial economy in the world by the time we got
there to see it.

It surely did look quite prosperous in the early 2000s. The
biggest thing in town (although quite invisible from the center) is the
Fabbrica Italiana Automobili Torino, whose initials define the name
of Europe's largest automobile company. Fiat was still largely owned
by the Agnelli family until the last male scion died at an advanced
aged in 2002. Loyal workers walked past the bier by the thousands
to honor the man who had brought such prosperity to their city. A
great deal of the current manufacturing of cars is now carried on in

factories in developing countries overseas. Homemade or not, we found the small- and medium-sized Fiats to be wonderful cars while touring the plains and mountains of Italy.

Torino has a reputation of being a busy town. However, it doesn't seem so when seen from the center of the city. The local industry is now quite high-tech, and even that is outpaced by fashion and design. From whatever viewpoint, prosperity abounds.

On our first night in this town we were favored to find dinner close by the Rocca and Cavour on the Via XX September at La Pergola Rosa (The Pink Arbor), an unprepossessing *ristorante* which turned out to be listed on the architectural tours of Torino because it is absolutely unchanged since the date of its opening in 1938. The decor is severe Art Deco, and the white tablecloths are accented by the same pastel-colored water bottles that were set out sixty-plus years ago. In one corner, a luminescent pergola on brick piers encompasses an only slightly larger table usually set aside for parties. The whole effect, down to coat hooks and inset tile decorations in a few spots on the walls, is reminiscent of the period of the New York World's Fair of 1939. On the other hand, I also remember something different of the Italian exhibit at Flushing Meadow in my childhood. It was done in the heavy, triumphalist style of the Fascist era, and pictures of Benito Mussolini decorated the walls. The little restaurant makes a much more agreeable use of the idiom. The veal served to Cathy with delicately fried polenta was obviously first-rate, but I chose the *fegato alla veneziana* (calves' liver and onions done to absolute perfection), always a good bet in northern Italy, with a bottle of Barolo, a fine red wine of Piemonte.

When we set forth to sample the museums of Torino, we didn't realize what a formidable task even a simple survey of these institutions would be. The attractive free handout in the hotel lobby, called *I Musei di Torino*, actually lists forty institutions in or around the city, conserving everything from painting, sculpture, and railroads to photographs of the mountain climbing of the Duke of the Abruzzi in the Karakorams of high Asia, or the art and ethnology of ancient Egypt. There are museums of furniture and natural history, as well as any number of *palazzi* which are examples of the high baroque for which the city is noted. Any museum buff will be happy here. We started on a misty and occasionally showery day, but the city is well prepared for inclement weather. There are many blocks of arcades lining the wide sidewalks all through the center of town. By scampering across the street crossings we managed to pass from arcade to arcade almost all the way to the Egyptian Museum.

Part of the mystery of Happy Charles was solved by a notice here that he was the well-advised monarch who purchased the collection of Egyptian antiquities of Bernardino Drovetti, who was an advisor to a certain Mohammed Ali in the early nineteenth century. Thus, through the good offices of these somewhat mysterious characters, an extraordinary wealth of Egyptian antiquities came to Torino over a century and a half ago. The treasure trove of other collectors and explorers was added, and in recent decades the museum has been rewarded for helping save various sites that were about to be flooded by the high dam at Aswan. They were given a large piece of a temple as a thank offering. The result of this combination of royal gratitude and private and civic collecting has been to provide the city with the best collection of Egyptian art this side of Cairo itself. Sculpture from Nubia, Thebes, and Heliopolis share star billing with the rock temple of Ellessya and a wonderful statue of Thothmes sitting imperiously and staring out above and beyond us from about 3,300 years before our time. For anyone used to the excellent collections of the Metropolitan and Brooklyn museums, the amazing size, breadth, and variety of this collection lifts acquaintance with this period of art and history to a new level.

Upstairs is the extraordinary Galleria Sabauda, which houses the painting collections of the kings of Piemonte and Savoy. Through a mixture of good luck and good taste, the royal collectors pulled together a group of paintings by the artists of northern Europe who flourished at the same time as the great Italian painters of the *quattrocento* and *cinquecento* that we had been following all about the peninsula. Here are works by van Eyck, van der Weyden, and Rembrandt, as well as an amazing Passion of Christ by Hans Memling, in which all the scenes from the Last Supper through the Agony, the Scourging, the Way of the Cross, the Crucifixion, and the Burial of Jesus are going on at the same time in the streets and alleyways and on the hills surrounding a fanciful Jerusalem. In other rooms are wonderful paintings of Madonna and Child by Fra Angelico, and sexy, wrestling nude gods and goddesses by Paolo Veronese. Among the most unusual is Bernardo Bellotto's hyperrealistic scene of the walls of the Palazzo Reale of Turino being built in the eighteenth century. The painting is done in a style that acknowledges Bellotto's relationship to the Venetian Canaletto. The detailed representation of the construction is in brilliant chiaroscuro, and shows one of the laborers pushing a wheelbarrow across rickety single-plank scaffolding over a twenty-foot drop into the moat. This one painting gave me a feeling of what a wonderwork it was to construct these huge buildings without a steam hoist, power saw, or backhoe.

After having spent most of the morning looking at famous works by name-brand painters, we became tired of pedigrees and began to relax and study the characters and actions of the subjects and their surroundings. Iconography is much less intellectually exhausting than the pursuit of art history. There were a pair of delicate predellas of

Catherine of Alexandria, lashed to a pillar, half naked to be scourged, the broken fragments of the steel-toothed wheel that failed to subdue her scattered about. In the second she has been beheaded but maintains a prayerful posture while her head lies beside her on the bloody sand. In another painting, St. Peter Martyr was peacefully praying before an image of the Madonna col Bambino. He wears a gold-chased meat ax lodged halfway through his skull. His golden halo is perched rather rakishly above the instrument of his execution. An elegantly painted dribble of blood runs down his forehead.

I wonder why these depictions of the heroic steadfastness of martyrs remained so popular so long after the persecution of Christians ceased in the fourth century. The only people suffering such martyrdom at the time these paintings were commissioned were the heretics being abused by the traditional Catholic Church. I know some Christians lost their lives in the period of the Crusades, but generally in acts of war rather than under threat of abjuring their faith.

The sixteenth- and seventeenth-century paintings were generally giant-sized versions of the subject matter better pursued by the earlier artists. The use of allegory or Scripture as an opportunity to paint the nude in sensual splendor makes for lots of repentant Magdalenes with their clothes off, frequent Lucrezias and Cleopatras committing suicide by applying stiletto or asp to their well-formed bosoms, Mother Eve coyly tempting Adam with fruit held alluringly before her naked body, and Susanna bathing while oblivious of the lascivious attentions of the elderly men who have discovered her. This period seems to have witnessed the origin of the rich and noble commissioning paintings for their homes and palaces rather than exclusively for their chapels and cathedrals. Hence, more succulent nymphs came to stand as caryatids in the corners and fly about the painted ceilings.

But perhaps the most charming of all the artistic treasures gathered together by the various Carlos and Emmanuels of the houses of Piemonte and Savoia are the royal children painted by van Dyck. The folder provided to help visitors find their way about the Sabauda has on its cover a chubby-cheeked princess who gazes regally at us while stroking the head of what looks like an adoring Irish setter.

The *duomo* of Torino is in the northern part of the old city center, a brief tram ride from our hotel. It is a rather plain church, but it is also the site of the famous *Sacra Sidone*, the Shroud of Turin, which purports to be the winding sheet in which Christ was wrapped before he was walled up in the new and unused tomb by Nicodemus and Joseph of Arimathea. The *Sidone* is a remarkable textile whatever one thinks of it authenticity. Radiocarbon dating seems to place it in the late Middle Ages, perhaps around AD 1200. The stains that make a lifelike pattern of the head, face, and body of a bearded man are currently not explained as being of divine origin. At the time of our visits it was not on display, but a large, color-photo reproduction was hung behind the altar. I had some difficulty making out the miraculous markings, but found it a sobering image nonetheless.

Besides the famous shroud, the Cathedral of San Giovanni contains some interesting paintings and altarpieces. To me the best of these is a remarkable assemblage of small paintings surrounding a *Madonna Alatante* with Saints Crispin and Crispinian by Defendente Ferrari, a wonderfully talented artist of the very early sixteenth century who only lived to the age of twenty-four. His image of Mary is set in an elaborate, Gothic gilded frame with two dozen miniature scenes from the lives of the two saints all around her. Crispin and Crispinian were Romans of distinguished lineage who went off to convert the Gauls in the late third century, a particularly dangerous task in 285, and well before Constantine made Christianity legal. They ran afoul of persecution and were subject to scourging, imprisonment, and other horrors of torture which seemed to give them no discomfort. In despair of any other way of defeating them, the Gauls beheaded the pair at separate sites. All these things are recorded in little framed pictures all around the larger representations of the two heroes and the nursing mother of the baby Savior. The shrine is quite beautiful and shows a style of representation that blends medieval decoration and Renaissance perspective drawing and portraiture. The saints were popular intercessors and the patrons of cobblers, tanners, and saddlers by the late 1500s. They also became fixed in the English consciousness by Shakespeare's rousing *ferverino* to the troops of Henry V on the eve of the battle of Agincourt.

Around the corner from the *duomo* is the Palazzo Reale, an enormous, rambling space which served as the largest and principal royal residence from its earliest construction in 1646. Many architects had a whack at it over time, but Juvarra and Alfieri of the eighteenth century did most of what is immediately visible today. Baroque it surely is, but somehow it has a warmth and even a simplicity when compared with Versailles or the Viennese Schloss Schönbrunn. All the monarchs of Europe seem to have built palaces that reflected their good opinion of themselves and their divine right to govern by whim, to make war as if it were a parlor game, and live high on the hog while doing so. But the House of Piemonte and Savoia seems also to contain the germ of political humility or resignation to the inevitable that graced some of the English kings of the same period. Both countries became constitutional monarchies by different routes. Thus they avoided the bloody revolution that was self-inflicted by the French.

Walking back south from these reminders of times past in Torino, we kept crossing the path of our own century. In the morning, the runners of a marathon had come coursing through the city, and encouraging fans held out paper cups of nourishing drink to the contestants as they went by. They trotted through Piazza San Carlo, a huge open square in the center of the town where a few gigantic advertising banners were hung over some of the baroque facades. Later in the day, the leaders came through at a great pace on their way to the finish line, somewhere farther downtown. At the south end of the piazza they passed between a pair of small but very baroque churches on either side of the Via Roma: San Carlo and Santa Cristina. In the former there was an image of the Madonna of the Seven Sorrows with seven silver swords piercing the golden heart she wore on the outside of her teal-blue gown. Grotesque as it sounds, the image of Mary was of such surpassing sweetness that the effect was quite devotional. Looking back at the two churches after we passed, I was startled to see that they had been clad in severe plain stone coverings from behind, presumably to make them harmonize with the more fascist-style buildings to the south. This is an area of fashionable shops, and the window displays featuring the current high style were greatly entertaining. We stopped to have lunch at a Brek, Italy's answer to American fast food. A little fresh pasta and a generous bowl of cream of carrot soup with salad, breadsticks, and cold mineral water *con gaz* were a fine repast. Wherever we went in Torino there were packages of *grissini* breadsticks, the very thin kind, baked by different companies, always crisp, fresh, and delicious. *Grissini* are, after all, one of Torino's contributions to international *cucina*.

Later, threading through the late-afternoon *passeggiata*, we were stopped by the sight of what appeared to be a collection of shiny new cars parked under a tent next to the arcade. The lead vehicle was a bright yellow Volkswagen New Beetle. Two girls in very short blue skirts and shiny tight boots were handing out folders illustrating the offerings of what turned out to be DiViesto, one of Torino's largest secondhand car dealerships. The four-color brochure presented sixty or more cars ranging from a presumably drivable Fiat Panda for the equivalent of $810 to a lightly used Mercedes with all the fixin's for $45,000. Lots of people stopped and climbed in and out of the various models on offer, jounced up and down on the seats, and did a little mock steering at the wheel. There was a carnival atmosphere to the display and the carefully made-up girls hawking the literature seemed to be having as much fun as their customers. Although scooters such as the original Vespa are still much in evidence, Torino has progressed far into the age of the four-wheeled vehicle. Unfortunately, the Italians have also discovered the Harley-Davidson and the various Japanese knockoffs. They seem all out of scale in the ancient streets of medieval cities, although I must admit they thread their way through with greater ease than our standard-sized car. There were very few SUVs in the spring of 2000, but I feared that this exemption would be short-lived.

We spent several afternoons just walking about and enjoying the window-shopping in this civilized town. After experiencing the rolled-down, crime-stopper steel shutters that close off the displays of upper Madison Avenue in New York or the Via Maqueda in Palermo, we were cheered by the more open style of shops in Torino. Perhaps it is the timing of the long lunch hour and the habit of late-night shopping that keeps the shutters up and the *commesse* on duty until well past nine in the evening. Starting from the vicinity of the Teatro Alfieri where we stopped for an *aperitivo*, we gawked along a great stretch of the Via Giuseppe Garibaldi, looking into book, bath, and bedroom shops that displayed the wares of the prosperous town. We had to make another bar stop for a glass of Prosecco to delay our arrival at Peppino's, where we had reserved for dinner. We barely arrived on time and were followed by what seemed to be a horde of hopeful diners who were turned away for lack of *prenotazione*.

Peppino's turned out to be a fortunate choice. White asparagus and *pesce spada* (swordfish) were delightful, and were followed by a *torta frutta* for dessert. As is usual in Piemonte and Lombardia, there was no sign of pasta on the menu. Starches in the northern part of Italy are usually in the form of risotto or polenta. I forgot to ask the designation of the white wine they served as *vino della casa*, but if we get back to Torino soon, I will again be happy to trust Peppino's selection. We walked back south through streets lined with the fantastic shapes of baroque palaces and reflected on the agreeable styles amalgamated in this city until we reached the Piazza San Carlo, the vast open space in the middle of the city where we had seen the marathon runners in the morning. The paper cups, emblazoned with the red-and-white insignia of the international Coca-Cola, had been swept up. The daytime traffic was gone. But along one side of the square, a crowd of a thousand or so was gathered around a newly erected stage with lights and amplifiers. An enthusiastic rock concert was about to begin.

X.

VERCELLI AND NOVARA:
Towns of the Pianura del Po

The flat *padana*, the plain of the Po valley of northern Italy, stretches across most of the outwash of the southern slopes of the Alps. It is studded with small cities between Torino and Milan. A few of them have personality and are attractive places to stay. We decided to experience more than the usual tourist locations in this part of the country and planned an excursion to Vercelli and Novara.

The Auto Europe pickup office for rental cars in Torino is in the Porto Nuovo railroad station, which was, as the Italians say, *due passi* from our hotel. Like many of these car-rental sites in Italy, they are only open in the morning and close for the day at 12:30 P.M.. If you are late returning the car at midday, you presumably have rented it for an extra day. In spite of this procrustean timetable, I have nothing but praise for Auto Europe. Their rates for a week at a time are reasonable and their cars are clean and new. Renting a small one through an American travel agent sometimes merits a free upgrade to the next-larger size. The only problem is that picking up a car at the airport merits not a discount but a *surcharge* of 14 percent, not just on the first day, but on the whole charter! Getting the car at the railroad station is worth the trouble, and city navigation in Italy is not as hard as you might imagine.

We escaped downtown Torino with ease and crossed the Po on one of the half-dozen bridges that span the broad, shallow river that flows beside the city. We progressed northeast and passed under the brow of the hill that was the site of Juvarra's Basilica di Superga in a park up above us. We elected not to go on this diversionary exploration so soon in the day, another of our frequent mistakes since the church is said to be a good example of late-eighteenth-century architecture. There is also a panoramic view of Torino, as well as an astronomical observatory up there. This provided us with another reason to return to this pleasant capital of Piemonte. Since we had decided to pursue a leisurely route to Vercelli, we avoided the E66 Autostrada and, we hoped, would also miss even the busy local Route 11 by sticking to the secondary roads indicated in the trusty *Atlante Stradale*. We followed the south bank of the Po toward Chivasso, but shortly came upon an even more rural road that promised to follow the river still more closely. This route rapidly became narrower yet and led us through some open gates into a barren wasteland ornamented by a few idle bulldozers and other desultory signs of a municipal landfill or sewage-disposal site. There seemed to be no way out in front of us, so we turned around in the narrow road and were just about to reverse our course when a rather official-looking pickup truck bore down on us. A scowling driver questioned us in brusque Italian, asking what we were doing in this restricted location. I replied in bland and impenetrable English that I didn't speak the language and had lost my way. This brought on laughter and good-humored hand gestures that soon set us right. There are times when an inability to speak the local tongue is an advantage.

Our eventual route to Vercelli took us through extensive rice fields, some filled with water in preparation for planting, others dry and surrounded by foot-high dikes which would turn them into shallow paddies when the rains came, or if the water of the Po was pumped up to fill them. This eastern end of the Po valley is the area of Europe's only rice cultivation, and the plain bordering the river (also known as the *pianura del Po*) is the source of the Arborio rice that makes a choice risotto in both Piemonte and Lombardia. There were no signs of barefoot peasants here or coolies with straw hats, only modern tractors and harvesting machines. Up on our northern horizon we could see the great barrier of the Alps covered with the gleaming snow of late spring.

Vercelli is too small to be described in either of the English-language guidebooks we were carrying, but it is listed in the *Blue Guide to Northern Italy*. Here we learned that the little city had a remarkable collection of paintings in the Museo Civico Borgogna, as well as an ancient church that would bear inspection. It was also just a few minutes east of Novara where there was a baptistery of an early date to be looked at. Being alternately liberated and encumbered by the car, we selected a hotel on the ring road around the *centro storico*, the Cinzia, which was distinguished in our new Italian *guida*[11] as providing laundry service. Contemplating such mundane things led me to wonder about how those traveling emperors, dukes, and cardinals of earlier ages were able to get their washing done on the road. I refuse to believe that the pretty d'Este sisters, Beatrice and Isabella, didn't

---

[11] By this time we were carrying four guidebooks, three in English and one in Italian. Each had some information that the others left out. The Italian-language Tuttitalia Alberghi & Ristoranti had excellent little maps incomprehensibly left out of the more-recent edition. In any case, it has a comprehensive listing of the facilities in each city large enough to support even one hotel. It gives information on bed and food rather than sights to see. On the other hand, it includes many more towns than the Let's Go or The Lonely Planet series.

change their lingerie frequently. It is a matter of historical record that Lucrezia Borgia, while on her way to meet the husband she had acquired by proxy marriage, required the whole caravan of her suite to stop every three or four days so that she could have the opportunity to "wash her head."[12]

Lunch at the Cinzia revealed that the rest of the guests were either long-distance truckers taking a layover, day workers not close to home, or commercial travelers settling in for a few days as drummers in the town. One was wearing a lime-green necktie and an ultramarine-blue shirt that caught Cathy's eye. The fare was appropriately substantial and excellent: a very thick bean soup and *bollito misto*, the selection of half a dozen boiled meats and sausages served with various mustards and sweet basil sauces. Even with a scant *quarto* of red wine, this is the sort of lunch that requires a postprandial nap in sequence.

Eventually we set forth to find our way about the town and locate the art gallery, the *duomo*, and the twelfth-century Cistercian monastery of San Andrea. The intaglio work in the choir stalls and chapter house is the sort of thing that in any other country would be a national landmark. Here it is merely some good thirteenth-century decoration. The church has a certain amount of Gothic detailing inside, but its blunt, late-Romanesque shape dates it firmly in the middle of the twelfth century. I subsequently learned that this was one of the very first examples of the new "Gothic" style to reach Italy from northern France. At the time I was too ignorant of the transitional detailing to know the difference. Always read a bit before you go; you will see more.

---

[12] On the other hand it was said approvingly of England's Queen Elizabeth in the late sixteenth century that she bathed every three months, "whether she needeth it or no."

But the real focus of Vercelli is the Museo Borgogna. Antonio Borgogna was what the town literature describes as "a learned gentlemen and a great lover of art." He established the museum in memory of his father, Francesco Borgogna. The younger Borgogna lived from 1822 to 1906, and after setting up the museum in his own palazzo, spent the final years of his life visiting the auction galleries to add to the collection so that his hometown could have a first-rate art museum. Eventually, the paintings from the local archaeological museum and the works of art from the Association for the Free Teaching of Drawing were added to the Borgogna, in the often-remodeled but still gracious house where the original donor had lived. He was a good collector himself, but the museum has not stopped with his gifts. The salmon pink and white-trimmed building houses paintings from the early *quattrocento* to the 1920s. There is also a considerable amount of sculptured architectural detailing, pottery, ancient glass, and elegant furniture on exhibition.

If the names of some of the Renaissance painters here are less well known than those in Milan, Florence, and Rome, their work is beautiful, and their treatment of the sacred subjects masterful. We found here again a brilliant enthroned Virgin by Defendente Ferrari who had done the elegant Crispin and Crispinian in the cathedral of Torino. She sits in regal majesty surrounded by an elaborate colonnade of Renaissance decoration, with St. Francis and a beatified companion who had not yet earned his halo on her right hand. On the other side is St. Margherita and St. Sebastian, who, for once, has his clothes on. Another very large-scale altarpiece by Ferrari clusters individual portraits of saints, holy women, and bishops around a shy Madonna, and a descent from the cross. This last, a lavish work, is set in a magnificent *quattrocento* frame with elegant classical detailing. There are also a number of paintings by Bernardino Lanino which were collected by the original Borgogna, as well as a wonderful Deposition from the workshop of Titian.

Vercelli was the birthplace of Giovanni Antonio Bazzi, who is known to us as Il Sodoma, a nickname he gained as a result of what my encyclopedia calls his "flagrant homosexuality." An openly gay lifestyle in the fifteenth century invited anything from censure to capital punishment, but Il Sodoma was so valued as an artist that he was sought out by other towns (notably Siena) and honored years later in his birthplace. Yet the Borgogna has only one of his paintings, a Holy Family with an angel and an infant John the Baptist. An orange-hued St. Joseph stares in amazement at the heavens and the infant Baptist reaches out to play with the baby. The angel stares with awe at the beautiful Mother who herself has eyes only for her child. Everybody in the circular composition is looking in a different direction around the tondo, which includes a pleasant landscape with a diminutive arched bridge, a river, and a patch of the distant sea.

In another gallery a muscular Bacchus by Ludovico Carracci is tempting a luminescent Ariadne. It is amazing how explicit the sexuality of Italian painting had become by the beginning of the seventeenth century. Close at hand is an eighteenth-century painting of "Gesu Bambino Adored" by cherubim, by Carlo Maratta, a far more beguiling baby than the greater masters of the earlier centuries were able to produce. One of the treasures of the gallery is a portrait of Domenica Volpato by Angelica Kauffman, the greatly talented eighteenth-century lady who really was the first of her sex to be recognized as a great painter in Europe. In this age when women are breaking through more and more ceilings, Angelica deserves a newer biography than the ones from fifty and one hundred years ago that are in libraries today.

Among the most curious paintings in the collection are the

late-nineteenth-century works of artists such as Giovanni Battista
Quadrone, who is represented by a masterfully drawn interior of an
artist in his studio contemplating his model. The room is full of bits of
sculpture, a stuffed owl, and a full suit of Japanese armor complete with
a sword, a pike, and a fan emblazoned with the rising sun. Arranged on
a blue silk drape is the model, her red shoes scattered on the Persian
carpet, her naked limbs arranged to prop her up to have a good view
of her employer. The artist has set his palette and brushes to one side.
He holds his chin in his hand and seems to be contemplating the
pretty thing with something more than aesthetic interest.

One of the most delightful paintings in the Borgogna is of the
traditional trio of the Madonna, the infant Jesus, and a playfully
attendant John the Baptist, attributed to David Ghirlandaio, who was
the brother and associate of Domenico, the better-known Florentine
painter of that family. To judge from this example, I would say that
David was quite up to his brother's standard.

On our way out of this attractive little museum, we stopped to
ask a question of a young woman who was walking busily through
the lobby with a sheaf of papers in her hand. She responded in
excellent English, and a few minutes' conversation revealed that she
was the director of the Borgogna, Lavinia M. Galli Michero, surely
one of the youngest museum directors in Italy, as well as one of the
prettiest. Angelica would have been proud.

Our *aperitivo* back at the Cinzia was a normal ration of gin
and tonic, but since it was served up in the sort of glass that
accommodated a double ice cream soda in my youth, it took a
while to get through it. The obliging *proprietario* directed us to a
ristorante called Il Paiolo, which was on the other side of the small
city on the Via Garibaldi. We followed the directions of our host
and several shopkeepers along the way with some difficulty, finally

realizing that the restaurant was entered through an alley that was almost completely obscured by pipe scaffolding and orange plastic netting. Much of Italy is always *in restauro*.

But once inside, we recognized that we had come to the right place. Little medallions of veal in a balsamic sauce were served with polenta. The large plates were decorated with morning-glory blossoms and were piping hot. The crusty bread was served with herbed garlic butter, the salad had been carefully chosen, leaf by leaf, and the *budino al cioccolato* at the end was a suitable complement to the whole. This restaurant merits a major recommendation. It is made up of a number of small rooms which are sufficiently separate to make for a sense of privacy. Service, cooking, and presentation are all first-rate. Along with the art museum, Il Paiolo provides sufficient reason for an overnight stop in (or a detour to) Vercelli.

The following morning we set out for a day trip to Novara, another of the midsize cities of Piemonte that receive scant attention in most guidebooks. But Novara has a history, which I suppose is true of almost any town in Italy. It was of Roman origin and undoubtedly tangled with the Cisalpine Gauls in the early days of the Republic. After the decline of the Empire, it was taken by the Langobards of Lombardy, who had the distinction of being almost the only "barbarians" who came to stay in Italy instead of grabbing what they could and moving on. By the early twelfth century, it had become a free commune by the uniquely Italian process in which the guilds and entrepreneurs of the cities took over control from the nobility who were preoccupied with war, show, and jealousy.

Not that the cities were spared the horrors of local war. Ludovico Sforza (known as Ludovico il Moro—the Moor—because of his dark complexion), the husband of the beautiful Beatrice d'Este, was actually captured by the French in one of these battles or sieges. He had rushed off to Germany to recruit a mercenary army, but the hired soldiers were ineffectual and the Duke of Milan ended up in a French prison, where he died. It would seem that Novara became French about this time, after 1500. Like much of Italy, the luxury of self-government eluded it for many years. Even the Piemonte kept but a slippery hold on the area, and the Austrian Radetzky took the town in 1849. But the eventual triumph of the *Risorgimento* established it as definitively Italian by the 1860s. These dates give us cause to reflect how relatively young a country Italy really is.

Driving across the flat *padana*, we soon observed the silhouette of a number of steeples and towers that had to belong to Novara. Tallest among these was a mass that reared itself far into the sky and dwarfed everything else in the little city. We eventually discovered that it was more than 450 feet tall, and was, of course, the work of Alessandro Antonelli, whose even taller *mole* rears above the city of Torino. The building is the church of San Gaudenzio, which was constructed in the seventeenth century. A couple of hundred years later, an ambitious bishop commissioned Antonelli to bring the church up to the best standard of the 1860s, thus conjuring up this second gigantic tower in the Piemonte. I have not discovered if Antonelli built still other priapic works in Italy, but I suspect that he did. He obviously had a fixation on huge vertical spaces, and an ambition like Ibsen's *Master Builder*, who completed his life's work by toppling from the tower of his ultimate creation. Standing directly under the cupola and looking up into Antonelli's soaring tower is an awesome experience.

The interior of the nearby cathedral is different. It was rebuilt by Antonelli in the 1860s and is decorated with various frescoes by Bernardino Lanino, which are, quite obviously pre-Antonelli, as are paintings by Gaudenzio Ferrari and Callisto Piazza da Lodi, neither of which impressed themselves on our attention as being able to compete with the gigantic architecture. Hanging about the interior are six sixteenth-century Brussels tapestries and an altarpiece by Gaudenzio Ferrari.

We went on to visit the baptistery which is pre-Lombard in style. Some of it, in fact, goes back to the first century, from which classical columns were rescued to build the octagonal building in the late fourth century, shortly after the time when Constantine made it legal to undertake any Christian worship at all. There we also visited the Broletto, where, among a cluster of ancient buildings, there is the Museo Civico. There is more than a morning's worth to see in Novara, but we headed back to Vercelli shortly after noon. In a village called Borgo Vercelli, we discovered a *pizzeria-pasticceria* diagonally across the street from a pretty church. A "toast" with *prosciutto* and *fromaggio* with a glass of wine revived us. The simplest sandwich shop in Italy can produce a delightful lunch.

Novara and Vercelli had provided us with fascinating architecture, churches and museums full of splendid paintings, and simple food along the byways as well as at that Lucullan dinner at Il Paiolo. It would seem that every town in northern Italy should be given a chance to captivate you. Sometimes the lack of touristic traffic in the lesser-known smaller cities makes them even more delightful than their famous neighbors. For us, they provided the inspiration for this book.

XI.

MILANO:
More than an Industrial City

Although Milan is among the more obvious places in Italy, especially since it has the second-largest airport in the country, there are some less-visited places there that seasoned travelers may not yet have seen.

Flying into Milan is a beautiful business. From the air the deep, dusty blue of the shaded side of the Alps stands out in sharply chiseled contrast to the gleaming snow and rich brown of the sunlit eastern slopes. The crests look amazingly steep, perhaps unclimbable when seen from ten thousand feet above their three-kilometer peaks. This land is truly insulated from the rest of Europe by the mountains that have only been pierced here and there by tunnels cut and drilled through them in the past 150 years. From our cozy perch in the warm cabin of a Boeing 767, we could see no sign of whatever route Hannibal took with his legendary elephants twenty-three hundred years ago.

Milan is Italy's third-largest city and well ahead of Rome and Naples in fashion, style, per capita income, and interest in the Bourse (stock market). It has always been the power center of the north, the Roman bastion against the Gauls and later invaders. After the reign of Diocletian, it became the capital of the entire "Roman" Empire for a couple of hundred years, until Constantine removed the center of government to his new city, Constantinople, on the Bosphorus, five hundred miles to the east. I have often wondered why the emperors moved out of Rome. The answer is that the Apennine chain isolates the original and eternal city from the action in the rest of the Empire. It could take the greater part of a week for a legion to march to the Po Valley from Rome, by which time the Goths would have ravaged the countryside. By the dark ages of the sixth and seventh centuries, contact with the power of Constantinople could only be maintained by sea, and Rome was on the wrong side of the peninsula for that; hence, the move of the capitol to Ravenna.

But Milan has remained the connection between Italy and the rest of Europe and the hinge of power until modern sea transportation made it possible to enter the boot from the sides after the Middle Ages.[13] Rome did not catch up to Milan until long after the popes came back from Avignon in the fourteenth century. Larger than Florence, its creative cousin to the south, and more combative than Venice to the east, it was an independent duchy and contended with France and with the German Holy "Roman" Emperors. Then, in the later Renaissance period, Milan settled into political and military mediocrity. But the artistic and intellectual achievements of the modern age grew here in their turn, and the work of Giorgio Armani and the late Gianni Versace turned it into the hub of European fashion from which America copies its styles. It is also the great center of Italian finance and commerce.

---

[13] European ships could not sail reliably to windward until they learned about the fore-and-aft rig from the Arab dhows of the Indian Ocean in the fourteenth century. Inside the Mediterranean they used oars to buck the wind. An argument can be made that the explosion of learning we call the "Renaissance" took place largely because of these improvements in rigging an ocean-going sailing vessel.

Aeroporto Malpensa is the arrival and departure point for overseas traffic; Linate is the smaller airport and serves mostly short-hop flights. It is closer to town and well connected by railroad. But Milan's major airport (pronounce it Mil-*ah*-no if you wish to be understood by the Italians) has recently upgraded its links to the city. The old (and still-surviving) method of getting into town requires an hour-long bus trip, which is admittedly less wearisome than taking public transportation from JFK to Manhattan. The bus deposits you at the Stazione Centrale, which is fine if your intention is to get through Milan and out again as quickly as possible. Unfortunately, the wonderful central station, the Ferrovia dello Stato, is several kilometers from the real center of the city, the major hotels, the opera house, the cathedral, and the great *castello*. But now at last there is a leisurely rail link directly from the airport to the Stazione Nord. We were deposited across the street from the Cadorna metro stop, next door to the Castello Sforzesca and a reasonably short walk west along the Corso Magenta from Leonardo's *Last Supper*. Locals and art critics refer to this most famous work of art as the *Cenacolo Vinciano*. It is there to behold at the church of Santa Maria delle Grazie.

This recently restored *ultima cena* was not originally on my list of top reasons for visiting Italy, or even Milan. To begin with, you have to make a reservation a day (or possibly two) ahead of time to be one of the chosen few who are admitted in groups of a couple of dozen with an Italian-speaking docent, some of whom also speak some English if questioned. If you ask your hotel clerk to make the reservation for you, it is possible to match up with an English-speaking guide. What with the procrustean scheduling and flummery of making a sacred icon out of a heavily restored sixteenth-century painting, I was not sure I wanted to bother with the much-reproduced mural that has been quietly peeling off its wall for the last five hundred years. But

Cathy insisted that we make the pilgrimage and see the real image of what is probably the most often copied and reproduced painting in all of Europe. As usual, she was right.

The most recent restoration work has removed all of the clumsy if well-meaning over-painting and saccharine apostolic faces with syrupy hairdos done in the last few centuries. Leonardo used the new technique of painting in pigments suspended in a medium of oil (probably linseed) and spirits of pine sap (turpentine). Unfortunately, the wall that was the ground on which he was working allowed dampness to seep through, and the painting began to detach itself almost as soon as he had painted it. Most restoration consisted of slathering more paint onto the surface of the picture, to the point that there was little of Leonardo's work left to be seen. But happily the painting was not beyond redemption. In the last dozen years the extraordinary Italian restorers have succeeded in lifting the entire painting from the surface and fastening it back on the wall, rescuing every flake of Leonardo's original brushwork and reassembling the scraps, slices, and chips of the great composition on a reconstructed surface that should last more or less forever. The colors are bright, almost as bright as the cleaned Michelangelo frescoes on the Sistine Ceiling. There are a few gaps of missing paint and some areas that had peeled away too completely to be rescued. But what we saw that day was Leonardo's work, and his great composition stood clearly in front of our eyes.[14]

----

[14] As in the case of the Michelangelo restorations, some critics have complained that the result isn't muddy enough and has lost the smoky charm of the over-paintings that most of us were brought up on. I fail to see how the real work of the original artist could be preferred to the dusty varnish that was obscuring it. And the colors were originally bright; the Renaissance painters did not color their work in brown and gray tints.

The room that houses the Last Supper was itself the dining room or refectory of the Dominican monks who commissioned the work in the early sixteenth century. The painting is as wide as the room and exactly fills one end of the space. As a result, when we stood in the middle of the room, the vanishing-point perspective of Leonardo's drawing matched our view of the walls, ceiling, and floor in front of us. From where we stood, the picture seemed to be an extension of the room itself. We were in the Cenacle, the "upper room," able to look beyond the figures at the table and through the windows where palm fronds reach upward from their unseen trunks below. Most of the apostles are recognizable from the symbolism of their poses: Thomas points with a raised and extended finger that suggests his later requirement that he be able to probe the wounds of Christ with his finger before he would believe in his resurrection. Jesus bears the face of the same model as James, "the brother of the Lord." Peter is old and bald-headed. John is boyish if not downright feminine.

The scene depicts the moment when Christ prophesies his betrayal by someone at the table with him. The figures all recoil from the possibility that each could be the terrible traitor, saying "Is it I, Lord?" The Iscariot alone seems unmoved by the shocked consternation of the agitated group. He is sitting in the midst of them, but somehow almost alone with other apostles conversing around his darkened presence. He clutches a small purse on the tablecloth: the thirty pieces of silver or more. He was, after all, the CFO of the original twelve.

Leonardo is well represented in Milan. Although originally a Florentine, Leonardo was hired by Ludovico Sforza, "The Moor," to be the military engineer charged with making Ludovico's city safe, and the *castello* in its center impregnable. It was later as an old man that he took up a generous offer of paid retirement made by Francis

I, King of France. He moved to Cloux, near the chateau of Amboise on the Loire, where he died.

The Science and Technology Museum (Museo Nazionale della Scienza e Tecnica) contains another interesting collection of Leonardo's work. A long hall in the museum is filled with beautifully made boxwood models of his theoretical constructions of airplanes, battle tanks, pumps, and various other engines of war. There is plenty to see in this museum, but the nearby collection of ancient musical instruments is in a pitiful state of decay and disrepair, especially in contrast to the wonderfully reverent conservation of the ancient violins and lutes which can be seen in the city museum of Cremona a few miles away.

Hotels in Milan, like those in Rome, are considerably more expensive than in the smaller towns along the Via Emilia to the east. Even rich old Bologna offers better bargains than Milan. A few years before the current century's collapse of the dollar, we found a small but adequate room at the London Hotel for around $120 a night. At a slightly higher tariff and in the same agreeable location on the Via Rovello is the Hotel Giulio Cesare, recently remodeled and close to the Via Dante, which leads to the Piazza Duomo. On an earlier occasion we found all the middle-rated three-star hotels booked solid with the inevitable trade-show participants. We were routed to the King Hotel, where there were considerably more sumptuous accommodations for around $170 a night.[15] As befits its cost, the King provided the most elaborate breakfast buffet we found in the North: besides several breads and preserves, there were three iced juices and

---

[15] Add 40 or 50 percent to these prices to estimate prices today (or you can check on Google).

a wondrous machine that would have done Leonardo proud by the automatic dexterity with which it selected oranges, sliced them in half, and carefully squeezed them into an onward-marching file of spotless glasses. As is usual in all of Italy, the coffee was delicious. In spite of the sophistication and cost of Milan, this, the center of town, is a lot less expensive than midtown Manhattan, and the restaurants are better and quite reasonable here.

We asked the gracious and pretty *impiegata* at the hotel for guidance in finding a modest place for dinner. She directed us to Al Cinque a few blocks away, and told us to say we came from the hotel. This house seemed to cater to a younger set and the food was fine: *risotto al frutti di mare* for me, and *vitello con funghi* for Cathy, as well as a shared artichoke salad decorated with *guana*, a mysterious shaved cheese. The lemon mousse and *torte con pignoli* topped it off nicely. The good dinner for two with wine and a tip came to 94,500 Lit, about $47 at the millennial exchange rate, probably equal to better than 50 euro today. That would be hard to beat on Cape Cod in the summer or in Mystic, Connecticut, while on vacation. For travelers, the bargains in good food do much to make up for the cost of relatively small rooms in a three-star hotel in most well-known Italian cities.

One of the advantages of our location at the King Hotel was our discovery of the neighboring Church of San Maurizio just down the Corso Magenta. We first entered this church after visiting the pleasant and interesting archaeological museum next door. We were unaware that there was a great profusion of frescoes by Bernardino Luini in the church. Luini was a Milanese and is justly valued here. His work at San Maurizio covers both the nave and the sanctuary, as well as a large chapel formed by the retrochoir, which can be discovered by exploring a brief dark passage behind the main altar.

I first went to search it out because I heard medieval music that stopped and started too irregularly to be a recording. Once we were located in the space behind the altar and reredos, we found a group of nine men rehearsing for the morrow's concert. We settled down to enjoy the show. The church was chilly and several of the singers wore woolen caps pulled down to their ears. Tenors, basses, and a few countertenors caroled away gloriously throughout the afternoon, bringing to life both sacred songs and secular canticles from the fifteenth and sixteenth centuries.[16] And all around were a wilderness of inspired painted figures by Luini: poor abused St. Agnes losing her breasts; Sebastian with his perfect physique studded with arrows; Christ clad in the purple robe that mocked his kingship; a tender deposition of the body of the Lord; and a Last Supper flanked on one side by the flagellation and Pilate's judgment on the other. The capture of the Lord in the garden of Gethsemane displays a typically ham-fisted Peter who has the servant of the high priest down on his back, about to lose an ear to the enraged apostle.

San Maurizio is mentioned in the better guidebooks but seldom shows up on anyone's must-see list. I have suggested to our friends that they not miss it. There are so many great collections in Milan that a short visit would not allow most tourists to see all of the first-chop locations. The Brea Gallery is one of the great ones which we saw on our previous trips many years ago. Mantegna's wonderful foreshortened corpus of the dead Christ is there, as are Piero della Francesca portraits of Federico da Montefeltro, the humanist Duke of Urbino, who some have suggested really provided the first home for

---

[16] At the end of their rehearsal, we found that the group was called the Ensemble Odhecaton. They had produced several CDs, one of which we were able to find at Buscemi, Milan's best classical music store, which turned out to be next door to the bar we later selected for our aperitivo.

the Italian Renaissance by welcoming scholars, artists, philosophers, and writers to his wonderful little hilltop city.

There is, besides the Brea, another Milanese gallery that was entirely new to us in the year 2000, the (at the time) recently reopened Pinacoteca Ambrosiana. This remarkable library and art gallery was created by one of the most brilliant young men to grace the post-Renaissance period of Italian history. Federigo Borromeo was a member of a distinguished family that produced a pope, a saint, and a number of scholars and several bon vivants. He was an aristocrat who actually took the teachings of the church seriously and lived a pious and celibate life. On the other hand, through the position and the eminence of his family, he became a cardinal at the age of twenty-three. This was in the period when the Council of Trent had done away with most of the simony—the actual purchase of bishoprics that had scarred the fifteenth-century church.[17] Besides doing whatever it is that cardinals do for a living, he began almost immediately to collect books, manuscripts, and paintings, using the considerable means that his family position afforded.

His cousin, St. Charles Borromeo, had sold his collection of antiquities to aid the poor after he had become a bishop. Federigo used his wealth to collect the best available literature and art (including some of the books piously sold to dealers by his cousin). He was a prolific writer as well as a scholar, an antiquarian, and an art critic. He once said he hoped to be remembered as having died

---

[17] Nepotism was another matter. In an age where the only agreed-upon legitimacy came from blood descent, even the election of popes by cardinals was a risky bet, and the appointment of nephews or even illegitimate sons to church office was a safer guarantee of security than was any "democratic" process that became popular in the eighteenth and nineteenth centuries.

with a pen in one hand and a crucifix in the other. He established the Ambrosiana Library in 1607. It is thus one of the very oldest libraries that was (and is) open to the public anywhere in Europe. He added his collection of paintings in 1618, as well as a wealth of prints and curios.

The Pinacoteca has some wonderful things in it that are not to be found in most museums. The only full-sized cartoon of a Renaissance fresco is here, and it is a giant: the original drawing of Raphael's *The School of Athens.* There is also the wonderful "Codex Atlanticus," the greatest of Leonardo da Vinci's notebooks, which was retrieved from the hungry arms of the French after the fall of Napoleon in 1815.

Today it requires some demonstrable scholarly purpose to use the library. Any part-time graduate student could surely get in, and the picture gallery is open to all anyway. Besides many great works by the local painter Luini, there are paintings by Titian, and the famous *Portrait of a Lady* by Giovanni Ambrogio de Predis. This regal princess was long thought to have been one of the Farrara beauties of the fifteenth century painted by Leonardo, specifically Beatrice d'Este, the young wife of Ludovico il Moro. Evidently she's not, but she is splendid in any case, and caught the eye of the young cardinal around 1607. He made her an early cornerstone of his collection. I grew up in a house where a good reproduction hung on the dining-room wall.

Leonardo, whose paintings are rare as well as beautiful, is represented here by the portrait of an elegant musician who is holding a folded scrap of a musical score. Sandro Botticelli is included in the shape of his *Madonna of the Pavilion*, as well as a tondo of the Madonna and Child. There are many, many others of both the Italian and Flemish schools, including a portrait of the donor's cousin, St.

Charles, whose large eyes and extraordinarily oversized nose proclaim a family resemblance quite clearly. But perhaps the most cherished painting in the collection is an exquisite little still life by Michelangelo Caravaggio, displaying fruit and leaves in a basket against a plain buff-yellow background. *Natura morta* was a new art form at the time. It is said the beauty-struck cardinal spent years searching for a companion piece to hang opposite Caravaggio's work, but never satisfied himself that he had found a worthy companion for the work of the scallywag painter, who spent much of his life keeping a few jumps ahead of the authorities who wanted him for assorted crimes that included at least one murder.

There are a number of works by Jan Brueghel here, including a tiny *Mouse with Rose (Topolino, rose, farfalla e bruco)* that also features an exquisite caterpillar and a moth. Brueghel also presents lots of flowers and a version of Daniel in the Lions' Den that shows the prophet at the bottom of a pit, surrounded by two dozen gentle if fearsome beasts while he says his prayers, unmolested. A huge crowd is gathered on the precipice of the den, their eyes filled with awe at the wonder of it all.

One of the most extraordinary things in the collection is a tiny vitrine mounted on a small slab of green malachite. Between the bronze-gilt framed pieces of glass is a wavy lock of lovely blonde hair, bound together with two twists of gold wire. It is a relic of the famous beauty of Lucrezia Borgia, daughter of Pope Alexander VI and eventually the wife of the Duke of Ferrara, and the sister-in-law of the two famous d'Este girls, Isabella and Beatrice. Lucrezia has gotten a lot of bad press through the years. I for one feel that she has been maligned quite unjustly. It is nice to see that the cardinal with such good taste and interest in public benefaction has saved this token of her beauty for us to glimpse almost five hundred years after her untimely death at the age of thirty-six.

But not everything in the Ambrosiana is so old. The collection has expanded since the early centuries and now extends well into the later nineteenth century, stopping just short of the Impressionist and Expressionist work of the last century and a half. Though many of the painters here are not the most famous that we are used to viewing in the small but choice collections at the Metropolitan and National galleries, this place is worth far more than the single morning that you will probably be able to spare it when you come here.

So many things in Milan are named for Ambrose that his person deserves a word. Born in Trier (in what is now France) in AD 340, during the rather flashy days of the later Roman Empire, he came from an upper-class family. He was sent to Rome to receive a fashionable, classical education, mostly reading the authors that later became the mainstay of secular schools all over Europe, right up to the nineteenth century. While still a young man, he was appointed by the emperor to be prefect of Aemilia-Liguria, the area which then included Milan. This was at the time of the Arian conflict in the late fourth century. The death of the local bishop had wrought a great uproar among the divided Christians in Milan, and there were bloody battles in the streets. By this time Christianity was legal in the Roman Empire, and Ambrose was meant to keep order among all citizens—even if it meant clubbing them into line on occasion.

Ambrose went to the church, the largest public gathering place, to calm the sectarian quarrelers, both Orthodox and Arian. He spoke to all about being peaceful and brotherly toward each other. The people were so persuaded by the young magistrate's eloquence that they immediately elected him their bishop. The emperor was delighted that his appointee was so successful in keeping the public order. Over his own protests, Ambrose was rushed through all the liturgical and sacramental preparations in eight days (baptism, confirmation, ordination, and consecration), and became Bishop of Milan. He gave his wealth away for the good of the poor and was devoted to the plight of prisoners. He wept so copiously when hearing of the sins of those who confessed to him, that the penitents also burst into tears. He ended up scolding emperors Maximus and Theodosius for their un-Christian behavior, and wore himself out doing good works. Although he died in 397, Milano has never forgotten him in the ensuing 1,600 years.

We went to explore the Basilica of St. Ambrose (Ambrose dedicated the original building to saints Gervase and Protase), a Romanesque church that has been much remodeled over the centuries. The colors of marble on the ninth-century altar ciborium and the Roman sarcophagus of Stilicho from the fourth century are purple and green. Stilicho, an Arian Christian, was the last of the great Roman generals. He came to a distressing end, executed at the order of the inadequate emperor who owed his throne to Stilicho's skill as a general. There seems to be some confusion as to the location of his elaborately carved Roman coffin. We saw it in one location and found it listed in a guidebook as being in another. Perhaps the one is a copy of the other. In any case, it is a remarkable Roman carving with enough Christian symbolism to have protected it from being broken up by iconoclastic followers of Jesus in the early Dark Ages.

The largest area of antiquity in Milan is the huge *castello*. Within its vast perimeter there were originally storehouses and wells enough to keep a small army in health and vigor for years. In fact, it once withstood a French siege of three years, although the rest of the town had been occupied. In the end the French simply went home and the lords of Milan reasserted their proprietorship. Today it stands as a memorial to the Visconti who started building it in the 1350s. It was rebuilt by the Sforzas a hundred years later. Like much Italian military engineering, looking imposing was almost as important as being truly impregnable; hence, the wonderful cylindrical towers at the corners and the huge tower that dominates the city. It is better than 250 feet tall. This habit of letting form rule over function reached its zenith under Mussolini, when the Italian navy built the most beautiful flotilla of destroyers and light cruisers ever seen on the breast of the ocean. They were the fastest in the world and breathtaking to behold, but, since they were designed with minimal defensive armor plate and few anti-aircraft guns, they were all sunk very early in the war by ugly British torpedo bombers.

But the *castello* was indeed nearly impregnable and designed not just as a defensive structure. Dukes and their duchesses, such as Galeazzo Maria Visconti and the "protector" who co-opted his realm, Ludovico il Moro Sforza (male), used it as a palace and an administrative center of government. The enclosed space within the walls is so large that it served as a military parade ground for the whole Milanese army. Stabling was adequate to keep, for example, seventy horses for the personal use of one duchess and her escort.

The art gallery in the Castello Sforzesco is large and well provided with printed explanatory sheets that gave us a lot of information about the profusion of statues, paintings, and the wilderness of inlaid furniture in the great collection. There is a towering medieval knight on horseback perched on top of a sarcophagus, which is itself supported by a grove of columns and a marble base. The knight is Bernabò Visconti who, as it is said, "flourished" in the period between 1360 and 1390. He looks very fierce, quite calm and settled on his giant mount. The whole memorial assembly must be close to twenty feet tall. Bernabò ordered this rather startling monument to himself to decorate a church in Conca. The church was subsequently demolished, but the impressive monument was taken down and moved to the castello where it now resides. A few rooms away is Michelangelo's final work, the Rondanini Pietà, an unfinished statue of the Virgin and her dead Son that has the quality of a piece of contemporary sculpture. Partially carved limbs and at least one other face are still attached to the block of marble from which the master was eliciting his final image.

Funeral Monument
for Bernabo Visconti
at Castello Forzesca
ordered by himself
6 meters high

The long morning in the *castello* introduced us to lots of armor and weapons, sculptures covering several thousand years, and a wonderful collection of furniture from the last four or five centuries, some of local design, some Venetian, some French. The collection ends up with eighteenth-century beds, sedan chairs, and clocks. There are also gems like the clean and startling bust of *The Negress* by Cristoforo Lombardi, a stunning portrait of a strikingly beautiful black woman that was carved in the early sixteenth century, roughly contemporary with the work of Raphael and Michelangelo. But perhaps the most impressive sculpture here is the somewhat earlier work, such as the tomb effigy of Gastone di Foix, looking almost medieval stretched out on his marble mattress with pillows under his head. It is the work of Agostino Busti (also know as "il Bambaja"), who was a new acquaintance to us.

One of the sixteenth-century paintings that presents the paradox of Italian art is the mannerist painting of Figino, showing St. Ambrose in full attack mode, mounted on a warhorse, flourishing a torch in one hand and his crozier in the other. In spite of the conciliatory stance he seems to have taken before he became bishop, here he is presented as driving the Arians out of Milan. He scowls most fiercely and unpleasantly in the direction of the presumably retreating heretics.

But paintings are far from the only works of art in the *castello*. There is a major collection of majolica, numerous golden altar vessels, and lots of ivories, glassware, and musical instruments—altogether a very worthwhile morning.

We made a sentimental stop at the *duomo*, reflecting that this gigantic, spiny wonder is rather more beautiful outside than in. Still, the piazza is one of the best in Italy. One of the currently interdicted adventures of Milan is to take the combination of elevator and stairs to the roof of the nave. Walking across the sloping limestone slabs to the western face, we got a wonderful sight of the city, the piazza far below, and the distant tower of the *castello*. On our final day in Milan, we walked past the face of the cathedral and sought out Biffi, a pleasant, nay delightful tearoom–cocktail bar inside the great iron- and glass-roofed Galleria Vittorio Emanuele, which splendid space provides a sheltered *passeggiata* for the Milanese, come rain or shine. The Galleria was the most modern of architectural wonders in the early days of recently unified Italy in the 1870s. It is actually a set of four city blocks where the streets between are roofed over and crowned with the lacy glass dome eighty to a hundred feet overhead. The whole set of interior streets would seem to be three or four hundred meters in length. It is the ancestor of all the malls that bring shops and restaurants together under one roof. Perhaps because of its proximity to the cathedral, the neighborhood has never declined, and the shops, banks, boutiques, and restaurants in the Galleria are still among the most fashionable in Milan.

We haven't exhausted the artistic, musical, and culinary pleasures of Milan as yet. We've got to go back some spring now that the great theater of La Scala, its restoration complete, is in full swing, presenting both opera and concerts. Soon, we hope—but there are so many places to see in Italy.

A presto!

XII.

BERGAMO AND
THE CHURCH AT CREMA

Bergamo rears up from the north Italian plain, an old fortified site high on a rock where a concentration of historic and artistic gems make it one of the best places for tourists to visit along the flank of the great Po River. Despite the riches of the collections in its small space, it is not overcrowded with visitors from other countries. It seemed to us that most of the people in the museums and restaurants were Italian. Not surprising. Italians know their own country, and this part of it is ornamented with sculpture and painting, studded with history, and full of good food and wine. We had enjoyed a preliminary stop in Milan and thus found that Bergamo felt like a more ancient place, probably because the larger city had been rebuilt in the nineteenth century and reconstructed after the bombing of World War II. Bergamo is still quaintly furnished with towers that reach back to touch the Middle Ages. Its memorials recall the heroes of wars of the Renaissance and artists who flourished in the nineteenth century, as well as the partisans of the 1940s.

The town is divided into the Città Alta, a small medieval town on the crest of the prominence that commands a great view of the Po Valley to the south, and a more modern town which is gathered around the feet of old Bergamo above it. Down here the streets meet at right angles, a rarity in Italy.

Besides its hilltop, the original settlement is further defended by a massive rampart that circles the Città Alta outside the Viale delle Mura. There are a limited number of entries from below; really, only two. We took the Porta Sant'Agostino, through an archway that was narrow enough to admit up- and downhill traffic only alternately, with an elegant system of traffic lights designed to preclude head-on meetings where the oncoming traffic turns a corner as it enters a darkened archway. Once up the hill, we sought the location of our hotel, the Agnello d'Oro, The Golden Fleece. We were soon entrapped in a courtyard from which there seemed no escape; it was decorated with *senso unico* signs that prohibited motion in any direction. Helpful natives guided us out in various directions with cheerful, conflicting instructions. We managed to nearly circle the upper city before we decided to abandon the car in an unoccupied car park in the center of things. Providentially this location turned out to be across the street from the hotel. I am still not quite sure how we came upon it.

The Agnello d'Oro is a perfectly satisfactory little hostelry. Rated at a modest two stars, it is a remodeled seventeenth-century palazzo where our tidy room was almost dwarfed by the grandeur of the bathroom. The management seems to have first dibs on the parking places in the stone-flagged courtyard across the street, even though a sign indicates that overnight parking was not to be suffered by the town authorities. We left the rental car there for three days and were not molested. Between the *parcheggio* and the *albergo* there is an *enoteca* titled the Donizetti, where we had a pleasant lunch of a seafood salad and a *panino di prosciutto*. (Why is it that a ham sandwich sounds and is so much more delicious when translated into Italian?) One can feel quite distantly transported from home here, although less than a half day's journey from Newark, New Jersey.

Like all Italian towns, Bergamo offers a number of churches to be explored. The cathedral itself and the church of Santa Maria Maggiore surround the Piazza Duomo, together with Palazzo de Raggione, roughly the equivalent of the county courthouse. Here we found one of the most charming monuments we have ever encountered: the memorial to Gaetano Donizetti, the composer who left us the sprightly *Daughter of the Regiment*, the yearning of *The Elixir of Love*, and poor, mad *Lucia di Lammermoor* among his sixty operas. A sad, white-marble muse droops on top of the monument. Below her feet is a bas relief of five or six weeping cherubs who bemoan the loss of the master by casting down their lyres and smashing their flutes and tabors, useless now that the great composer is no more.

Next door is the cathedral, connected to the memorial chapel of Bartolomeo Colleoni. The little chapel presents an elegant wedding-cake style of Renaissance decoration, tucked into a corner of the medieval architecture of the church. Inside, a gilded statue of the mounted professional soldier struts his warhorse in front of a blue background. He is in the company of a serene, sleeping effigy of Medea, his favorite daughter, who predeceased him by seven years. The old man was deeply moved by her death and he commissioned the best sculptor he could find, Amadeo, to memorialize her.

Bartolomeo Colleoni lived from 1400 to 1476. He was a legendary warrior who worked for hire, usually for the Signori of Venice. Unlike most of the *condittori* of the *quattrocento*, he never double-crossed his paymasters to earn a higher fee from their enemies. He won all of his battles. The Venetians rewarded him with a huge salary and, most unusually, a commission as commander of their armies for life.[18] When he was on his deathbed, living in retirement in Bergamo, he counseled their ambassadors (who came to do him honor) never to give such power to any man again. "I could have done you much harm," he said, and then expired, leaving his huge fortune to the *Serenissima* from whence it had been derived, for he had no living heirs. The surprised Venetians were grateful for the largesse and also had a mounted statue cast in his memory. That one, in Venice itself, is by Verrocchio and stands in the Piazza Zanipolo, in front of the huge church of Saints Giovanni e Paolo. He looks quite ferocious in Venice, more noble in Bergamo.

The Piazza Duomo is a short climb up into the center of the town. It is ringed by shops, little restaurants, and bars. Along one side there is a great outdoor stair that gives access to a hall that housed an interesting collection of sculpture during our visit. The head of the stairway also gives a good view of the stone-flagged Piazza Vecchio. In the center of this splendid public space is the wonderfully ancient Contarini Fountain, where three small pools are surrounded by a set of small sphinxes, serpents, and lions. But what lions! We were familiar with Wiligelmo's massive, cheerful beasts whose backs support the columns of the porticoes of the cathedral doorways at Modena. We had also seen the great brutes that flank the facade of Pedrocchio's classical coffeehouse in Padua. But these Bergamasque lions are something else. They are sized like domestic dogs and have the sweet expression of contented house pets, holding the chain that circles the fountain in their teeth, happily begging a pat on the head from the passersby.

A brief shower of rain forced us to take refuge in the Caffè Tasso for an *aperitivo*. The day's excursion eventually included three or four

---

[18] The Venetians almost never fought their own wars, preferring to hire the lusty warriors from other parts of Italy to wield the sword for them. They paid very well, presumably to lessen the possibility of bribery and treachery.

churches and a chance meeting with an articulate and gracious art history professor, Joan Bernstein, from Mills College in California. She pointed out to us the frescoes that Tiepolo had done for one of the ceilings we were walking under. Later we found an old *trattoria* with coral tablecloths and ancient graffiti on the ceiling. We reveled in the *polenta taragna*, a local specialty which included rabbit, chicken, and veal slices, each in a different sauce, with porcini mushrooms. There were two distinctly different polentas, one plain and one made with Branzi, a most special cheese of Lombardia. The waitress was very pleased with our choice, evidently a matter of local patriotism. We topped it off with new spring strawberries with lemon juice and a touch of sugar.

We set out on the following day to explore the Città Basso on foot. We were told that the trip was all downhill and we could find our way back via the funicular. The descent was along a cobbled, narrow

path that brought us back to the Porta Sant'Agostino and eventually onto the flat land of the Città Basso, where we found the Accademia Carrara. It is now the municipal museum of Bergamo. The original academy was founded by the Count Giacomo Carrara, who set up the museum to house his own private collection of artwork and a school of painting in the late eighteenth century. When he died in 1796 he willed it all to a foundation to be maintained for the use of the town. After a century and a half, the city council took it over and looks after almost two thousand paintings, as well as drawings and prints. The original building provided by the good count has been enlarged over time, but the facade unifies it all behind a lovely pale-buff and gray neoclassical set of four columns and a dental pediment that reminded me of something Thomas Jefferson might have derived from the books of Andrea Palladio.

The portrait of Carrara, the *fondatore*, although contemporary with our retrospective paintings of the American Revolution, is presented in a steel cuirass and a velvet throw over his shoulders, giving him the look of a grandee of the age before the invention of gunpowder. I suppose it is no more anachronistic than Jean-Antoine Houdon's version of George Washington pretty much mother-naked under his Roman toga. But despite the time warp of the costume, I have to hand it to Giacomo. He made a great gesture to the people of his post-revolutionary time and inspired a host of followers to continue the enrichment of the public institution he set up two centuries ago. The collection is a rich one. Vivarini, Botticelli, Pisanello, and Donatello are all here. There are paintings by Jacopo Bellini, his sons Giovanni and Gentile, and his son-in-law, Andrea Mantegna. The younger Bellini's *Madonna di Alzano* with its distant vistas in the background and a ripe pear on the balustrade also presents as lovely a Virgin as the fifteenth century provides. Bellini signed this work with a painted trompe l'oeil label tacked to the spandrel, giving his name in Latin. Carpaccio, Morone, and Crivelli are also well represented among the *quattrocento* painters here.

Fast-forward a century and you will also find works here by Lorenzo Lotto and Titian, El Greco and Raffaello. The collection extends to dreamy Venetian water scenes by Francesco Guardi and some lovely canvases of the late nineteenth century. There is nothing here from the last century, but the whole is a catalog of beauty that reaches back through the recent ages. Perhaps the most charming is the work of Giovanni Battista Moroni who was a local talent in Bergamo in the sixteenth century. His *Ritratto di bambina*, a portrait of a little girl, reveals a solemn-faced five-year-old wearing a richly brocaded rose-colored gown, a dainty white ruff, and a scattering of pearls in her necklace, her earrings, and the ribbon that secures her Pebbles Flintstone hairdo. The amazing thing about the painting is that the child looks completely confident and comfortable in the museum-piece costume.

We left the Accademia Carrara and walked farther down into the Città Basso, until we eventually found one of those archetypically Italian places to eat quite well for very little, a neighborhood bar. While waiting for our order of *insalata di tonno* with bread and butter, we looked about the half-dozen tables. At one there was a dignified man with a disfiguring growth on his nose. His security and presence reminded us of Ghirlandaio's old man with the cancerous deformation of his nose, smiling at his grandson who is returning an approving smile. The Italians seem to have internalized the Christian belief that the afflicted are somehow more beloved by God than those of us not so put in the way of derision, avoidance, or scorn.

Lunch and a glass of white wine restored our will to explore, so that we could work our way through several churches and pleasant nineteenth-century squares on our way to the foot of the funicular that took us back up to the rim of the Città Alta, just down the street from the little fountain-adorned square at the entry to the Agnello d'Oro.

Later I followed the signs pointing the way to the Rocca, where I found the heroic remains of the great fortress that allowed Bergamo to dominate the area in the Middle Ages. Unoccupied now, it serves as an almost inaccessible public park and a site for monuments to the memory of those who died when the Italians turned on the Germans in the final year of World War II. It is a place of solemn stillness, surrounded by the towers of the churches that sprout up from the old town beneath. There were three or four other visitors on the Rocca that sunny May afternoon, but it still seemed a lonely place.

Perhaps Bergamo's greatest contribution to the arts is its primal role in the Commedia dell'Arte, the immensely popular improvisational theater that flowered here in the sixteenth century. This extraordinary early form of modern drama had a significant influence on Shakespeare and Molière, Lope de Vega and Goldoni. The plays generally began with an improvisation known as an *imbroglio*, in which the members of the company acted and made up their lines according to their stock character. Prominent were Harlequin, the valet who spoke pure Bergamasque (ancestor of Figaro); Pantaleone, a merchant of Venice; Columbine, the lively lady's maid who marries the best zany in the end; the learned quack doctor from Bologna; and the lovers who spoke elegant high Tuscan. It must have been a startling babble of local tongues, but then, as now, Italians could understand many languages besides the dialect they used at home. They mocked their neighbors, such as Scaramouche (from Naples), and threw themselves about a simple platform stage doing prearranged tricks (known as *lazzi*), and always providing fun and a happy ending. Commedia troops traveled all over Europe for several hundred years and surely provided the structure of Mozart and da Ponte's *Marriage of Figaro*. It all began in Bergamo.

On our final night in Bergamo we went back to the Caffè Tasso for the cocktail stop required to space dinner late enough to accommodate the schedule of a good Italian *ristorante*. There we met an English couple similarly occupied; he was a professor of mathematics from Hertfordshire doing a two-week lecture visit at the University of Bergamo. We parted company to seek other dining spots, but, both being frustrated by day-off closing of our intended places, by chance wound up at adjoining tables at Il Cantinone, where the proprietor dedicated himself to our gastronomic education. He served us many small portions of most of the things on his menu; polenta with dainty sausages, tortellini with an eggplant sauce, Gorgonzola gnocchi, veal, chicken, and pork slices, and not a smidge of salad or greenery. Despite the lack of vitamins, it was delicious. The accompanying conversation in English was a nice change, until we bid our companions farewell as they departed for Venice and we prepared to go to Piacenza on the morrow.

We left this pleasant town and, abandoning the Autostrada, headed south across the grain of the country. In an hour we passed through the outskirts of the town of Crema and almost went by a midsize basilica. It was such an intriguing building that we stopped, backed up, and dismounted to explore and photograph it. It turned out to be named Santa Maria Della Croce, and that day, featured an accomplished organist practicing inside. There was a scattering of small chapels and side altars with ornate decoration, and one obviously significant shrine under the center altar. For an investment of 500 lire, a coin-in-slot machine produced the story of the origin of the church in any one of four languages. The tale is one of the mixture of cruelty and sweetness that seems so common in Italian stories: A young man who was already wanted for murder took his bride into the woods to steal her jewelry and do her in as well. As he struck at her, she raised her arm defensively and her hand was cut off. The miserable desperado ran off, and the girl cried out to Santa Maria to come to her aid. An old woman appeared and took her by the arm, which immediately stopped bleeding, bringing her to a nearby hut. Villagers found her there on the following morning and nursed her until she expired quite peacefully on the following day, in her prayers forgiving her terrible husband. A cross was erected at the spot of the attack in the woods. It became a site of devotion, and when a crippled boy asked his mother to take him there to pray, the defining miracle took place and the lad was cured. The village responded by building this large and splendid church. Crema is a small town today, and the amount of the public wealth that was put to this end is impressive by any standard.

We were joined by a young Italian who lacked change for the recorded lecture and who spoke no English. We were quite out of coins by now, and his interest resulted in my recitation of the grisly tale of faith, treachery, and devotion. I did my best in halting Italian, and he suffered my language patiently. He seemed particularly impressed with the forgiving spirit of the uncanonized saint, and very grateful to us for the translation. We waved good-bye to each other as he mounted his delivery van and sped off in the direction of Milano.

XIII.

NAMING THE BAMBINO

When it comes to naming their children, Italians have had a hard time with their military and political heroes through the centuries. Julius Caesar, and Augustus who followed him, turned out to have destroyed the Roman Republic. Most of the later Caesars were contemptible brutes, and not a few were mad. After their time, the records of the next few centuries of Roman history are lost in the mists of legend, but the Gothic, Vandal, and Langobard leaders were surely a rough bunch. Names like Alboin, Zotto, Liutprand, or Grimoald are not heard much today.

The early popes were acknowledged to be holy fellows and often martyred, but it is hard to name your firstborn for Anacletus, Zephyrinus, Simplicius, or Symmachus. After Constantine they soon became the real political (and often military) leaders of the fifth, sixth, and seventh centuries. All are listed as saints, even if next to nothing is known about most of them. I have wondered what dreadful activities can be attributed to Boniface II, whose pontificate ran from 532 to 535. Nearly half a millennium after St. Peter, he is the first acknowledged legitimate pontiff not to be accorded the title of "Saint." From then on that designation becomes considerably more rare. In fact, after the death of St. Pope Nicholas I in 867, there followed seventy-eight successors to the Holy See, only one of whom (St. Gregory VII) was ever declared to be indisputably among the blessed. That was Pope St. Gregory X, who died in 1276 and was recorded as the next one to have definitely died with the aura of sanctity.

Frederick II Hohenstaufen, who lived mostly in the twelfth century, was born in Sicily and eventually ruled virtually all of Italy, and most of Germany as well. He was the grandson of the crusading Frederick Barbarossa Hohenstaufen, and was a man of extraordinary ability, intelligence, cruelty, and sexual appetite. He seems to have been most often on the side of the angels in Italy, but politically he was not on the side of several popes who, although they seldom defeated him in the field, pulled out the canonical heavy artillery and had him declared a heretic and an excommunicate. But there have been so many Fredericks (Federigos) in European history (thirty royal or imperial enough to merit inclusion in my small encyclopedia) that it is hard to figure out which one is honored when a child receives the name. Someone that was a hero, for sure. I think this Sicilian devotee of hawking and friend of Islamic and Jewish scholars won the battle of popular history with the Holy See.

The intellectual, political, and military leaders who ruled during the nineteenth century, and throughout the upheavals that resulted in the *Risorgimento*, were too mixed a bag as heroes to hold up as role models for the young. Mazzini, Cavour, Garibaldi, and the earlier apparition of Lord Byron all displayed a certain lack of filial piety or moral probity that made it a risky business to name one's *bambino* after any of them. (Streets and public squares were another matter, however.)

Perhaps as a result of a plethora of such leaders, the Italians seeking their mythic identity have for years turned to the saints of the church. Joseph and Mary (Giuseppe and Maria) are the most common names given to children to this day, although Mary is often embellished with the name Rose. Americans' cyclic fascination with Kimberly, Kelly, Karen, Kyle, and Kevin must astonish most Italians, especially since their alphabet lacks the letter K.

But how sensible the old-fashioned choices are! Politicians seem always to fail as models of heroism. Generals have always been risky; they often prosecuted the wrong cause or the wrong side (with the exception of Montefeltro of Urbino, another Federigo, the one with the notch chopped out of his nose). Just consider Benito Mussolini, surely the most popular Italian leader of last century, who, after a promising start, turned out to be a moral disaster. No; apostles, martyrs, and penitents are safer mythic personalities to look up to. Exceptions can be made for Dante, his Beatrice, or the great and kindly lady of the house of Este in Ferrara, Isabella. People who loved a lot (like la Madelena) are best of all.

A nice thing about Italian saints is that they seem quite like the Italian people, which is not to say that Italians are particularly saintly in their daily lives. But their spiritual heroes, canonized by the Catholic Church, seem generally friendly, gentle, not very aggressive, and, unlike the blessed of other nations, not fanatical. This is in stark contrast with the Spanish, who have venerated Sant Iago Matomoro (Saint James the Moor Slayer), who presumably lasted long enough to be both an apostle in the first century and a scourge of the Muslims sometime after the origin of Islam in the seventh.

The English have a canonized king, Edward, while the French have Louis, also a monarch and a warrior, among their most popular. Sir Thomas More was a humanist to be sure, but also a royal chancellor and a burner of Lutheran heretics; thus, a riskier popular exemplar of modern British virtue. The English often let their royals pick

out names for their next generation of children, which explains the
spate of Alberts a century ago. Now there are lots of Dianas and no
Edwards (since Number Eight, who abdicated to marry an American
divorcee).

The Italians, by contrast, seem to have beatified few if any
political leaders and hold the gentle Francis (or Francesca) most
dear, next to Mary. They greatly love Catherine of Siena, who prayed
so hard it is said that she rose several feet off the floor, managed to
convince the pope to come back to Rome from Avignon for a while,
and nursed the sick poor, who suffered from "the most revolting
diseases." Giorgio rescued maidens from dragons. Perhaps most of
all, they depend on kind and eloquent Anthony of Padua, the patron
of the poor, the travelers, childless women, and the legendary finder
of lost objects.[19]

Along with their saints, the Italians venerate their artists. Tiziano
and Raffaello are buried in Venetian and Roman churches in tombs
that would do honor to a martyr or a king in any other culture.
Giuseppe Verdi is much revered. When Federico Fellini died, that
robust nonbeliever was buried at an almost pontifical requiem
mass. I wonder if he will someday be memorialized with a marble
sarcophagus in his hometown cathedral.

Some Italian choices for little boys' baptismal names might strike
English speakers as falling somewhere between the sublime and the
ridiculous; for example, two that grew up to be famous musicians:

---

[19] When a sometime golfer in my youth, I learned to pledge 25 cents to St. Anthony
when a drive sliced into the rough. The bargain had to be struck as an act of faith before
you left the tee. The saint, after all, had to be given a fighting chance and not be called
upon only when the odds were down after a five-minute human search had proved
fruitless. This method was never known to fail.

Arcangelo Corelli and Muzio Clementi.

Anyway, it is certain that there will be many more Federicos and Federicas in future generations of Italians. And since there are fewer Italians who are actually practicing Catholics in an era when the pope has created a huge number of saints, it would seem that for the young, nonbelieving parents, there must be other possibilities to pursue. We know of one young Italian man named Leonardo for the scientific spirit of the man from Vinci, and another lovely girl given the originally Arabic name of a star: Altaira. Her sister, however, has the archetypically Italian honor of being known as Beatrice, the perfect girl-child worshipped by Dante.

And who cannot understand the pride with which an Italian mother names her newborn son Massimo: the greatest!

PART III

THE TYRRHENIAN COAST AND WEST

XIV.

LIGURIA:
The Home of Pesto

The northwest coast of Italy is cut off from the rest of the country by coastal Apennine mountains, but looks as though it should be quite easily approached from the French Riviera or, quite obviously, from the sea. Its centers of population have all been seaport cities since the beginnings of time. Because there were special fares from home to the second-largest French airport, Nice Côte d'Azur, we decided to come in from the west. Since all of these countries are members of the European Union, there are no border checkpoints to be navigated. The only difference between Italy and France would seem to be that a shiny new Renault Clio rented in France was a bit less expensive because the Italian branch of Auto Europe insists on collision-damage insurance and the same company trusts your gold Visa card to cover it if you start in France. We escaped Nice via the inevitable maze of airport roads continually subjected to reconstruction—something that seems to be inflicted on all countries. We sped to the east with blue bays down below the Autoroute along the shore on our right. We made rapid progress except for a worrying moment at a tollgate when I remembered that we had no francs, only a few leftover lire to give to the pretty attendant in the booth.

She asked if we had a card, accepted my Visa, handed me a receipt, and waved us through with a ravishing smile.

I had often wondered why Hannibal went so far to the north into the Alps before crossing into Italy when he came this way in 250 BC, instead of taking a pleasant stroll along the beaches of the Riviera. Taking the modern French Autoroute or its connecting Autostrada in Italy made it clear. There are dozens of mountainous fingers of rocky ridges stretching down to the cliffs along the sea. Today the narrow valleys and near-vertical ridges are pierced by dozens of tunnels, some quite long, others measuring only a few meters. The cliff faces where they emerge are far too precipitous to urge elephants or men up to the summit or down the other side without the possibility of some dreadful disaster. The Carthaginians surely had enough trouble around the Val Chisone or the Val di Susa, fifty kilometers inland, where they most probably got through the mountains, somewhat higher than at the coastal ranges, but presenting less-rugged topography approaching the high valleys and passes. Along the coast road there are about forty tunnels between the airport in Nice and the small Italian city of Imperia, which was our destination.

We chose Imperia as a first-night stop because it would give us a short first excursion after the usual sleepless night on the airplane from the American South and a hectic change of planes and airports between Gatwick and Heathrow, where sheep graze in the English countryside. It turned out to be a drive of about an hour and a half from the airport to Porto Maurizio, the western sector of Imperia. This and Oneglia used to be separate towns divided by a torrente, a shallow stream that can become a serious river when the Alpine snowpack melts in the spring. Mussolini decreed that a bridge be built between the two towns and settled the rivalry of the new town's name by calling the amalgamation "Imperia."

We had selected a hotel, the Corallo, by faith in the Tuttitalia guide, the sensible handbook of accommodations published by Gambaro Rosso. It proved to be a good choice, even though parking in front of the hotel seemed impossible. Being used to Italy by this time, we ran two wheels up on a neighboring sidewalk and left the car more or less off the street, although slightly at a tilt. The hotel manager later inspected this arrangement and decreed it to be quite satisfactory. Our room faced the Ligurian Mediterranean, and from a small balcony we looked down at a patch of sand, some cabanas, and a pebbly beach where modest surf broke into stunning white banners over the tops of the deep blue swells that rolled in from the restless sea to the south. To the northeast, just visible by a neck-stretch from our balcony, there was an extensive seawall that protected the two harbors—one for yachts and the other for a few large commercial fishing vessels. Yet even in March, this part of the Mare Ligure is studded with hardy souls in wet suits who compete with each other on Windsurfers with red, white, and bright-green sails. It was obvious that summer on the Italian Riviera must be both pleasant and crowded.

The hotel was perched on a cliff over the ocean, and our room, one flight below the reception, was still three floors above the beach access and the restaurant. Being well out of sync with local time, we decided to dine at home, and were pleased to find that the *pizzeria-ristorante* offered an extensive menu from which we chose linguini with shrimp, various versions of zucchini with tomato, and finally, a grilled red snapper with a bit of eggplant. We reflected that it was nice to be back in Italy where the simplest supper is quite often a Lucullan feast.

This part of the Italian coast is noted for its production of both olive oil and flowers. Signs of the Riviera dei Fiori had been visible all along our route from France. There were dozens of greenhouses beside the highway, facing south where they could gather light and warmth in the winter months and nurture a great harvest of flowers to be shipped north to the markets of Paris and London. The olive trees are prettier than the metal-and-glass structures that house the roses and snapdragons. But olive oil also requires the hand of man and his machines to make it available to us. The process is both old and arduous. At the hotel desk we found elegantly printed brochures describing olive culture from the Museo dell'Olivo, an interesting and extensive institution in Oneglia, the eastern half of the double town of Imperia. Built and sponsored by the Fratelli Carli, the Olive Tree Museum turned out to be quite wonderfully informative. We learned, for example, that Athena and Poseidon, god of the sea, disputed as to who should rule Attica. Zeus decreed that the dominion should go to the one who gave the greatest gift to mankind. Poseidon beat the waves into foam with his trident, and his horse leapt out of the sea to the land. He claimed victory because the horse is greatly useful both in war and peace. But Athena offered the sapling of an olive tree, telling the gods that the twisted little plant would grow to everlasting life and give mankind shade, warmth, medicine, ointment, perfume, light, food, and condiment. She obviously won the contest, and her tree became the symbol of the goddess of wisdom and her city, Athens, the place where she was worshipped.

Finding the Museo required a couple of reversals and, finally, a request for directions from a woman carrying a load of laundry balanced on her head. She understood and answered my Italian with dignity and the manners of a duchess; we had come too far and must go back to the driveway just before the corner.

The museum exhibits point out that the wild olive, originally small, bitter, and almost devoid of oil, was cultivated all around the Mediterranean from 4000 BC. By 2000 BC, selective cultivation had made it juicier, and ointments and perfumes were being made from the squeezing of the fruit. By the high point of the Greek and Phoenician civilizations, olive oil was being made and shipped all over the great inland sea to the newly sprung cities, where it was required both for cooking oil and lamp fuel. Today it continues to be a major export of Italy and Spain. What would a salad be without it?

There were examples of all the stages of olive oil production, from the stone-rolling mills that reduced the olives to a paste, to the presses that made the greenish-golden liquid flow into reservoirs for bottling. There were examples of all these tools, both ancient and modern, as well as a mock-up of the hold of a first-millennium ship packed with the pottery amphorae that were used to contain the precious fluid. The extensive lesson was completed by the presentation of a small bottle of the oil. We brought it home for a salad, noting that the Carli Brothers who sponsor the museum gave away samples of good oil, but not the very best extra-virgin oil that we favor. (On the other hand, it *was* a free gift.)

Back in Porto Maurizio, we stashed the car after lunch and set out to walk the streets to the cathedral and the Museo Navale Internazionale del Ponente Ligure, which translates as the "International Naval Museum of Western Liguria." It turned out to be a reasonable climb with wonderful views of the sea at each turning of the road, as well as glimpses of the well-tended backyard gardens that are the delightful characteristic of any Italian town. If a family has ten square meters at their disposal, they will fill it with fresh vegetables of all sorts. If they have twenty, they will also grow grapes and make their own wine.

The square at the summit had the *duomo* in pale-yellow stucco on one side and the town hall and *questura* in matching color on the other. The church was modest and attractive, but I admit to being distracted by a great horde of the *polizia* in full-dress uniform with various cars and emergency vans. I never did figure out what event they were rehearsing. We left them possession of the piazza sounding occasional choruses from their brass band while we sought out the Museo Navale. That institution turned out to be on the third floor of the Palazzo Pubblico, the town hall (also in pale-yellow stucco), and up long flights of stairs. The rooms at the top were sequenced by hand-drawn arrows on pieces of white cardboard that routed us through an extraordinary collection of ship models and fascinating maritime junk that varied from twelve-foot facsimiles of mid-twentieth century ocean liners to some of the elegant destroyers of the Italian navy that were sunk by British torpedo bombers in the early months of World War II. There were diving suits, gyroscopic compasses, mysterious marine machines whose utility I could not fathom, and as large a collection of ship models as I have ever seen in one place. It spanned examples from the Renaissance to the modern era.

In the process of exploring the museum, we happened on the director of the museum, Comandante Flavio Serafini, whose name seems a nice combination of the power of the Roman Empire and the angelic choirs of the later history of Italy. He explained that this attic of naval history is soon to be moved to larger quarters near the shoreline below, where it will also be more accessible to both scholars and tourists. In any case, the collection is worth a detour for any sailor who passes through Liguria. We exchanged cards, and I promised to bring his good wishes to the Mystic Seaport Museum where I volunteer in the summer. The mention of Mystic brought out rapid and cheery greetings in just barely understandable Italian, and a couple of copies of a Columbus poster to bring home and deliver to his counterpart at Mystic.

We walked down a precipitous *scala* and eventually got to the oceanfront, where we found a side-street pizzeria that provided a fine supper. When we asked the waitress about a less-vertical route back to the Corallo (which by now was fifty or sixty feet above us, about halfway back to the museum), she set out to show us the way by walking along the pretty brick *lungomare* with us. We eventually sent her back with great thanks. That Italian helpfulness and courtesy keeps showing up wherever we go.

Genoa, or rather, Gen-*o*-va, as it is pronounced in this country, is in the center of the arc of Liguria, a city strung out along the curve of the shore, backed up by close inland mountains and seemingly possessed of virtually no level ground. It is the largest port in the Mediterranean, a rank it has held since the maritime republic shared the honors with its rival, Venice, in the twelfth and thirteenth centuries. It has an excellent natural harbor, an advantage which put it ahead of *La Serenissima* in the sixteenth century, when the discoveries of its adoptive favorite son, Cristoforo Colombo, and others caused a redirection of shipping, and the spice trade began to enter the Mediterranean from the West rather than from the Levant.

We saw this ancient and interesting town at a touch less than its best. In an attempt to avoid the most traffic-clogged entry, we came in from the east and were easily able to reach the Stazione Brignole, which seems to be a good point of entry to the area of hotels. The Brignole is a handsome building of a Beaux-Artes style, reminiscent of a combination of the facade of the Metropolitan Museum in New York and Grand Central Station. From this logical location, a chaos of redirected traffic and torn-up streets ensued. Genova was preparing for great events in the new century; and thus, streets, avenues, water mains, electrical conduits, and other mysterious subterranean vessels were being operated on by crews of leisurely laborers who keep at their tasks in a desultory fashion, right through the evening until well after midnight. All the directions we received to find the Hotel Viale Sauli were thwarted by temporary signs forbidding our entrance. The little Clio climbed part of the medieval walls of the city and descended an almost-perpendicular cobblestone reentry to the quarter we sought. An agreeable English-speaking man with a bemused attitude tried to give us directions to find our way back to the Viale Sauli.

"Well now, this is going to be difficult," he began with a grin, and then proceeded to give us precise and clear directions. We found, however, that on that very day, the *senso unico* (one-way) signs on the neighboring streets had been temporarily reversed. We plunged on, violated various city ordinances, and found ourselves behind several other cars trying to traverse the courtyard of no less than three *lycei* (high schools), both classical and technical, all of whose students and faculty were leaving early for the weekend on Friday. No one had any intention of giving way to a French-licensed car on their school property. I could see an exit that went in our direction not twenty meters ahead, but we eventually had to wait for four or five hundred students and a fair gathering of their teachers, some on motorcycles, to pass through before we could make the turn. Down the hill and into the viale, we saw the sign for our hotel. Since the end of the street was blocked by an excavation, I parked comfortably in the middle of the street and went into the hotel. There we found a gracious and capable *padrone* who carried our bags and then seized the key to deposit the car in a neighboring garage. He also pointed out the Ayers Rock Australian Cafe, which turned out to be a *pizzeria-ristorante* decorated by a large color picture of the great landmark of the Australian outback. Two hours after we had found the Stazione Brignole, we were quite hungry and felt quite at home.

The Sauli was a midsize, comfortable hotel and charged us a bit less than $75 a night in the then-prevailing low season. We set forth to inspect the town. We soon realized that our three-day stay would allow us only a superficial tour of Genova, but would include the flavor of the town nevertheless. We progressed through the classically styled nineteenth-century Ponte Monumental and proceeded up the Via XX Settembre inside of a great series of colonnades that sheltered sidewalks paved with large, golden-orange terrazzo squares ornamented here and there with mosaic fish and dolphins. If the whole city is a bit run-down, it has an air of past elegance, and we saw signs of recrudescence and rebuilding all around us. We shortly reached the Palazzo Ducale, the classical site of the power and authority of the ruler of the maritime republic. We were disappointed to see the usual signs of reconstruction, but optimistically entered the lowest level of the palace, following some encouraging posters. We eventually learned that the Ducale had no collections of artwork of its own, but puts on exhibitions of paintings and other *objets d'art* that they borrow from other institutions.

And what a collection of borrowed paintings and documents they had brought together! There were paintings from Corot and Carracci to Titian and English watercolorists of the nineteenth century. There were letters of the great personalities of the Renaissance, from Pietro Bembo to Isabella d'Este, and a little vitrine enclosing in crystal a lock of Lucrezia Borgia's famed blonde hair.[1]

I was as excited to see the letters and books as the drawings and paintings. After the original Johannes Gutenberg, the next most

---

[1] As mentioned in chapter 11, we had a chance to see this memento of the famous papal daughter's loveliness a second time in the Ambrosiana Library in Milan, to which it had been returned when the show was changed in Genoa. Considering Lucrezia's fame, it is not surprising that a number of cities would want to exhibit the relic.

famous printer and publisher of the Renaissance was the Italian, Aldo Minuzzio, who established his Aldine Press in Venice before 1490, all his books marked with the colophon of the dolphin curled about an anchor. In the last years of the fifteenth century, he established a tradition of intellectual liberty that kept the strictures of the papal censors and the newly founded Inquisition at bay. Here was a perfect of copy of his *Hypnerotomachia Poliphili*, a book concerning an erotic dream whose typeface, original at the time, remains in use today, five hundred years later, looking as clear and legible as ever.

Nearby was a manuscript copy of *The Book of the Courtier* by Baldassare Castiglione, the behavior guide for the "Renaissance Man." There were also life portraits of Niccolo Machiavelli and the historian Francesco Guicciardini, whose works describe the horrifying sack of Rome by the Burgundian French and Germans in 1523. From this same period were letters from Isabella d'Este in her own elegant italic hand, and letters from her correspondents.

I have a long-standing interest in the career of Lord Nelson and his famous affair with Emma Hart Hamilton, the beautiful if lowborn wife of the British ambassador to the Kingdom of the Two Sicilies. She was often painted by George Romney,[2] who was enchanted by her beauty. Here we found one portrait of Emma by Romney and another by a painter named Hugh Douglas Hamilton, who represented her as the classical Three Graces, fully clothed, all at the same time in the same canvas. Was the painter a relative of Sir William? There were paintings here arranged from the sixteenth

---

[2] Some said he was so "besotted with her beauty" that all women he painted later looked just like Emma . . .

century to the nineteenth century, hung in small rooms where they were observable at close range without the competition of hordes of other viewers.

Somewhat drugged on the combination of the Italian triumphs of the Renaissance and the conquests of the early phases of the British Empire, we emerged into the square that fronted on the opera house which was, unfortunately, dark of any gig while we were in Genoa.

There were, however, a number of other sights to behold. Genoa has a world-class aquarium recently constructed on a waterfront pier. We reached it by bus and managed to dodge most of the groups of schoolchildren who were pressing the patience of their chaperones to get in and see everything as quickly as possible. Besides the usual exhibits of beluga whales and medium-sized sharks, this impressive collection had a good number of harbor seals and penguins to be seen, as well as various fish and marine mammals.

The Via Garibaldi was obviously named something else in the sixteenth century, when it was the site of the palaces of the greatest Genovese families who had grown rich on the extensive trade of the maritime republic. Two of these magnificent houses are the Palazzo Bianco and the Palazzo Rosso, the Red and White palaces. Both are museums today, and although the Red has more lavish contents than the White, both are worth visiting. One of the more startling portraits in the Rosso is that of the tough old admiral, Andrea Doria, who managed to turn back the Saracen fleet in various Mediterranean wars from 1530 to 1560. In the process he became the dictator of the city, even though he kept the forms of the republic intact. Peter Paul Rubens painted him as the protector of Genoa, presenting an allegory of the city in the form of a rather amazed young woman of very fair skin who seems to be sitting in the old warrior's armored lap while they both fondle his helmet. His free arm and hand encircle her neck and clutches her right breast as he stares into her face. Various cupids and a leering Bacchus join the two in the canvas.

The *duomo* of Genova originated in heaven knows what era. It was rebuilt around 1100 in the black-and-white-striped fashion that later became the favorite style of Pisa and Siena. Dedicated to San Lorenzo, it is an imposing structure with a pleasing irregularity of design. It has various oddities on the outside, including a sundial entangled with a medieval knife grinder, whose sculpture is one of the very few secular images in this statue-studded city. An early tradition of ornamenting the corners of buildings here with small statues of the Virgin led to some competition among the great families, who strove to commission the finest images of the Madonna in various parts of the city. They are generally at the second-story level, and you have to look up to find these charming works of art.

There is plenty to see in Genoa. Any city which has collected such wealth for so long a time is worth far more than the three-and-a-half-day stay we were able to allow it. Perhaps a return during the opera and ballet season would be a sensible plan.

Immediately south of Genoa are a series of interesting small cities and towns, connected to each other by railroad and good second-class highways that stretch all the way to La Spezia, the principal Italian naval base on the Ligurian Sea. About midway along this pretty stretch of the Italian Riviera is the charming small city of Chiavari, which had been recommended to us by an Italian oceanographer as a base from which to explore the whole area. We set forth to find it.

XV.

CHIAVARI:
A Comfortable Base for Visiting the Cinque Terre

By judicious use of e-mail and surface post, we acquired a brochure to research this town before we embarked. It was unknown to us, and not even listed in the index of the Lonely Planet guidebook. The center page of the modest *opuscolo* bore a few illustrations of the "beautiful people" enjoying the town, among them a snapshot of the late Duke of Windsor and his American wife, Wallis Warfield Simpson, skulking quietly under a colonnade. Although we met no celebrities during our stay, we felt that they could have easily popped out of any of a number of the *trattorie* that graced the narrow streets of the town. They certainly would not go wrong making this charming little city their next haunt.

Seeking less than royal accommodation, we had booked ourselves into the Albergo Monte Rosa, which was surprisingly easy to find when we descended toward the shore from the alternately elevated and tunneled route of the coastal road of Liguria. Olga, the receptionist, was pretty, formal, and efficient, but also absolutely insistent that we postpone our plan to find a modest restaurant for dinner. We simply must sign on instead for the Monte Rosa's once-a-month Saturday-night special, a gourmet's delight, the *Serata del Bongustaio*. It required about $40 to subject the two of us to what turned out to be an elegant exercise. The price for dinner with wine would just about pay for a modest supper in Wilmington, North Carolina, or barely cover the cost of lunch for two in Connecticut.

Ristorante Monte Rosa
SERATA DEL BUONGUSTAIO
Aperitivo con stuzzichini caldi
Polpo pressato agli aromi con gamberetti marinati e insalatine novelle
Pappardelle al rosmarino al sugo tipico d'agnello e timo
Trancio di dentice in crosta de olive con calamaretti saltati e piccole vedure
Crème brûlée ai fiori d'arcioconcroccantezze
La sorpresa del Maitre

VINI
Degustazione: Prosecco de Valdobbiadene
Pigato Az. Masseretti
Moscato

Illycaffé e Digestivi[3]

Despite diligent note-taking, I am unable to recall what the Chef's Surprise was for dessert. It was surely, like everything else, delicious, as were even the wafer-thin slices of octopus. The whole experience was a matter of being engulfed in a gastronomic ballet.

──────────

[3] Epicurean Evening:
Hot Hors d'oeuvres (on toothpicks!)
Garlic-Flavored Octopus with Salted Shrimp
Ribbon Pasta with Rosemary in Sauce of Lamb and Thyme
Slices of Olive-Crusted Squid with Tender Vegetables
Crème brulee with the Archbishop's Crust
The Chef's Surprise
Wines, both red and white, cordials, and Illy Coffee

The sense of it being like a musical composition was accentuated by the striking fact that one of the elderly waiters was an exact double of Arturo Toscanini.

Although the dining room was crowded with patrons, it appeared to us that we were the only non-Italians in the room. The *Serata del Buongustaio* would seem to be a secret well kept from most of the foreign tourist trade. In fact, the whole of Chiavari seemed innocent of the American and German, or even English, tourists that we mingled with along the Cinque Terre on the following days.

And the Cinque Terre are not to be neglected; just don't expect too much from what some have called "terminally cute" villages along the coast. They almost seem constructed to be photographed. Besides, the travel to and among them is an adventure in itself. There is a rail line[4] through the cliffs that links the five tiny "fishing" villages. There is a cliffside path for the young and strong as well, but there is no real road to these towns, and thus, no cars. We took the train to Vernazza (the one in the middle of the five) and walked down the single street to the shore where there are colorful beached boats and the little church of Santa Margherita, which is said to be built in the 1100s. Unlike many other small churches in Italy, it is still in active use. There is a pretty gilded Madonna next to the simple altar. The ecclesiastical furnishings are contemporary, but the architecture is better than a thousand years old. I am sure there are fewer than five priests for the five towns, and Sunday morning must see some rapid transit on the FS, or require the *reverendissime* to be loping over the hills to the next sacramental appointment.

----

[4] Built, of course, by Mussolini in his heyday as dictator back in the 1920s.

Vernazza and its four companions are built to be photographed. The Ligurian Sea is, as the Italians say, "Blue blue." The stucco of the houses is pink or yellow, and the ancient stones of the quay and the church a deep basaltic gray. Pretty, bare-legged girls with packs on their backs and blond-bearded companions were strewn about the waterfront stones, eating peaches in the sunshine. We retreated up the single street in search of lunch, and entered a little *trattoria* which might have been the one shown in one of Rick Steves's films about European travel. It was completely devoid of diners, and the *proprietario* welcomed us with enthusiasm. A very fresh seafood salad, a hearty wedge of *pecorino*, bread, and a half-bottle of wine made a fine lunch. The recorded music was by Rossini and Verdi. I would risk the combination again without anxiety.

We climbed part of one of the hills that separated the five towns, took a few compulsory photographs, and headed back up the single street to the Stazione FS to catch a train back to Chiavari.

Later we set forth to explore the beachfront and yacht harbors of Chiavari. The area was full of families with small children in strollers, and slightly larger ones looping by on Razor scooters (or their knockoffs), which seem to have burst onto the Italian scene about a year after they first infested America. There were also a number of elderly with canes and a few in wheelchairs. We took up people-watching from under an umbrella for a leisurely time, and concluded that Chiavari was indeed a town much to be recommended to our friends.

That evening we found the Trattoria Tagemme inside one of the arcades. All the other patrons seemed to know the lady who ran the place, and we found the rapid Ligurian dialect much beyond our comprehension. Nevertheless, we acquired a wonderful dish of spaghetti with a gamberetti sauce and a fish with fresh tomato and cream in its presentation.

In North Carolina we had met a charming oceanographer named Alessandro who recommended Chiavari to us, and told us that his friend, Alberto, ran an excursion boat out of Santa Margherita Liguri, by which means we could visit the legendary Portofino. The drive from Chiavari was a short one. We asked along the docks for the location of Alberto's boat, and soon were told that it was tied up close by. We called up from the wharf that we were friends of Alex's. Immediately there were shouts of welcome up and down the waterfront, to the effect that Alex's friends were here. We were surrounded by well-wishers and waved aboard by Alberto, the captain, who explained in fluent English that he was conducting the excursion to Portofino himself today rather than setting out on one of his newly advertised whale-watching expeditions.

The day was sunny, bright, and not too cool. Portofino turned out to be almost hidden in a cleft in the rocky coast where the picture-book town seems only slightly larger than the more isolated villages of Cinque Terre. Its harbor, however, accommodates a dozen or more sailboats that I would judge to be close to sixty feet overall, if not more. In the late twelfth century Richard the Lion-Hearted set forth from this tiny harbor to joust with Saladin in the Third Crusade. Today there is still a distinct aroma of wealth, if not of royalty, at Portofino. Our Tuttitalia guidebook lists four hotels of four stars, one of which, the Splendido, charges something in the range of $800 for the night (bed and breakfast). Use of the garage is extra. The guide calls it *"Un prestigiso albergo in splendido posizione."*

Not so the final stop on the excursion, San Fruttuoso. This tiny settlement is completely isolated from everything but the sea. Neither rail nor highway connects it with the rest of Italy, and the hiking trail over the mountains is steep and used only by the most athletic of tourists. There are fewer than thirty houses here, and an ancient abbey that was rebuilt in the thirteenth century. A single restaurant set on the side of the hill looked promising, but we used our time to explore the church. The mountainous land hereabout is part of a national park that was established sixty-five years ago, and the waters immediately around it are off-limits to commercial fishing. We saw the seriousness with which this prohibition is taken on our way back, when a fishing boat was pursued by a coast guard helicopter, and later by an official Zodiac, presumably because he was dragging his nets inside of the one-kilometer limit.

Back in Santa Margherita, we had a pizza in the afternoon sunshine and reflected that ocean voyaging is always good for the soul, and an excellent way to explore a new part of the world.

Before we disembarked from his boat, Alberto suggested that we visit the basilica of San Salvatore dei Fieschi before we left Chiavari. This handsome, austere building, not readily apparent from the coast, is situated above the town in the inland hills that provide a backdrop to all of Liguria. The direct road was blocked by the visual delight of a village day market, where dry goods and vegetables were being displayed under tents and umbrellas. A considerable detour eventually led us up a narrow defile to a weedy parking lot from which we could see the church, a severe gray-stone building with a Gothic spire. We climbed to the little cluster of buildings around a sloping square paved with geometrically patterned stones. We tried the door of the church and found it open. There was no one inside.

But the church was far from untenanted. Displayed against the dark gray stone was an icon of Christ Pantocrator. The thirteenth-century design is cool but somehow embracing. Although it has always been possible to find simple towns and great religious sites on the Ligurian coast, it seemed odd to find such a lonely and spiritual location so close to the egregious wealth of today's Italian Riviera. But that, of course, is part of the charm of this country, which is both ancient and contemporary. It is a country of the farm cart and the Maserati; of the peeling stucco of the *trecento* watchtower and the glass-and-stainless-steel surface of the contemporary buildings of Milano and Torino; a land for young women in bikinis and for those in the habit of the nuns.

XVI.

MASSA MARITTIMA:
A Delicious Medieval Town

Massa Marittima is one of those places in Italy which are not only hard to find but also hard to pronounce. It is accented on the second of its four syllables, as in *Ma-RIT'tima*, sort of ignoring the nearby presence of the Tyrrhenian Sea, which made me want to sound it like "maritime." The town snuggles into the hills thirty kilometers inland from Falonica, north of Grosseto, and boasts neither rail connection nor auto-rental agency. In an attempt to avoid navigating a car in Rome itself, we took a train from the Fiumicino Airport shuttle to Roma Ostiense, and thence caught the first available Intercity train for Grosseto, where we had reserved a chunky little Fiat. Unfortunately this connection (called a *coincidenza* in Italian) missed the mandatory two-hour lunch break of all Italian offices by fifteen minutes. Hence the affable and polite clerks were disconnected from their master computer at the central office until later in the day.

Then it began to rain.

A couple of hours later, everything came back to life, despite an interval in which I, depending on the position of the sun for direction, became hopelessly lost among the non-rectilinear crossroads and corners of the medieval city. Everyone was very helpful, including the proprietors of several bars that looked exactly like the one where I had left Cathy to await my return. Eventually we found our separate ways to the Auto Europe office, and were rewarded by the presentation of a shiny, black, rain-sprinkled Fiat Punto that did good service for the next several weeks.

We followed a good Michelin atlas and the characteristically informative Italian road signs inland and up the hills to Massa Marittima. We were almost immediately confronted with the cheerful pink stucco of the Hotel Duca del Mare, where we were enthusiastically greeted by Roberto and Mario, the brothers who had inherited the sizable inn from their father. They had a fire burning in the waist-high hearth of the bar, and we were soon warm and dry, our thirst and good humor restored.

Massa Marittima is a small town in the far western corner of Tuscany, the area known as "the Maremma." I'm not sure how we came to visit here, except that we had been in the nearby surrounding areas of Siena and Florence where we enjoyed a restaurant called La Maremma, which suggested that the food might be very good there. We were disappointed to find that although the Duca del Mare had an excellent bar and a very pleasant breakfast room, there was no *ristorante*. As always in Italy, not to worry. Roberto pointed out that there was a clutch of *ristoranti* eight hundred meters up the hill—*un breve passeggiata* to the central *piazza* of town. We inspected the rugged build of the two brothers and studied the uphill route to dinner. Those boys had spent their youth running up and down hills and ravines. We also learned that after five o'clock, the tariff in the municipal parking lot became one euro for the rest of the night. The piazza turned out to be surrounded by a number of *ristoranti* and *trattorie*. Following the brothers' instructions, we soon found ourselves at the BoccondiVini, a jolly *enoteca*, one of those most Italianate places of refreshment where there are a hundred wines to choose among and only two or three dishes for dinner. It was the first of a number of excellent meals we found in the Maremma; in this case, chicken and garbanzo soups, salad with fresh Sicilian tomatoes, and a flaming Spanish *caramella catalan* for dessert. After more than three thousand miles and adventures with aircraft, railroads, and the nice little Fiat Punto, we slept very soundly at the Duca del Mare.

On one side of the Piazza Garibaldi stands the elevated *duomo* of St. Cerbonius,[5] an imposing church in a small town, but in the fashion of Italian places of ecclesiastical antiquity, governed today by a full, four-stripe bishop. Cerbonius was a fifth-century shepherd of his flock who was in the habit of rising at three in the morning when he was wakened by angelic voices calling him—and thus, his congregation—to prayer with bells and, perhaps, with trumpet blasts. His parishioners, tired of this interruption of their rest, sent word to the pope that Cerbonius was a heretic. Summoned to Rome to defend himself, Cerbonius suffered the embarrassment of being too poor to bring a suitable gift to the pontiff. Providentially, a large flock of white geese joined the bishop, followed him on the road to Rome, and into the presence of the pope, who was so moved by the piety of the birds that he declared Cerbonius innocent and restored him to his see with honor. This event is recorded in a charming, circular stained-glass window high up in the west wall.

---

[5] The square was for centuries called the Piazza Duomo, but was renamed for the unifier of modern Italy, presumably after Pius IX excommunicated him for liberating the Papal States and creating the nation of Italy. Pius retaliated by declaring it a matter of mortal sin to vote in an Italian election. The people of Massa returned the compliment by naming the center of the town for Giuseppe Garibaldi.

The fourteenth-century window only shows five or six geese, but the glass oculus is only five feet in diameter and the general effect is quite appropriate.

The church has a modest scattering of rather good, pious works of art, including a Duccio Madonna and Child and a splendid crucifix by Giovanni Pisano. The baptismal font is a huge construction done and signed by a Lombard sculptor, Giudetto da Como, in 1267. It is lavishly ornamented with images of John the Baptist and a full panoply of saints and prophets carved out of a single block of travertine. While we were examining these remarkable works of art, the greater part of a pre-wedding warm-up was taking place around the main altar. A capable organist was starting to pitch the Schubert "Ave Maria" in a proper key for a robust contralto. Her voice filled the lovely old church with a rich and appropriate melody. After all, the marriage of Maria and Giuseppe, consummated or not, is the very model of fidelity and extraordinarily good parenting.

Then the wedding party arrived, delivering a pretty bride, a strong young contadina, in an elegant and obviously one-of-a-kind wedding dress. The intermittent rain showers had made the many steps (thirteen, I think) up to the cathedral doors wet and muddy. Cathy was horrified to note that no bridesmaid stepped forward to hold up the sparkling-white train which was being dragged through the puddles. Someone later explained to us that the dress was designed to be worn but once; the marriage bond is supposed to be permanent. And besides, there is an old Italian saying: "*Sposa bagnata, sposa fortunata!*" ("A soaked bride has good luck!")

Contemplating the dozens of beautiful blind arches that flank the sides of the fine church of Cerbonius, and the elegant, seven-story tower that rises behind this cathedral, it occurred to me that only in a country with such a surfeit of great works of architecture as Italy could

Massa Marittima be known as less than "worth the entire journey." Yet somehow this town is listed in only a few of the guidebooks.

There are many things to be seen in the Piazza Garibaldi. On Sunday morning a colorful parade of costumed citizens came across the square to reach the cathedral. A beautiful ragazza in gorgeous dress and bearing a double handful of lilies in her clasped hands came up the steps to enter the fine old building. She wore a flower headdress in her long, swept-back hair, and was attended by dignified children in elegant costume. Behind her were a double rank of drummers and a skein of trumpeters, followed by a small squad of crossbowmen shouldering their vicious-looking weapons. Getting a closer look at the medieval militia, I noted that the crossbows were modern adaptations of the thirteenth-century arms and had sighting crosshairs that could be adjusted with micrometer screws to make aiming more accurate for long-range shooting. I eventually concluded that those acting the parts of the ancient marksmen were members of a current-day hunt club that sought deer and wild boar in the neighboring mountains.

There are associations and clubs for almost everything in Italy, from bicycling, hunting, and fishing, to touring according to the excellent maps and directions of the "Touring Club of Italy." One popular sport in Ferrara and in Massa Marittima consists of flipping brightly colored silk flags on short staves in the air between several ranks of skillful young men, who toss them ever higher in the air. We never caught them in full exhibition costumes in this town, but one evening we heard the summoning rattle and boom of the drummers while we were enjoying a well-made martini produced by Mario. Quickly drawn out to the large parking lot next to the hotel, we found a skeleton band of four musicians there, providing the rhythm, while a dozen neophyte flag tossers were flinging their plain white practice banners to each other across a space of ten to fifteen meters. They were not completely proficient at the ancient art as yet, but the spirit with which they pursued their practice session bodes well for future exhibitions.

Although Massa is small city, it is very well equipped with a great number of small restaurants, most of which can accommodate about two dozen guests. We ate in six of them, and were always delighted with what we found. A little place located up a narrow stone alley was called Il Gatto e il Lupo ("The Cat and the Wolf"), and was

Author at
massa marrittima
"The Cat and the Wolf"

possibly named for one of Aesop's fables. Despite its diminutive scale and modest prices, it seemed to us to be worthy of our own private designation of lots of stars.

There are a number of extraordinary works of art of religious devotion in other parts of Massa Marittima. The *Stele del Vado all'Arancia* is one of the most mysterious and ancient of these. It is a roughly triangular slab carved primitively with eyes, a nose, and arms folded over the belly. This crudely carved figure looks like a modern anthropomorphic devotional statue, but is actually about three thousand years old. In another location is an unusual fresco of a group of women, busy harvesting startlingly realistic symbols of largely erect male genitalia from a tree. It would seem to be a fertility charm from a few hundred years before the Council of Trent banished the remnants of pagan symbolism from Italy.

We set forth one day to sample the coast of the Tyrrhenian Sea, but noting that the car was quite dirty, we pulled into a self-service car wash and began to fumble with unfamiliar knobs, vernacular instructions, and coin slots. As usual, Italian manners came to our rescue. Two excessively muddy and somewhat desperate-appearing, fiercely scowling young men on motorcycles took a five-euro note from my hand, showed me which slot it fit, and proceeded to wash the car for me. They rejected my attempt to tip them and waved good-bye as we departed for the neighboring town of Falonica. We have often noted that next to carrying a very small child, the best talisman for getting the best service in Italy is a head of white hair.

This part of the Tyrrhenian coast is largely parkland, and as a result is heavily forested with a number of coniferous trees. There are sequestered car parks and a few anchorages for sailboats. We eventually returned to the center of Falonica to spend a pleasant morning inspecting the beach, and eventually found a small restaurant which was full of delicious smells but void of untenanted places to sit. An accommodating senior citizen told us to wait while he settled his *conto* so he could gather up his family and turn their table over to us. The complex stew of fish, clams, calamari, octopus, tomatoes, a variety of vegetables, and a handful of pasta with chewy bread and butter, along with a slightly rough red wine of unknown variety, was much better and surely healthier than the fried New England "shore dinner" we'd left behind in Connecticut.

The seaside towns of western Tuscany extend from the Cinque Terre all the way to Rome. They were fought over quite fiercely in the Middle Ages, and Massa Marittima came under the sway of Florence and Siena in different periods. To protect its extensive real estate, Siena built a great fortress in the upper or "new" part of the city, most of which still stands, with towers and bridges of connecting stonework ramparts. These upper reaches of Massa are worth exploring, with a number of interesting churches, a small collection of archaeological remains, and a mining museum. The "metalliferous" hills provided iron ore to be smelted in the times of the Etruscans, and led to the great technological change from the Bronze to the Iron Age. East of Massa there are rosy heaps of what I took to be iron mine tailings in many of the valleys extending toward Siena. There are also valleys full of pipes and penstocks which give off plumes of steam from underground sources of geothermal energy, which provides quite a lot of cheap electricity without burning any fossil fuel at all.

On one of these excursions to the east of Massa, we took the road halfway to Siena to visit the Abbey of San Garfana, its abbey church a fourteenth-century Gothic skeleton standing in solitary beauty in a green meadow. The abbey had housed thirty or forty monks for several centuries after its founding in 1185 by a warrior, St. Garfano, who forswore arms and plunged his sword into a stone, vowing to live a peaceful life henceforth. It was an early example of "I'm gonna lay down my sword and shield, down by the riverside / Ain't gonna study war no more!"

The sword is still there, stuck in the rock in a glass-enclosed niche in a chapel at the top of the neighboring hillock. This is the famous Spada nella Roccia which made the monastery a pilgrim's goal until it was abandoned when the great scourge of the Black Death descended on Tuscany in 1348. The plague killed almost half the population of Italy. The peaceful and helpful monks were not spared despite their prayers and good works. All but two died, and that miserable pair abandoned the beautiful site. They walked to Siena where they joined what was left of another Cistercian house.

The great abbey church suffered the same ruin as Tintern Abbey in Wales. The lead roof was later stripped off for bullets; the roof beams, thus exposed to the weather, rotted and fell. Leaded windows suffered the same decay until, in a couple of centuries, only the soaring Gothic stonework remained. There is green grass where the nave was once located. Portals and lancets of elegant embrasures beckoned us to enter the house of prayer, where once the silent and peaceful brothers chanted their office.

PART IV
THE CENTRAL PO VALLEY

XVII.

PARMA:
Realm of an Austrian Princess who Became a French Empress

We knew somewhat more about the ham and cheese of Parma than about its art or history when we first put it on our agenda. The richness of all four Parmesan sources of fame made the town a very worthwhile stop on our journey.

Parma is a small golden city set where the Parma River is crossed by the Via Emilia, the Roman road that parallels the Po River as it runs from Rimini and Bologna in the east almost to Milan in the northwest. Midway along this ancient straightaway are Parma and its near neighbors, Modena and Reggio Emilia, two of the best (and least-frequented) destinations for tourists in northern Italy. We arrived at the Stazione FS and took a cab for the short trip to the Piazza Garibaldi. We found that the driver was delighted with our attempts to communicate in Italian, and quite willing to slow down and speak *più piano, più lentamente, per favore*, when his enthusiasm for his hometown led to a torrent of rapid-fire description.

We stayed at the Hotel Button, a sort of standard, small commercial hotel just off the Piazza Garibaldi, an unbeatable location that cost us just $68 a night at the time (but closer to $85 in euro a few years later, when the dollar began its collapse). It is about what we are used to paying at a "plastic motel" along I-95 in the U.S. The Button also has an attractive breakfast room, but we passed it up for the chance to explore the perennial delight of the coffee bars located around the piazza.

Here, as I point out elsewhere, one of the great pleasures of Italy is breakfast in the neighborhood "bar." The professional coffee apparatus that dominates even the smallest of these establishments is a wondrous collection of valves, pressure gauges, tubes, and stainless-steel reservoirs for boiling water. Delicious gurgles and hisses accompany the production, one cup at a time, of the best-tasting brew you can imagine. Despite the fact that an overly scrupulous cardiologist convinced me to change to the decaffeinated stuff at home, I have never had the slightest problem in Italy with the real thing, the high-octane essence that fuels all of Italy and is the basis of *caffèlatte*. Mixed in a proportion of about four to one in favor of scalded milk, it is a wonderful beginning for the day. With a *spremuta* of freshly squeezed orange juice and any one of a number of breakfast breads or jam-filled buns, the first collation is a joy, and promises further gastronomic pleasure to follow throughout the day. And while you are enjoying your meal, you can observe the grizzled workmen taking their coffee with a good shot of Fernet Bianca, and the pretty office girls accepting a thimbleful of espresso without adornment.

Parma's history, like that of all of northern Italy, is a long account of war, domination, treachery, and brilliant artistic production. The opposing parties of Guelphs and Ghibellines kept it in turmoil in the late Middle Ages, as the influence of popes and Holy Roman emperors waxed and waned. During the Renaissance, the French got a foothold when the Constable of Bourbon came through to successfully besiege and sack Rome in 1527, but in the longer run, Pope Paul III Farnese scooped up the little city along with a bunch of other northern Italian towns to provide duchies for his natural sons and nephews. Paul, as mentioned above, was originally named Alessandro. He was a brilliant young man who became a cardinal at twenty-five, and pope when he was sixty-five, in 1534. In his fifteen years on the job, he excommunicated Henry VIII of England (for the second time), established the Inquisition to deal with the "Protestant Heresy," called the Council of Trent to reform the Catholic Church, and brought about the final and complete alienation of England from Rome. He thus created the setting for the bloody struggle between the religious followers of the half sisters, Mary and Elizabeth Tudor. He was also the pope who hired Michelangelo to be his chief sculptor and architect; a mixed legacy for sure, but not without significance.

The papal dynasty of Farnese dukes stayed in charge of Parma from the days of Ann Boleyn in England until the early career of Benjamin Franklin, printer of Philadelphia. After that, the Spanish Bourbons acquired the duchy by marriage. Napoleon took it in 1802, and when he was finally disposed of after Waterloo, the great powers of Europe gave it to his second wife, Maria Louisa, known locally as Maria Luigia, who originated as an Austrian princess and was deemed to be in need of some sort of principality befitting her high birth and late rank as Empress of France, as well as most of Europe. When her husband was first sent into exile to the island of Elba, she stayed home in her new duchy. In portraits she appears wide-eyed, demure, coquettish, and slightly simpleminded. Although she is referred to by one historian as being "devoid of political sense," the *Parmagiani* thought she was just fine, and honor her memory to this day.

Walking about the city is a pleasant affair, even though there is little architectural distinction to the eastern portions of the town. We did discover, however, that the huge bulk of the Cittadella, a great pentagon of Renaissance military architecture, has been turned to peaceful purposes. The interior green has become a park, and there are children's swings and sandboxes where the emplacements for guns and bombproof magazines were originally designed. On the day we visited, balloon and ice cream vendors tended their carts under large and spreading trees. From there we turned west and soon reached the elevated banks of the Torrente Parma, which seemed lacking in sufficient water to live up to its title. I later discovered that it was indeed likely to be a torrent in the spring when the first of the Apennine snowpack melts down to feed the River Po. In more agricultural weather, the Parma torrent is tapped for irrigation water for a large area of the plain of the Po, *la padana*, the most productive agricultural area of all Italy.

Perhaps because of Maria Louisa, Parma has a French style of elegance that seems to have lacquered over the more brutal power of the descendants of the Farnese. The stucco walls of many of the downtown buildings are lemon-yellow with pale-ecru trim, and give something of the impression of a disordered Parisian drawing room turned out of doors. The church of San Pietro in the Piazza Garibaldi is a jewel of this exuberant color scheme, as is the towered building that displays three sundials on its southern face across from the tram-car stop in the very center of the square. My view of the sundials kept getting interrupted by the graceful silhouettes of the delicately long-legged *Parmagiane* gliding by on their bicycles with their chic and expensive pocketbooks slung over their shoulders. Some purred through the square on the latest model motor scooters.

Fortified by a good breakfast ration of blood-red orange juice and a large *cornetto con marmellata*, we set forth to visit some of the extraordinary buildings scattered around the city by the various pampered nobles and ecclesiastics who have enjoyed owning the town through the centuries. We began with the most unusual, the enormous Palazzo della Pilotta, which Duke Ranuccio I Farnese put together as a stronghold and power center of the family authority. A huge second-floor arms magazine and horse-training space was converted in more peaceful times to a magnificent theater, reached by a ceremonial staircase that still seems to cry out for the presence of costumed baroque figures coming or going to a celebration.

This Teatro Farnese seems the very essence of seventeenth-century magnificence. Built as a three-dimensional backdrop for the court, it was filled with mechanisms for changing scenery, flying actors, and artificial lighting. The huge theater was created for the private enjoyment of the prince and his courtiers. His location at the very front and center of the curving tier of seats made him a part of the action that his entertainers were commissioned to present. In some of the plays, the prince was supposed to rise up at the end and, taking on the role of one of the gods of antiquity, settle the fractured affairs of the mortal lovers and warriors on stage by his command.

The theater is reminiscent of the famous Teatro Olympico (on a much larger scale), designed by Palladio and Scamozzi at Vicenza. But unlike the earlier model, this one has no permanent structural set before which the actors are to perform. Here the backstage is deeper than the theater itself; it is several hundred feet from the proscenium arch to the rear wall, a vast depth, all of which could be clothed in backdrops and ground cloths that were raised into the flies far above and out of the sight of the audience. Designed for the most elaborate staging that the sixteenth-century mind could imagine, it has only been used for three or four productions in its nearly four-century history. It was started to provide a setting for a really proper party when Cosimo di Medici was invited to come for a long weekend. The Farnese family was trying to arrange a marriage for their prince Odoardo with Cosimo's daughter, Margherita. Unfortunately, the two young people were in no hurry to be paired off, and Cosimo canceled the date; thus, the huge room remained empty and not quite finished for ten years, until the bride and groom were finally brought together in Parma. It was used a few more times, but last held an audience in 1732 when Charles of Bourbon took over as duke.

Although much of the theater was bombed during World War II, reconstruction has re-created the great space almost exactly as it was, utilizing every scrap of the painted woodwork that could be reassembled. Regrettably, the very accuracy of the reconstruction has perpetuated the disuse of the theater, since there are inadequate fire exits to accommodate a modern audience. It stands today as an enormous wooden sculpture that we may explore, its seats filled with hundreds of costumed figures provided only by our imagination.

But the Palazzo has other and even livelier things to see as you go on up. The reconstructed spaces of the Pilotta also contain the National Gallery of Parma, where the great Farnese collection of artworks was once assembled. Charles of Bourbon took them off to Naples when he became the King of the Two Sicilies. He took most of the furniture, too. We were favored, however, with a brief return of the paintings during a hometown celebration in the spring of 1995. We also met them several years later at the Capodimonte museum up above the Bay of Naples, where the earliest and this most-famous of the Farnese collection is usually located.

Despite this distressful wholesale removal of the entire museum's contents, a later duke put together a pretty good replacement collection by starting out with a very good Correggio as the keystone of a group of paintings displayed to train young artists. Napoleon stole most of these paintings in his turn, but Maria Luigia brought some back with her when she took over in the early nineteenth century. Among other wonders in the gallery is one of the few great drawings by Leonardo da Vinci, the sepia chalk portrait entitled *Testa di Fanciulla* ("Head of a Young Girl"). But above all, there are a handful of wonderful works by Francesco Mazzola who came to be known as "*Il Parmigianino.*" His Turkish Slave (actually a portrait of a young woman), *The Marriage of St. Catherine*, and a small self-portrait are among the works assembled in a series of modern galleries that were remodeled after being bombed during World War II.

Besides a good set of galleries and churches to be visited in Parma are such things as the house where Arturo Toscanini was born. It now functions as a small museum, displaying many of the events of the great conductor's long life.

Parma's *duomo* is a great example of the Lombard Romanesque style. It was begun in the middle of the eleventh century, but had to be started over again sixty years later when a devastating earthquake hit the town. Marvelously, it has stood through all further shaking ever since. Since medieval man looked on natural disasters such as *terremoti* as acts of God justly punishing sinners, they lacked the knowledge that the fault line might spring apart again. Considering the almost-miraculous preservation of the lofty towers of Modena and Siena, as well as Parma, it seems quite possible that they might have been right. God has surely visited enough destruction on the cities of Italy to make knocking down their piously reared church towers seem an act of superfluous correction.

There is an extraordinary fresco in the interior of the dome by Correggio that took him from 1524 to 1530 to complete. But great though Correggio is, I was far more moved by the Descent from the Cross by Antelami, which dates from the late twelfth century. He also designed a wonderful early-thirteenth-century baptistery just to the west of the cathedral. Why the north Italians went in for these freestanding baptisteries when all other parts of Christendom had given up baptizing in separate buildings, I do not know. There are wonderful examples of these usually octagonal buildings in Florence, as well as Padua and Cremona. The biggest of them all is the round one in Pisa, which dwarfs the scale of the cathedral, and whose dome is actually higher than the famous leaning campanile. Parma's baptistery is among the best of them all.

Just west of the town there is Maria Luigia's own palace in a park just across the Ponte Giuseppe Verdi. Next to the Palazzo della Pilotta is the Teatro di Reggio, one of the great opera houses of Italy. We had no luck in finding opera here, but were rewarded by a fine evening of Beethoven when we visited. There is also a famous conservatory in the town, as well as attendant shops for finding musical instruments and published scores of music which are hard to find elsewhere. Walking back to the Button one afternoon, we passed through the neighborhood of the music school and came upon a shop window displaying a spectacularly beautiful viola da gamba, gleaming, pale-blond, lightly grained spruce with a rich purple fingerboard fashioned from some tropical hardwood. Although neither of us could play it, and it obviously cost *un occhio della testa*,[6] we were momentarily seized with an irrational desire to own the beautiful thing. But fortunately the shop was closed for the midday three-hour *pranzo e pisolino*, and by the time we had found our own lunch, the spasm had passed and we were sane again.

On another daylong excursion, we took the local train fifteen minutes out of town to visit Maria Luigia's country retreat, a few kilometers to the north. We walked through pleasantly untrimmed

---

[6] We would say it cost an arm and a leg in America. The Italians, with a nicety of value, require an "eye out of the head."

grass to a luxurious but moderately proportioned building. Here, the lady entertained guests and whiled away the hours of her eventual widowhood after her former husband was translated to the desolate rock in the south Atlantic, where he died somewhat prematurely, some think of poison.

Parma violets are not much in evidence in this town now, although elegant cosmetics are displayed in the apothecary shops and department stores. The great cheese of Reggio and Parma is made in the country here around. The Parma ham is cured by salting (without smoke) in the very chilly environment of huge walk-in refrigerators at the Consortio del Prosciutto. Be sure to order the best *prosciutto crudo* while you are enjoying this pleasant town. Whether you have it with melon as an antipasto or with thin slices of buffalo mozzarella, it is a very special experience. Wash it down with a glass of Prosecco, northern Italy's dry, bubbly white wine.

Parma has lots of good restaurants of every price range. As is often the case, *Let's Go Italy* gives a good list of *trattorie* and *pizzeria-ristorante* in the town. At one modest step up in price from these, we particularly enjoyed the Gallo d'Oro, which was close by the Hotel Button. We found this by quizzing the locals, coffee-bar keepers, and hotel desk personnel, to help us find *un buon trattoria a buon mercato*. The town has an unrushed and tranquil style—a wonderful place to rest up before or after the more hectic pace of Venice or Florence.

XVIII.

PIACENZA:
Verdi's Hometown

Piacenza is a beguiling town, very much neglected by American tourists and very much worth a leisurely visit. It has all the ornaments of a modern Italian town: a great palazzo, a fine art gallery, an opera house, an elegant central piazza, plenty of good places to eat, and easy access to the rest of Italy.

What was in Roman times the next-to-last stop on the Via Emilia, Piacenza is now nestled alongside the confluence of two of the great Autostrada of modern Italy—the A1 and the A21. Although it is within sixty-five kilometers of Milan, it is not at all a bedroom community to its great neighbor to the northwest. It has, however, provided a refuge from the big city, and was the location of the country farmstead of Giuseppe Verdi in the satellite village of Sant'Agata. The great composer lived there while his newest works were being introduced at the opera house of La Scala, "in town."

Ignoring the logical Roman directions, we descended upon Piacenza from the north; spurning the superhighways and thus crossing due south from Bergamo, we came to a town full of the memories of the great composer. We put up at the Hotel Milano, a middling walk north of the center of town. We found lunch in a splendid "Self-Service," where the *insalata di tonno* was cheap and nourishing. This chain luncheon spot, another of northern Italy's response to Wendy's or Burger King, was cheerfully patronized by lots of students. After a brief tour of the town, we progressed south with a brief stop at a very baroque Church of San Antonio, and came to the square of the opera house where we had learned there would be a *spettacolo* that evening.

The box office would not open until an hour before the show, which was to be Verdi's very early opera, *Stiffelio*. There was an underground restaurant across from the theater, and by ducking out between cocktails and dinner, I was able to procure two unnumbered tickets for the circle. The house is a delightful, small-sized affair that Cathy compared to a pint-sized San Carlo di Napoli. Besides, any chance to hear live opera for the equivalent of $20 a head should be taken. Yet the great maestro did not seem to have totally gotten the hang of his style at the time he wrote this one. *Stiffelio* is a gloomy tale of the adultery of a Lutheran priest and a married woman who comes to within an ace of being stoned by the townspeople until the principal dies and they all decide to forgive her and sing a chorus of reconciliation. The opera seemed an appropriate Lenten production in spite of murder, revenge, and illicit sex in the plot. The house was full, principally because Verdi is the national champion and the piece is rarely performed.

We approached an attractive Japanese couple at intermission, assuming they might speak English. They were music students who had come all the way from Verona just for the opportunity to hear it. The soprano (Dimitra Theodossiou) was quite wonderful, but the tenor had to be replaced by a brave understudy at the end of the first act. (He was generously applauded by the sympathetic house after his first aria.) We have since wondered what has become of that promising young prima donna. She seemed a cut above some of the singers we have heard on the radio broadcasts of the Metropolitan Opera in subsequent years. Perhaps she just hasn't met up with the right impresario.

Taxis being unavailable at the late conclusion of the opera, we took a long walk back to the Hotel Milano at close to midnight and slept well. Walking in the lonely dark late at night in northern Italy is, from our experience, a perfectly safe thing to do.

Reclaiming the rental car from the hotel *parcheggio* the following day, I backed into another vehicle, rather gently, and scratched his fender. The owner bounced out of a nearby bar and was upon me in an instant. He began in rapid Italian to bemoan the irreparable damage to his car. I offered a fistful of lire and an apology. He was not about to accept conciliation or be pacified by my offer to provide the equivalent of ten dollars for a dab of paint.

"Ma c'e niente! Niente!" I brayed at him, rubbing the offending scar with my fingers. After a few minutes of this sort of monoverbal explanation, he decided to take the money and return to the bar from whence he had appeared.

A fifteen-minute drive out into the country brought us to the tiny village of St. Agata, where Verdi had his country home and where he lived with his mistress Giuseppina for many years.[7] Villa Verdi is a small hacienda, and while it is set near the road, it has a sizable grove of trees around and behind the house, many of them exotic species planted by Verdi himself. Son of a farmer, arboreal culture was one of the composer's principal hobbies. At a simple guardhouse, we found a guide warming herself by a cheery open fire and were

---

[7] He eventually married her, and the scandal of their relationship died down.

greeted in very clear but much too rapid Italian. Shortly we were joined by two other couples and set out to visit the property, all the while listening to her pretty but unintelligible commentary rather as background music.

After the gardens, replete with fountains and pools, we were led to the house which is longer than it is broad. Its division down the length of its structure has resulted in two long, thin apartments, one of which is occupied by descendants of Verdi's extended family. The other side is a museum, almost a shrine, containing his bedroom (small and narrow); his studio, with a large piano; his mistress's bedroom, featuring a large and luxurious double bed hung with a green velvet canopy; and a chapel with an altar for mass and an alcove with an elaborately carved confessional. This latter was presumably for her to use when atoning for her irregular relationship, rather than his, since Verdi was more of a freethinker than an orthodox Catholic. When they were eventually married, and after he wrote his spine-chilling Requiem, he was buried in the Cathedral of Milan with the sort of honors more usually reserved for a bishop or perhaps a pope.

Verdi was in Milano attending an opera when he breathed his last in 1901, by then one of the most famous men in Europe. The central room in the home-museum has been equipped with the furniture of the Milanese hotel room in which he died, including the monogrammed ashtrays of the hotel and his nightshirt, embroidered with blue and white flowers.

He had not always been so famous or so sure of himself. His first few opera met with minimal success. But when he composed *Nabucco* in 1842, everyone knew that he had a hit on his hands. At that time all of northern Italy was governed by Austria, and the great *Risorgimento* to create an Italian nation was just beginning to gather steam. The soldiers of Franz Joseph (beloved in Austria but not at all so in Italy) would crack down on any political demonstration and would have prevented any *spettacolo* that they felt was politically incorrect. But somehow they missed the popular interpretation of the chorus of the Hebrew prisoners on the banks of the Euphrates, who sing of their longing for their homeland in the words *Va, pensiero, sull'ali dorate. . .* ("Go thoughts, on golden wings!")

When the chorus and orchestra first performed this song in rehearsal, the workmen building the sets (who were normally a hardened corps of lower-class workers) put down their hammers and stood transfixed at the soaring power of the melody. Common laborers in Italy know a piece of great music when they hear it, and then there was the obvious parallel of the situation of the Italians held in thrall by Austria to the Hebrews in the Babylonian Captivity. The anthem became the theme of the *Risorgimento*, often sung under the very noses of the Austrian thought police. Several of his later opera also had political interpretations, and Verdi's name eventually became an acronym for Vittorio Emanuele Re d'Italia, the monarch of the first unified Italy since the emperors of Rome.

"Va Pensiero" is not the only beauty wrought out of political oppression today in Piacenza. The Farnese extended their sway over this town when that wily old pope Paul III[8] made a duchy for his bastard son Pier Luigi out of the free communes of Parma, Piacenza, and a couple of other towns along the Po. Holding on to this choice real estate required some muscle, and the family set to work building

---

[8] Paul's given name was Alessandro. His sister Julia was the mistress of the Pope (Alexander VI), which gave him sufficient clout to be named a cardinal at the age of twenty-five and elected Pope as a bearded old man in 1534. In his later years he became a stickler for religious orthodoxy, and established the modern Inquisition and the Index of forbidden books to keep freethinkers in line. He also commissioned a lot of really classy art.

a huge fortified palace in Piacenza which would serve as a home for
Pier Luigi, as well as a military headquarters to keep the townspeople
in line. The magnificent work of oppression was never finished, but
the great bulk of it was made into a civic museum in a later era. Thus
we now have the Palazzo Farnese, which is vast and fascinating.

The day of our visit, we were required to go in the company of
an attractive young conscript who wanted us to follow a prescribed
route. Cathy was firm and skipped ahead, ignoring the portraits of
the lesser Farnese to wander the rooms below and the vasty halls. She
managed to get separated from the official presence when she slipped
past a screen and into a section of the museum that was officially
closed. We both succeeded in finding the Etruscan *Fegato*, a bronze
model of a sheep's liver several thousand years old, marked with
indecipherable symbols of the *auspici* that guided the pronouncements
of the Etruscan soothsayers.

Eventually, two guards reunited us and steered us back into the
parts of the museum that were meant to be legal for tourists on this
day. They seemed to be on our side, and allowed us as much time as
possible to examine the interdicted areas of the collections until we
descended to a collection of coaches and carriages, and eventually
found our way out of ancient times into the pleasant Piacenzan
spring, where we walked south to the open-air market in front
of Il Gotico and the Piazza Cavalli, so named for the large bronze
equestrian statues of a later Duke Farnese (another Alessandro) and
his son, Ranuccio. The great amount of bronze in these castings and
the fact that they still stand today would seem to be evidence that
the later Farnese got on well with their subjects; at least their effigies
have never been overturned since they were first sculpted and set up
in the seventeenth century, in spite of some revolutions and a change
in taste for royalty that measures its descent from a pope. The Gothic

Palazzo Pubblico where they stand dates from 1280 and is splendid. Piacenza became a firmly republican center in later centuries. It was the first province to join the kingdom of Italy by plebiscite when Italy became a nation in the nineteenth century.

The nice people at the Hotel Milano directed us to the Trattoria Carozzo, where we enjoyed a really nice supper (in spite of having arrived a bit early for the usual hour of service): polenta with speck for an antipasto, *tagliatelle con funghi*, well-roasted pork, and divergent desserts, fresh pineapple, and *panna cotta* with berry sauce. Everything in Piacenza left a good taste in our mouths.

XIX.

PAVIA:
And an Experience with Italian Medicine

Heading southeast from Milan, we had approached the first of the string of cities that follow the course of the Roman Via Emilia to the southeast coast at Rimini and the Adriatic. It is the very archetype of the Roman roads that held the great republic together. After Milan, Piacenza and Pavia are first in the sequence. Like many small, flourishing towns of the Renaissance, they gradually lost ground to their slightly larger neighbors and then became virtually eclipsed by them. But these were the heart and center of the Lombard occupation in Italy in the Dark Ages of the sixth and seventh centuries. Pavia was the sight of their coronations and in every way a rival to Milan. Today Milano is the capital of the entire north, the business capital of Italy, and now seems to have displaced Paris as the capital of fashion. Little Pavia is a steady little satellite, prosperous and busy, but no one would believe today that it was once the chief city of all of Lombardia.

This part of the world was once known as Cisalpine Gaul, a country of the first of the northern and eastern peoples to despoil the city of Rome. "Cisalpine" refers to the Gaul on the Roman side of the Alps. A thousand years before the incursions of the first "barbarians," Rome was still small and virtually unwalled. These fierce northern

Italians were able to burn and conquer the "eternal city" in the years of the early republic. The date is uncertain, but is thought to be 378 BC or thereabouts. Rome was rebuilt in due time, and one of the major tasks its consuls undertook thereafter was the subjugation of their ferocious northern neighbors. This conquest required several centuries to complete, but eventually gave Rome control of all of the land north of the River Po. They linked it to the capital by the long military highway of the Via Emilia, stone-paved and bridged over swamp and river, providing a firm and direct footing for the legions. This area soon supported fifty cities and towns. The encampment of Ticino was one of these. It became Pavia.

A thousand years after those early troubles from the people of the north, the city of Rome was in the hands of the Goths. Its empire had come and gone, ruled from the east by Byzantium. Among the last of Italy's destructive invaders were the Lombards—also called Langobards or Long Beards—presumably recognizable by the luxuriance of their hirsute adornment. Unlike most of the other barbarians of the preceding centuries, these Germanic northerners decided to stay in Italy after they had despoiled it. Milan and Pavia were their principal locations, although they established duchies in Spoleto and Benevento farther south. But it was in little Pavia that they established a sacred site where their kings were invested with the "Iron Crown of Lombardia."

Guidebooks had told us little about the small city, focusing largely on the Certosa di Pavia nearby, which is rated as a "must-see" by all the commentators. A *certosa* (or charterhouse) was actually a monastery of strictly self-governing monks known as Carthusians. These were usually scholarly men who lived in elaborate isolation from each other, as well as from the rest of the world. They emerged from their cells twice a day, once to celebrate the conventual mass together after the hour of terce (the short mid-morning prayer). Later they dined rather sparsely in a common refectory while one read from a spiritual text to the gathering. To this day, Carthusians are strict vegetarians and seem to subsist largely on beans, bread, and watered wine. Since water was often a disease-bearer in the Middle Ages, putting some wine in it was a salubrious practice that effectively killed off the various destructive bacteria. Such prophylaxis as this may also be the origin of their development of the deliciously alcoholic after-dinner cordials, green and yellow Chartreuse. In some charterhouses each monk cultivated a small garden outside his cell. Men are usually not accepted into the group until well past fifty, and they are reputed to live to an average age of better than eighty. Like most other tourists in Pavia, we had come to visit this famous place.

We approached the town through rain showers on the Autostrada as we came from eastern Liguria. With a newly rented car at our disposal, we selected the Hotel Excelsior which was equipped with a garage deep underground. There was an *ascensore* from the underground car park to the lobby, but none from the lobby to the bedrooms above. The sad-faced manager carried our bags up the two flights to our room. Cathy thought his face must resemble Sisyphus in gloomy contemplation of perpetually carrying things uphill. The hotel was comfortable and generally up-to-date in its fixtures.

We set out to discover the town and shortly found ourselves in a large and pretty piazza in front of the cathedral. The building is under repair from a discouraging event of 1989, when the tower simply fell down and killed four people who happened to be in the wrong place at the wrong time. The nave has been walled off and was then in use as a shortened, crosswise place of worship. There was a rather businesslike Holy Thursday liturgy that evening. The bishop, obviously directing his attention to the future, washed the feet of a set of elementary school children rather than the more usual dozen prosperous businessmen. The singing of modern Italian hymns was lusty, and the people in our area helpful when we seemed hard put to find the proper place in the paperback hymnal.

Feeling neither religiously nor aesthetically stirred by the experience in church, we went in search of spiritual reinforcement at a clearly marked "American Bar" on the Corso Cavour near the Piazza Minerva, where late-day sunshine and a scattering of tulips made a very pleasant setting. As is usually the case in Italian towns, there was a convenient *ristorante-pizzeria* that provided us with a splendid supper of gnocchi and tomato salad.

Up early the next day we experienced our first contact with Italian medical practice. I noticed while shaving that an old mole under my arm had suddenly become enlarged and turned black. Mildly concerned by the color of the growth, I asked the (much-cheerier) day manager at the desk in the morning about seeking a consultation in Pavia. He said that his friend, a doctor, came every morning to have coffee at the hotel and that I should ask her. The young lady was charming and full of information—mainly that I should go to the Policlinico San Matteo and see someone at the dermatological unit. The prospect of a lengthy and bureaucratic encounter with the specter of socialized medicine was daunting, but it seemed the sensible thing to do. We parked outside the gates of the Policlinico and I left Cathy with a good book to while away the morning while I plunged through the portal.

The attendant at the uncrowded *sportello* heard me out in my limping Italian and rattled something into his computer. A map emerged from the printer and he drew bright green lines to direct me across the considerable campus of the Policlinico to the Dermatologia Clinica. The whole institution was arranged like a small college campus with separate buildings for the various specialties. Once in the "derm unit," I explained myself at another window and was given a sheet of paper to take to a numbered room. Finding no one there, I came back to the source of instruction and was then led to another room where a nurse said *il dottore* would see me in a few moments. Five minutes later, a tall, black-bearded man examined me, diagnosed it as a necrotic "skin tag," and suggested that he remove it. The operation was completed in about *un attimo* and capped with a Band-Aid. When I asked him about paying for his services, he said it should not cost much more than 30,000 lire ($17) at another building on my way out to the exterior world. The whole adventure took about thirty-five minutes, surely far less than having anything to do with the medical world in the United States. Maybe the Italians are onto something. After all, the oldest medical school in the western world is in Bologna, just down the Via Emilia to the east. When I asked the doctor how he learned to speak such fluent English, he replied that after graduating from Bologna, he spent a postgraduate year at Massachusetts General Hospital.

I skipped out on my responsibility by leaving the campus by the gate from whence I came and mailed a check later from the States. I made the check considerably larger than the doctor's estimate and said that the extra amount should be considered a contribution to the estimable Policlinico San Matteo. Three months later I received a letter telling me that I owed the clinic nothing at all, and enclosing my uncanceled check. So much for socialized medicine.

Reassured by this intimation of immortality, we set out to visit the Certosa, a short drive north of the town. Gian Galeazzo, one of the later inheritors of the Visconti name and power, first established it in 1396 as an oversized private chapel for his family and a home for a dozen monks. The wealth of the pious warrior family was poured

into the building over the next several hundred years. Eventually
there were cells for two dozen monks and a cathedral-sized building
fit to crown and bury the kings or dukes of the country. It began as a
Gothic building, but successive generations went on building during
the Renaissance years, eventually adding baroque styles, until the
whole breathtaking mass became quite hard to characterize. I would
say that the guidebooks are right: It must be seen, if only because
there is no rational way to describe this richly decorated building.

In the north transept there is a lovely set of tomb figures where
Ludovico il Moro Sforza lies as on his nuptial couch with his bride,
Beatrice d'Este, the young princess of Ferrara, sister of the more
famous Isabella d'Este, who was the wife and widow of the Gonzaga,
Marquis of Mantua. The d'Este girls were surely two of the most
famous women of the Italian Renaissance and, if the artists are to be
believed, two of the loveliest. The tomb effigies at the Certosa show
the husband and wife somewhat idealized, since he was in fact close
to fifty when he married the teenaged beauty. Their marble figures
carved by Cristoforo Solari are shown as innocent young age-mates,
side by side, heads pillowed on embroidered cushions, dressed in
elaborate court costumes. Her bodice has an attractive, deep *scollatura*,
and she wears not high heels, but platform shoes that would have
elevated her diminutive stature a good three inches.

At the opposite side of the crossing is the vastly more elaborate
tomb of Gian Galeazzo, whose effigy rests under an elegant loggia
ornamented with Roman swags, Corinthian pilasters, and acanthus
leaves. It is the duke's third resting place. He left instructions as
to the general shape of his tomb at Pavia, but he was buried and
dug up twice before finally being settled here in the late fifteenth
century. Work on the decoration of the monument went on for
some time thereafter.

One of the most delightful and curious of the many sculptures at the Certosa is just outside of the transept where the monks would come into the church for mass. Having possibly been digging in their gardens or merely in contemplation of their own imperfections, it was appropriate that they should wash their hands and say a few prayers. A large, ornamental lavabo placed here is an intricate piece of cream-colored marble carved into a horizontal water tank with six bronze spigots where the ablutions could be performed. Above the water source is a pair of luxuriating dolphins on either side of a bust of an unknown man. A benefactor? The sculptor?

All around this washroom are the Visconti duchesses of Milan and the ladies of the Sforza family, seven women in all, placed here in charming if unusual profusion in the all-male celibate purview of the monastery.

The entire church is decorated with frescoes and paintings to a degree of richness really unmatched in any other interior in Italy. They are truly too much to describe. One of the most charming is an elegant little piece of trompe l'oeil painting high up in the nave where it seems a monk is peering down at the visitors below from the half-open shutters of a secret attic. Up above, the groined ceiling is painted a brilliant, star-studded blue.

I was startled to learn from the literature in the bookstore that this beautiful place was still a monastery, but no longer for Carthusian monks. It was despoiled by the anticlerical soldiers of Napoleon who shot up the frescoes, cut up the tapestries, and stole the golden and jeweled ornaments of the church. Ah, the visits of the French! Paintings were stolen and the lead roof requisitioned to be recast into bullets. The order was suppressed, the altars desecrated, and the furniture sold at auction. After the French withdrew, a few priests were allowed to work as caretakers to prevent the tombs of the rest of the Visconti from being opened and robbed. The Carthusians were allowed back and pushed away several times in the nineteenth century, and again under the terms of Mussolini's Lateran Treaty with the pope. Most recently the Cistercian monks took over the care of the national monument in 1968.

We were shown through the building by a young Cistercian, a tall and elegant black who lectured in rapid Italian and was obviously well informed about both the art and history of the charterhouse. His order is almost equally strict, but slightly more loquacious than that of the founders of the Certosa. Unfortunately, he seemed to speak no English and we were forced to resort to the guidebook. In spite of the language barrier, he was a charming man who stopped occasionally in his tour through the great buildings to pause before various altars and shrines and lead his guests in a few prayers.

There are ten of these brother priests in residence now, living in the cells constructed for their Carthusian predecessors. The quarters seemed quite comfortable. Each of the little residences surrounding the "Great Cloister" was in effect a small, three-room house composed of a kitchen, a study, and a bed chamber. Each cell has a small walled garden behind it where part of each monk's food supply was provided by his own effort. For a solitary scholar with access to books and writing materials, it appeared to be a rather pleasant hermitage. Surely the good fathers then and now were surrounded by beauty as wondrous as the combined talents of a half-dozen generations of Italy's greatest artists could provide.

Since it was now Good Friday, we felt faintly guilty seeking a good lunch in such close proximity to the home of holy men who ate so little on any given day, and still less in such a season of penitence. We need not have worried. Just outside the gatehouse and gift shop of the convent is La Bruschetta, a tidy little pizzeria that provided better-quality food and service than anyone has a right to expect from the snack bar at a major tourist attraction.

Back in the town of Pavia itself, by late afternoon we went out to visit the church of San Michele, an early Romanesque building that seemed in much more vigorous use than the available fragment of the cathedral we had attended the day before. A solemn service was just getting under way amid the remaining banks of Holy Thursday flowers. A layman and a priest collaborated in a dramatic reading of the Passion. It is amazing what familiarity with the story will do for one's understanding of a foreign language, especially when it is declaimed in a loud, clear voice in an area of good acoustics.

Continuing to stroll through parts of the city almost depopulated by the holy day, we passed the Church of the Carmine, where the warm brickwork glowed in the sporadic sunshine and the deep blue of the sky. We found an office building that looked almost as though Brunelleschi might have designed its lofty interior rotunda. Kids used the elegant space for roller-blading, and since we were threatened with a shower of rain, we took advantage of a convenient coffee bar to settle in for an *aperitivo*. The bartender was sociable and not very busy on this holiday afternoon. A young father with two attractive sons dropped in to provide the boys with mountainous cones of *gelato*. Later we found a simple restaurant where we dined on risotto con pesce and a mushroom pizza. We were amazed at the dimension of the dinner being served the people at the next table: slices of pizza, a half ball each of fresh mozzarella, a platter of fish, spaghetti *alla mare*, bread, wine, and, finally, a macedonia of fresh fruit. As always in Italy, dinner in even the simplest circumstances can be a memorable affair.

We departed Pavia the next morning, hoping that we might come back someday. There is more here than a couple of days can encompass. We had missed the Visconti Castle where there is a museum of the *Risorgimento* and a gallery of modern art. The university also boasts distinction of age (1361) and a number of famous graduates, including Cristoforo Colombo. I wonder if he dreamt of those fabulous realms of the Far East while being bored during irrelevant lectures while Lorenzo the Magnifico ruled in Florence and before Michelangelo was just a talented beginner. No less than Rome, Pavia has sent out her sons to change the world.

XX.

REGGIO EMILIA AND CANOSSA:
Good Food and the Memory
of a Powerful Contessa

There are two Reggios in Italy: Reggio Calabria at the very toe of the boot, just across the tide-racked Strait of Messina from Sicily; and Reggio nell'Emilia, about an hour west of Bologna on the broad plain of the Po Valley, next door to the other half of the great cheese partnership. The word *reggio* means either the rule—or perhaps the support—of something. The *reggipetto* supports the bosom; the regista is the director of a film; *reggia* means royal palace; and *Reggiano* refers to a native of one of the two Reggios. Italians are sparing with place names, and there are very few that share a single designation. It is not at all like the United States, where there is a Salem in perhaps forty of the fifty states. I think the name reflects a time when this small city swung more weight politically before the turn of the last millennium. In any case, the city and province of Reggio Emilia have seen a lot of history, a bit of which is still visible and much of it well remembered.

It is not surprising that a simple river crossing could grow to become a municipality in the early years of the Roman republic, when the citizen soldiers were unifying all of Italy but were not yet embarked on foreign conquest. The Roman Regium Lepidi was a fortified camp of the army which here protected the bridge over the Crostolo, a tributary of the Po which cut across the road along the south side of the greater river. At that time the Ligurian Gauls were still a menace in Italy proper.[9] Like many of the standardized Roman camps, the settlement expanded quite rapidly. The fertile plain of the Po was intensively farmed, and a city established in the relatively few hundred years of the Empire before the coming of the Goths and the later domination of the Lombards. The gradual collapse into feudalism in the sixth, seventh, and eighth centuries led to castle building and the isolation of the few remaining towns. The revival of cities (and thus of civilization) began shortly after the bishop-ruled towns developed a middle class and the guilds developed a corps of skilled artisans. The successful mercantile population built city walls and developed the client towns into the free communes that became the cities of the Renaissance.

Emilia Romagna is reputed in Italy to be the locus of the finest food found on the peninsula. Reggio is also the other half of the true designation of the world's most popular cheese: Parmigiano-Reggiano. In America it is usually grated when dry and sprinkled on almost any kind of pasta, vegetable, or salad to its benefit. In Italy it is often eaten in chunks whacked off the wheel, with fruit or by itself, still slightly moist and sweeter than the shaved or grated variety vended in supermarkets from the Atlantic to the Pacific. The town is also famed for *prosciutto*, the finest Parma ham. A century ago Parma violets were made into perfume, but there seems little of that industry

---

[9] History shows that the French and their Gallic predecessors have been coming south with lascivious designs on disunified Italy for thousands of years. The only Italian to have made an invasion in the opposite direction would seem to have been Julius Caesar. The Germans have done a fair amount of Italian invasion as well.

left in the area, its place having been taken by organic chemistry.

In Reggio, the east and west segments of the old Roman road are designated Via Emilia San Pietro and Via Emilia San Stefano. There are lots of one-way streets, and finding our landing place at the Albergo Cairoli took patient application. The attractive little hotel is off a tiny parking court a block and a half west of the Piazza Martiri VII Luglio, convenient to the Teatro Municipale, for opera and also ballet, which have a flourishing season in Reggio. It is one of the most prosperous towns in Italy, despite the fact that restaurants and hotels are modestly priced. We paid about 45 euro at the Cairoli for a good room with a modern bathroom. The hand laundry in the next block was, however, the most expensive of all that I ever found in Italy. (On the other hand, if you really want to have your socks ironed, they do it rather well.)

We explored the town and discovered the Piazza Grande where the *duomo* and the Palazzo del Comune present fifteenth- and sixteenth-century facades, although the cathedral originated back in AD 857 and has plenty of Romanesque evidence about it. The town hall contains the lofty and elegant room where representatives of a quasi-independent Italy wrested from Austrian control by Napoleon III's imperial republicans designed the three-colored flag that is today the emblem of the nation. We also worked our way east for a ten-minute walk to find the Piazza San Prospero, where a half-dozen splendid stone lions crouch before the entry of the basilica. The lions have saddles to support the bases of columns on their backs, but the church, started in the tenth century, has been so often and so completely remodeled in the styles of many centuries that it is impossible to tell today what the handsome rose marble beasts supported in their original orientation. But one should not miss this piazza; it is part market and part processional site, to my mind the best show in town. Walking around the cathedral we passed through arcades with the lighted windows of an extraordinary number of lingerie shops and came at length to market stalls of fruit, vegetables, cheese, and sausages.

Later we chanced on the Nuovo Boiardo, one of those wonderful Italian institutions that bear the modest title *pizzeria-ristorante*. Armed with a bottle of excellent Sansovino, we both ordered the gnocchi with buffalo mozzarella and a fresh tomato sauce, as well as a bit of *risotto asparagi* and *panna* with garlic-spiced spinach on the side. Sharing from each other's plates is the only way to get the true benefit of Emilian food. There are so many things to sample that eating a full portion of each would be gluttonous.

The name of the restaurant piqued my curiosity, and I subsequently learned that Matteo Maria Boiardo was what we would call today a Renaissance man, a poet of the new learning that so excited the *quattrocento* poets. He was Count of Scandiano. He wrote in both Latin and Italian and translated Greek and Latin classics in that period, which was the dawn of the age of printed books. He was a favorite of the great d'Este family of Ferrara when that distinguished house was at the peak of prestige and power. Boiardo's most popular work was a restructuring of a medieval epic poem, "The Song of Roland"—the legend of the perfect knight who was lost, slain by the Muslims while in command of Charlemagne's afterguard at Roncesvalles in the Pyrenees. Roland died romantically because he would not acknowledge weakness or distress and blow his mighty horn to call upon the king for reinforcement: "*Roland, Roland! Sonnez vostre cor!*"

Boiardo's version is more romantic, entitled "Orlando Innamorato." He shifts the scene to the walls of Paris and creates a charming Chinese girl named Angelica to distract the hero from his duty. Matteo never finished the mock epic, but Ariosto later picked up the thread and ran with it in the still more popular "Orlando Furioso," in which the hero is driven mad by the love of the daughter of the King of Cathay. Like the current writers of cinema and television, the romancers of the Renaissance borrowed material from wherever it lay handy, spinning tales of delightful improbability. It is interesting that his literary obscurity has not prevented Boiardo's name from being commemorated in the title of an excellent restaurant in this, his old hometown. Presumably the *clienti* catch the reference. In spite of the literary pedigree and the excellent food, the bill for our dinner and house wine came to just 76,000 lire, around $45 at that day's exchange—considerably less than most of the mediocre restaurants along the shoreline of Connecticut. Prosperous and industrialized northern Italy demanded about the same prices for books, automobiles, and most clothing, before the dollar sank, in comparison with the euro, but gasoline is more expensive and good food very much cheaper.

An English-speaking couple at the table next to ours introduced us to two of a number of teachers of early childhood education from Australia. They seemed especially pleased to be in Reggio, which we discovered later to be world-famous for the quality of its programs for preschool children. Later, we noticed another couple who had economically ordered a modest half-liter of a simple wine. Not being able to finish our larger bottle of a more pretentious vintage, we put it on their table as we left, asking them to please finish it for us. Such largesse gives one the feeling of being *un signore*.

The following day dawned gray and threatened rain, one of only two such days during a five-week spring tour. We set out from Reggio to explore in the hills to the south where it was said there were castles. The countryside is rolling and lumpy south of Reggio, and soon there were sizable hills ahead of us, the beginning of the Apennine barrier that cuts diagonally across the boot (*il stivale*) from Liguria to the Marches. Getting through these mountains via infrequent passes gave early importance to Parma and Bologna, for Reggio's southern accessibility was through narrow defiles and zigzagging hill roads that were easily dominated by castles on the hilltops. Quattro Castelle on the map and on signposts is an area where each mist-shrouded mountain seems to bear the ruin of an ancient stone fortification. Not knowing quite what we were looking for, and being somewhat frustrated by intermittent rain, we were surprised to come upon a sign pointing downhill to Castello Canossa. The story about the emperor who stood in the snow to do penance remained in the attic of my mind, so we turned in pursuit. The downhill path soon turned up again, and then down and around the sides of the green and dripping hillside. After ten minutes and perhaps five hundred feet farther up in the mountains, we emerged in a stone-paved area at the foot of a large ruined fortress that reared above us. Signs proclaimed that it was chiuso—for the time being, at least. But across the stone-flagged court there was a modest tower three stories high, where the door stood ajar and there was some sort of building activity going on. We ducked through the rain and poked our way inside.

The room was not large, but contained a cheerful open fire burning scrap lumber and builder's leavings. Seated at a broad table beside it was a handsome elderly man who welcomed us in clear and articulate Italian. He spoke with such distinct pace and pronunciation that it seemed to me the most intelligible Italian we had yet heard. He had evidently purchased the tower quite recently and was remodeling it according to plans approved by the government to make a lunchroom, or *tavola calda*, to cater to tourists who would come to seek the more important ruin up the hill. The source and history of this most noticeable example of the struggle for authority between church and state was a few yards away. He knew his history and brought us up-to-date. When bishops were the political leaders of large territories, to whom did they owe the ownership of their demesne? To the king or emperor as liege lord, or to the pope as their spiritual superior? Who had the right to appoint them to office? To the emperor it was absurd that a distant pope should appoint the civil authority within his empire. To the pope it was anathema that anyone but the pope should select a bishop. This conflict was in full spate in the years after Charlemagne, who had himself crowned by the pope to lend authority to his newly invented office of "Holy Roman Emperor."

To me the most fascinating part of the eleventh-century story is not the position of Pope Gregory VII or his rival in power, the Emperor Henry IV of Germany, but the hostess who brought the two together and is said to have had much to do with their reconciliation.

Her name was Matilda. She was the daughter of the Duke of Lorraine, and in spite of the murder of her father and the captivity of her mother, she was a countess in her own right, and far better educated than most young noblemen of her time. She read widely in Latin as well as Italian and French, and was piously devoted to the church. The murder of her husband (it was a childless marriage with her stepbrother) left her with a huge possession of land and castles all the way from Tuscany, south of the mountains, to Reggio and much of the plain of the Po in the north. Canossa was dramatically and strategically situated to dominate the routes from Germany to the prosperous central and southern Italian cities. From her own fortification as well as from the castle of Rossesa on a neighboring hill, Matilda thus governed a vast territory that extended from Florence to Mantua. In a spirit of mixed shrewd self-protection and piety, she gave the whole thing to the pope, who gallantly ceded it back to her as a fief with the right to direct its descent. Her court at Canossa welcomed artists and intellectuals. Her era in the eleventh century was another of those renaissances that came before the "Italian Renaissance," with which we are more familiar.[10] Her castles are all in ruins now and there is relatively little of that civilized center of culture to see today.

But if the buildings are gone, their historical location remains, and the echoes of what happened there are still with us. In 1076 Henry IV and the German bishops convened the Synod of Worms where they defended lay investiture of bishops. After all, without the right to appoint these ecclesiastical landlords, governing the empire would seem to be impossible. The synod moved to depose the pope and even found some support among the north Italian bishops. Gregory deposed and excommunicated the emperor. Henry, seeing that he was about to lose the battle, came south to where the pope had taken up residence as Matilda's guest at Canossa. But the pontiff refused to even meet with the emperor, who did penance by standing in the snow in the palace courtyard from dawn to dark. Matilda and the Abbot Hugh of Cluny (Henry's godfather) finally persuaded the combatants to settle the issue: Henry would invest with legal power the episcopal candidate selected by the pope, and the pope (or his nuncio) would approve all candidates. The king came in from the snow without frostbitten toes. But the pope really won, and the right

---

[10] Our whole idea of the Renaissance seems really to be the invention of a brilliant Swiss scholar, Jacob Christoph Burckhardt, whose book, The Civilization of the Renaissance in Italy, published in 1860, makes good reading even today. There is a Penguin edition in English currently in print.

of the Bishop of Rome to intervene in political matters and the right of succession among the powers of Europe stayed around until the nineteenth century. The American constitutional division between church and state has some of its origin in the lack of a clear-cut victory of civil over religious authority at Matilda's castle.

Of course, there was no way either man could have won a decisive showdown in eleventh-century Europe. Bloody wars echoed on for centuries thereafter before the American and French revolutions began to show the way toward the modern secular state.

But the lady's power made a difference. On postcards she is seen sometimes mounted, sometimes regnant, but usually holding up an orange by the stem. I assume this is some sort of symbol of hospitality and nourishment that refers to her providing bed and board to pope and emperor while they quarreled.

Our host, who helped fill me in on many details of the winter of 1076, was a veritable fountain of medieval history.[11] It was a delight to sit by the fire in the cheery old stone room with the rain pattering outside and discuss things that happened so long ago with a scholarly innkeeper who cared about them. He had a bundle of ancient keys that had surfaced during his work remodeling the little tower. Evidently none of them matched existing doors, and he presented me with one as a souvenir of our visit.

We drove back to the more northerly area of Matilda's great fief, passing among the imposing ruined stumps of castles of indeterminate age while looking for lunch. Here we came across the town of Ciano d'Enza, where the bar-trattoria Il Giglio welcomed us for a splendid

---

[11] For example, he maintained that the pope gave Henry absolution for his sins but refused to give him communion at mass at Canossa.

midday meal along with most of the workmen of the town. We had a thick minestrone, *penne arrabiata*, and various vegetables topped off with wonderfully chewy bread, wine, and two or three great hunks of Parmigiano-Reggiano.

In the continuing tradition of Emilian gluttony, when we got back to Reggio we followed advice given by our hotelkeeper at the Cairoli and sought out a restaurant across the lovely opera-house square, which turned out to be closed for this one day of the week. In its stead we were lucky enough to find a neighboring *ristorante* on the Via Roma, not unusually entitled the "Canossa."

Here we found that the great tradition of the *bollito misto* was carried on by the proprietors, the *fratelli* Caro. A steaming trolley was wheeled to our table, and by maneuvering various levers, the waiter raised from the boiling broth a breast of capon, a beef tongue, a cotechino sausage, a haunch of beef, a loin of pork, a *zampone* (stuffed pig's trotter), and a chunk of prosciutto. After the *salami maigro* and *mortadella* we had for antipasto, one might wonder what else we could add. We rejected the mashed potatoes that the locals seemed to prefer and accepted a small slice of fried polenta and a green salad along with the meat. Cathy could only manage three of the boiled offerings; I asked for slices of five. Two sauces were served with the *bollito*—one yellowish-brown that appeared to be a mild mustard; and best of all, a green sauce made from virgin olive oil, balsamic vinegar, minced artichokes, lots of basil and parsley, and a couple of mystery ingredients that must have been specified by the Caro family some generations ago.

It was our last night in Reggio, and it turned out to be an appropriate salute to the legendary cooking of Emilia Romagna. Wine and all, that extraordinary meal cost the two of us 83,000 lire—about $46 by prices in the late 1990s. Restaurants like the "Canossa" are in

XXI.

A WEEK IN LUCCA
AND A DAY IN PISA

Lucca, ringed by fierce, intact medieval walls, is nevertheless a very approachable town. On one trip we were fortunate enough to come to Lucca by air into Pisa Airport, and found that there is a spur of the state railroad just outside the air terminal. The train took us through the downtown Pisa station and then directly on to Lucca, which we reached about twenty-five minutes after our plane landed.

Traveling economically as usual, we had booked at the Hotel Moderno, which we found to be located on the wrong side of the tracks from the little city itself. But we soon learned that there was an overpass stairway which bridged the railroad only a hundred meters west of the station. The Moderno is neither among the better nor the worst of the places we have patronized in Italy, but it was, at least, convenient, and cost $54 a night for a fair-sized room with a perfectly adequate bath in a season when the lire stood at 1,680 to the dollar. Since being pegged to the euro, it has become even a bit cheaper, but surely not more comfortable. Its location outside the historic walls, however, turned out to be an advantage. If we had been on the better side of the tracks, we might never have discovered some of the delights of modern Lucca, which has overflowed the old bounds of the city and created new neighborhoods to the south and east of the old town.

The great walls of Lucca evidently worked as a defense, but I don't think they were really tested in the age of high Renaissance artillery. Such walls are monuments to the mangled bodies of the thousands who must have died while attacking and defending these towns. What it must have smelled like in the weeks after a siege attack! For all its beauty, the Renaissance was a bloody time of slaughter.

But this old city has seen longer stretches of peace than most in Italy by substituting diplomacy and guile for powder and ball. As a result, much of the medieval architecture is intact, and the entire circuit of the city is here for us to walk upon. The crest of the wall is twenty or more yards wide, and expands into ten or more bastions, each making a mini park almost half the size of a soccer field. The whole perimeter is planted with a double row of deciduous trees, which look to me like sycamores and maples but are a related species of European tree, the London plane tree.

Walking the wall is a favorite occupation of young lovers and elderly couples in this town. Access is gained by ramps near the various gates to the city. Young mothers push their prams up to the encircling path with ease. Although there is no real parkland in the center of town, this green sash about the hips is everywhere close at hand in Lucca. It provides a location for the traditional Italian *passeggiata*.

As in most small Italian cities, the Piazza Duomo (or cathedral) is both a place of worship and public gathering as well as the site of the principal museum of the area. Lucca's biggest church was built in the eleventh century and is dedicated to St. Martin, the young Roman officer who gave his cloak (or perhaps just half of it, cut off with his sword) to a poor man of Tours. Martin appears on the facade in full relief, the legs of his horse standing square on a pair of elaborately carved corbels between the two left-hand arches of the front doors of the great church. Above him are rows of narrow, delicate arches that decorate the whole front of the building. Surely the sculptors of these elegant spans were among the best artisans of their time. Most of the stone carvers' names are unknown, but there is reason to believe that the great pre-Renaissance master Nicola Pisano did the reliefs over the left doorway inside the open-air narthex. The style of the rows of arches is characteristic of the churches of Pisa and Lucca, which set the fashion for all of Italy in the twelfth and thirteenth centuries.

The building is literally stuffed with small artistic treasures of the late Middle Ages. One of the finest is preserved in a little *tempietto* of its own done by Matteo Civitali. It is the *Volto Santo*, a greater-than-life-sized sculpture of the crucified Christ. Said to be far older than it can possibly be, the *Volto* is reputed to have been made by Nicodemus, the bystander who, with Joseph of Arimathea, lifted down the lifeless body of the Lord from the cross. This splendid and obviously ancient icon is taken out of the cathedral once a year on the thirteenth of September and carried in procession through the town in the gathering darkness. Like so many Italian traditions of piety, the firm belief that the corpus and its supporting cross are much older than they could possibly be is easy to accept when you are present in the church with others who gather around the little interior temple on their knees and tell the beads of their anachronistic rosaries.

The cathedral also houses one of Tintoretto's *Ultima Cena* paintings, which he usually drew in accordance with the then-current decrees of the Inquisition and Holy Office, showing Christ giving a communion wafer to each apostle by placing it in their open mouths in the prescribed manner of the mass of the Counter-Reformation.

The amazing thing about Tintoretto is that he is so good at what he does that the almost silly fundamentalism of his subject matter does not detract from the majesty of his conception and the great detail with which he tells his visual story. Even so, there is something almost excessively concrete about some of the later art of Lucca.

But there is a great exception to this literalism in the spirit and style of the greatest gem of the cathedral collection. This portrayal is not of a saint, not the Redeemer, but a beautiful girl, Ilaria del Carretto, who was married to Paolo Guinigi, the lord of Lucca in the first years of the *quattrocento*. She died in her early twenties. Her heartbroken husband commissioned the young Jacopo della Quercia to do a tomb effigy in the costume of a wealthy young princess of the time. Della Quercia presents the young beauty in a long, flowing robe with a high standing collar and a turban-like hat decorated with flowers in high relief. He surrounded the sides of the sarcophagus with shy *putti*, naked little cherubim, boys who hold drooping garlands of flowers that encircle the marble coffin. A pet dog looks up from his position warming her feet. The almost sentimental tribute to love and beauty is firmly a work of the new dispensation, one of the initial sculptures of the Renaissance. Its date, 1405, is amazingly early for a work bearing so many signs of Roman paganism and the humanism of the coming age. Shortly after her entombment, Paolo remarried. His first wife was disinterred and her sarcophagus moved three times before it settled in its reverent location: a must-see site when you visit.

There are many churches in Lucca, as there are in all Italian cities. Here, however, almost all seem to be open and in use, although one which we visited had been converted into an art gallery. Another, San Michele in Foro, is second in magnitude to the cathedral, its grand facade topped by a great archangel pitchforking Satan into hell from the very crest of the church roof. Inside, San Michele is noted for a particularly lovely Madonna and Child by Andrea Della Robbia. The innocence of the Virgin is accentuated by the faithful sculpture of a model who can have hardly been more than a fifteen-year-old when Della Robbia made her immortal in a masterwork of white glazed terra cotta outlined against a deep cobalt-blue background. She is probably a century younger than the marble tomb figure of Ilaria in the duomo, but the two girls could be sisters.

While in Lucca we breakfasted each morning outside the walls at a comfortable bar-*pasticceria*, the Planet Café, two blocks south of our hotel across the railroad tracks, about five minutes' walk from the center of town. Their breakfast pastries were delightful and their *caffelatte* and cappuccino the usual delicious Italian brew. There was an *edicola* across the street where I could find my morning copy of *La Repubblica*. Paying an extra premium for the coffee gave me the lease of a table on which to spread out the newspaper and translate the morning's news with the assistance of a pocket dictionary.

The excellence of the coffee shop made me bold enough to search farther to the south down the Viale Concordio toward the location of the old church of Paolino, which was marked on the map as being of "secondary" interest. A few streets farther along I came upon a large and busy *pizzeria-ristorante* which seemed to function mostly as a take-out shop. I saw no sign of a restaurant, so I asked. The obliging counter girl drew aside an accordion door at the end of the shop and revealed a restaurant of what appeared to be twenty tables set with peach-colored tablecloths and stemmed wineglasses. It opened, she explained, at 7:30 in the evening. Making note that the place smelled good and was obviously a great bargain, I explored further to see what this new quarter of Lucca had to offer.

In another fifty yards I came upon a huge, modern brick building

settled in the space near an underground parking lot. It bore a set
of letters six feet high that proclaimed it to be a SUPERSTORE
with free parking. Now, we Americans are used to setting the style
for retailing all over the world and are accustomed to our large-scale
Stop & Shop, Wal-Mart, or Harris Teeter offering us groceries along
with a variety of services such as a pharmacy and a bank. We have
something to learn from Italy even so. The Luccan Superstore with
the American-English name boasted a row of about twenty checkout
lines that led the departing customer to a great transept paved with
creamy Bottocino marble and giving access to a bank, a pharmacy,
an optician, an upscale ladies' boutique, a men's haberdashery, and a
store that specialized in high-quality lingerie of minimal surface area.
The market itself contained not only all sorts of food and delicacies,
but also all the less-expensive lines of sweaters, T-shirts, underwear,
sneakers, and the like. Italy is largely motorized now, and this store
welcomed those who drove into town from country residences to
park in the subterranean garage beneath the store and take the lift
to a complete shopping experience with the children in the stroller.
At the end of the west end of the transept was a complete bar that
served coffee, gelato, soft drinks, wine, and spirits from eight in the
morning until past nine at night. The pleasant bistro was positioned
to allow the patrons to survey the other customers coming or going
from the ranks of registers. It seemed to be a very popular place to
meet a date.

We went on to find San Paolino. The reconstructed church is in
the southern quarter of the expanded town. The pleasant elderly pastor
was bidding affectionate good-byes to the children who had come for
religious instruction after school. He told us much about the church,
including a remarkable story of the return of the tower bell which
had been removed by the Fascists and for years was thought to have

been melted down during World War II. But the bell had been placed in another city and a long negotiation got it returned to Lucca just a few years ago. In terms of Tuscan sites, the little church may well be of "secondary" interest, but only in comparison with the eleventh- and twelfth-century ecclesiastical architecture that is in the center of town. Anyplace else on earth, it would be a city landmark.

We walked back toward the central city in the late afternoon and stopped at the Superstore bar for our customary *aperitivo* of a gin and tonic and a martini. We found Schweppes and Gordon's available in generous measure and with plenty of ice at a price of £2,500, less than $1.50 at the prevailing exchange. The barmaid was anxious to please and generous with her dishes of peanuts and oyster crackers. The Italian dinner hour is always late enough to require that we find some such bar to kill the pangs of hunger while we wait until the requisite 7:30 P.M. for entry to *ristorante* or *trattoria*. People-watching in the Superstore made this interval a pleasant one until we repaired to Al Viale Pizzeria-Ristorante, which I had investigated earlier. We were almost the first to arrive, but it filled up quickly and we soon realized that we were the only non-Lucchese there. The pastas listed among the *primi* all looked quite wonderful, and we learned that the best the restaurant had to offer (for we returned again on a later night) was the most extensive buffet of *antipasto* I have ever seen. The huge selection of appetizers and a simple plate of pasta made a wonderful meal. The house wines, both red and white, were fine, and the *conto* came to around $24.70 for a superb dinner with wine for the two of us. We toddled home to the Moderno feeling that we could afford to stay several more days in this pleasant town.

The proximity of Lucca to both Florence and Pisa made it almost mandatory to visit both of these more-famous cities for day trips. The two journeys were of forty minutes in one direction or twenty in the other. We chose Pisa first because we had never been there and knew that the Campo dei Miracoli where the Leaning Tower stands is one of the great sights of Europe. The bus from the Pisan Stazione Centrale was easy to find and delivered us right to the archway that led to the "Field of Miracles."

We had, of course, seen pictures of the tower and knew that there was a cathedral close by. However, we were not really prepared for the stunning collection of buildings in the famous Campo. The lush green of the seven-acre lawn that surrounds the buildings is like a brightly colored cushion laid out to display the jewels. Far bigger than the famous Torre Pendente is the baptistery, a circular building splendidly surmounted by a huge dome whose summit rises higher than either the dome of the cathedral or the top of the well-known tower. Between the baptistery and the campanile is the cathedral which was begun in 1064, a few years before the Normans invaded either England or Sicily.

The cathedral is an extravagant and wonderful piece of architecture which was decorated by the best artists of each succeeding age. Cimabue did the apse mosaic of Christ in Majesty, finishing it in 1302; Giovanni Pisano made the pulpit in the early fourteenth century. The pulpit is probably the best such you will ever see. Scenes from New and Old Testaments encircle the whole, but the four supports of the pulpit itself are caryatids that stand as allegories of the arts. The figures are real precursors of the Renaissance, Grecian ladies and gentlemen draped and naked in the best style of two thousand years before Pisano's time. The ages are bridged in this cathedral where the late Middle Ages seemed fused with the art of classical Rome and Greece.

Alongside the *duomo* is the Campo Santo, a long, enclosed cemetery in which Pisans were buried for hundreds of years. Much of the earth in which they were interred is supposed to have been brought back from Calvary itself by crusaders serving in the armies of this wealthy trading city. The whole of the Campo Santo was burned to a dismal pile of wall-enclosed trash in the aftermath of an errant Allied bomb in 1944. Again the Italian genius for putting things back together after a seemingly irretrievable disaster won out over the heartbreaking destruction that has affected this country so often. There is much to see here, including the tomb of the Countess Matilda, who reconciled Pope Gregory and the excommunicated Emperor Henry Hohenstaufen, who stood in the snow doing penance at Canossa in the late eleventh century. Besides the tombs, there is a whole building full of the *senopia*, the sepia drawings that underlie all frescoes. They were covered with wet plaster into which the painter brushed pigment to create his design. Where the tinted plaster has been removed to be stabilized and preserved on a new backing, the original drawings have been recovered from their underlayment. These have been carefully lifted from the wall and presented here as works of art in their own right. These free-hand drawings of the great masters of fresco seem wonderfully contemporary. In some cases they are all that remains of the work of art, since time, moisture, and wartime bombing often destroyed the colored fresco itself.

Any of the great Pisan buildings are worth the journey to this city. We felt we were well served by buying the perforated tickets that admitted us to everything for a single charge. The Museo dell'Opera del Duomo is a fifth place to be seen. There are more of Giovanni Pisano's great sculptures here, as well as a mini course in the art history of the last half-millennium.

But the ultimate gem of the Campo is the campanile, *Il Torre Pendente*—the Leaning Tower itself. The tower, begun in 1173, was originally designed by the architect and artist who also did the doors for King William of Sicily's great abbey of Monreale in Palermo. Bonanno Pisano[12] originated the exquisite design, and supervised construction as it grew. It began to lean before the first three tiers of arches were in place. The soil is slippery and shifty down below. Nothing seemed able to deter the list to the southeast. Lots of concrete pumped into the subsoil did no good, but in 1994, six hundred tons of lead blocks were strapped to the north side of the foundation and the whole mass was brought into balance. All was well until one night, a year later, the tower suddenly gave an unobserved lurch in the middle of the night and straightened itself up a couple of centimeters all at once. The engineers peering through the theodolite were terrified at the possibility that the whole thing would pull itself to pieces, but after a reduction of the weight of the counterbalance, things have pretty much stabilized. There is no plan to make it perpendicular, just constant in its tilt. At whatever angle, Il Torre Pendente is an elegant and masterful creation. Today it is again possible to climb its 294 steps and retrace the route of Galileo with his lead and wooden balls in his pocket.

Whatever else Pisa is known for, it will forever be the city of Galileo. Born here and sent to the local university to study medicine, he did not earn a degree but took up the study of mathematics and physics. His father, who was both a physician and a musician, supported his independent study. By the time he was twenty-five,

---

[12] So many of the early artists are named Pisano that the mind conjures up an image of a huge and talented family of architects, sculptors, and painters. Actually, surnames were not much in use for commoners before the fifteenth century. Anyone who traveled outside his hometown got to be known by his place of origin, so there are lots of artists known as Pisano, Perugino, or Romano. Others are known by such names as Il Sodoma for their lifestyle or sexual orientation.

Galileo had applied for a position as a university professor. Bologna and Florence turned him down, but his hometown offered him the chair of mathematics, and he spent the next twenty years teaching in Pisa. Going to the cathedral (he was a devout Catholic despite all of his later trouble with the pope and the Inquisition), he noticed that the suspended chandelier near the pulpit swung gently back and forth with the same rhythm, whether the swing was broad or narrow. Presumably distracted from paying close attention to the sermon, he pieced together the theory of uniform pendulum beating and the beginnings of a theory of gravitation that completely refuted the physics of Aristotle, which was the revealed truth of the day. From there he demonstrated the uniformity of the descent of falling bodies and conducted experiments with inclined planes, presumably measuring velocities and rates by having a musician play a steady beat that allowed him to calculate time intervals to a fraction of a second.

The bell tower of Pisa, quite aside from its beauty and angle of repose, would be a monument to science if only for being the location of Galileo's experiment to show that falling bodies accelerated at a constant rate, irrespective of their weight or density. He truly established the modern science of mathematical physics, and demolished the wholly theoretical physics of the classical philosophers and the medieval school men. His experimentally derived mathematical laws set up the conditions for Isaac Newton's formulation of the law of universal gravitation, only a brief lifetime after the great Italian physicist's discoveries. For Newton, who seems a recent, modern Cambridge professor of mathematics, was actually born in 1642, the year in which the church-bedeviled Renaissance Italian, a professor of the University of Pisa, died in retirement, still under the threat of the Inquisition. What a collision of historical periods is that!

In the eighth year of Harvard College, shortly before the beheading of the last personal monarch of Britain, the great old man who had seen the moons of Jupiter and demonstrated that the Bible is not to be read as science, dies after being humiliated by the fundamentalist forces of obscurantism and superstition. His place on earth and in the pantheon of science is then taken by the astonishing Englishman, whose flexible mind fashions a new physical law that describes the three dimensions of the then-known starry universe in an exact mathematical relationship: It is all held together by a force directly proportional to the product of the masses and inversely proportional to the square of the distances between them. This was the work of the giants on whose shoulders stood James Clerk Maxwell, Max Planck, and Albert Einstein.

Feeling that we were far from being sated on Pisa, we returned to Lucca and continued to explore the town for several more days. We made forays into various quarters of the old city. There are streets full of the shops of bookbinders, frame makers, and other artisans, as well as bookstores and shops full of statuary. On regularly scheduled days there is a huge open-air market curving around the eastern quarter of the town. Like all such areas of commercial enterprise in Italy, the market seems to present our century in the fashion of the Middle Ages. Food, clothing, art, and even ironmongery are presented in tented booths. Prices are negotiable within a broad range. Everything seems affordable.

We went on to visit the small museum that the family has made of the home of Giacomo Puccini. It contains some interesting exhibits and the piano on which he picked out the haunting melodies of "Che Gelida Manina" and "Mi Chiamano Mimi." It is said that he finished *La Bohème* at dawn, having worked all night with the tears streaming down his face as he created the final sobbing chords that accompanied the death of the heroine. He had obviously fallen in love with Mimi ever as much as Rodolfo had. The museum gives a feeling of the great composer, but it seemed to us to make too much of his relatives and not enough of his music. Still, it was fun to tour the house.

Outside the house, a half-dozen blocks to the south, is the town's honorific statue of the great modern composer. He is shown in regal relaxation in a comfortable armchair with his legs crossed, characteristic cigar between his fingers, and broad-brimmed Italian hat jauntily on his head.

We found a number of good restaurants in Lucca during the six nights we spent there. Best known is the *bucadisantantonio*, or St. Anthony's-hole-in-the-wall (or bistro). Here we had an elegant Sunday dinner surrounded by well-to-do Lucchese who were honoring the Lord 's Day with a celebration of good food. For a *ristorante* with paneled walls and a fireplace glowing in the bar, the *buca* turned out to be surprisingly affordable.

One of the most charming (and most touristic) sights in Lucca is the imprint of the old Roman amphitheater, which is outlined by the buildings constructed over the years on its foundations and from its building stones. Rather like a miniature of the Piazza Navona in Rome, this sunny, oval space has been a constant location for the restless reconstruction of the city for 1,500 years. Today it has ranks of comfortable plastic chairs set out in the sun where visitors can refresh themselves. Around the piazza is a circuit of little shops and trinket stands to provide visitors with mementos of their day in Lucca. We settled down for our customary refreshment and enjoyed it, but had to take note of the fact that this location caused the price of a gin and tonic to rise to £9,000 per drink, or $10.80 for the two of us, in comparison with the $3 worth of lire the same service cost us the night before at the congenial little bar in the Superstore outside the walls.

But despite the costly *aperitivi*, we remember Lucca fondly for the children in the Piazza dell'Anfiteatro who blew soap bubbles in the late-afternoon sunshine. As the curved shadow of the Roman space grew and the sunny crescent shrank to a smaller and smaller area at the far side of the piazza, the children and a pair of frolicking dogs moved with it, like performers staying in their spotlight, until the illumination mounted the far wall and left the area in shadow. The evening grew chilly quite soon, and we all left to join the *passeggiata* back to the center of town and the promise of a good supper. There are plenty of places to eat at all levels of price in Lucca. One of the more elegant hotels[13] on the Piazza Napoleone had a public dining room that offered a "touristic menu" which provided an excellent dinner of limited choice for £20,000, including the house wine (less than $17 per person at the time).

Quite a bit later that night we climbed the stair to the railroad overpass that took us back to our hotel. The darkness had been accentuated by the Ferrovia Statale having thoughtfully turned off the floodlights of the railroad yard for a few hours to aid naked-eye stargazers who were seeking the latest astronomical wonder. We searched the sky and were about to give up when a young Italian couple stopped to help us in our obvious quest. They pointed, and there it was—Comet Hale-Bopp hanging misty in the western sky. Then felt we like Keats's watcher of the skies when a new object swam into our ken, silent upon a railroad bridge in Tuscany.

---

[13] On a later visit we put up at this hotel and found it a considerable improvement over the Moderno, but with a considerable increase in tariff.

XXII.

PISTOIA:
Just Next Door to Florence

Pistoia is about twenty miles from Florence, too close, perhaps, for the town to have developed a distinct history and personality of its own. Even today almost no tourists seem to spend the night here. There are no four- or five-star hotels, but a half-dozen rated at three stars, most of them in the *centro storico* around the Piazza del Duomo, good bargains in comparison to most of the hotels of Florence. The proximity to the more famous town accounts for the fact that Pistoia is often overlooked by tourists. There are also historical events that led to its being dominated by its famous neighbor. It was, oddly enough, founded centuries before Florence, created as an army camp by the Romans who were in the process of subduing Liguria to the northwest. The town is probably even older than that, since modern civic repairs have uncovered a couple of Etruscan burial markers in the very center of the city. An ancient Roman road, the Cassian Way, ran through the city to the hills beyond and provided direct access to the capital at Rome.

There came a tumultuous time in the first century BC when the constitutional stability of the Roman Republic was giving way to social instability in the face of a rising number of slaves and disenfranchised plebeians. Rule of a strong man became popular, and power was seized by Marius, Sulla, Pompey, and, eventually, Julius Caesar. Sallust and Cicero (who was a politician-warrior as well as a writer and orator) recounted the events of the time, giving their own spin to the activities of the characters and assessing their motives. Catiline, the famous conspirator, was one of the prominent actors in this period. His life ended in the fighting at Pistoia. He was a fire-breathing warrior, and the town remembers him still. Many Italian cities are still psychologically close to things that happened several thousand years ago.

The chaos of the Ostrogoth invasion came along a half-millennium later. Shortly thereafter the Langobards took charge of the whole area, from Lombardy all the way south to Spoleto and Benevento, where they established great independent duchies. It was only in this feudal period that city walls were built around Pistoia for the first time. But the city was prosperous and powerful, and even issued its own coinage. In the late eighth century Charlemagne and the three Ottos brought a semblance of central government to this part of Tuscany, but after the eleventh century, the various cities developed a style of self-government, establishing *comunes* headed by oligarchic societies of nobles—the beginnings of an entrepreneurial class and guild masters.

Religious pilgrimage was one of the sources of trade and wealth in the Middle Ages, and Pistoia was well situated to be a stop on the journey from Rome to both sea and land routes to Santiago de Compostela in northern Spain. A relic of St. James himself was acquired in 1144, and other signs of prosperity appeared in the good repute of the metalworkers of the city. One of these young apprentices was Filippo Brunelleschi, who went on to make his fortune and fame in Florence by creating the dome of its huge cathedral. But

Florence did more than just lure away the most talented sons of Pistoia. The town lay between Lucca and Florence and was a prize to be fought over until, during the fifteenth century, both towns came under Florentine rule. In the age of gunpowder, Pistoia developed its industry of swords and daggers into the high-tech field of lethal novelty, the handheld piece of portable, small-scale artillery. It came to be known as the pistol.

We came to Pistoia by the modern tourists' route—the half-hour train service from Santa Maria Novella station in Florence. Although it was a beautiful day in early April, we figured there would be plenty of walking during the day, so we treated ourselves to a taxi that brought us to the somewhat-elevated Piazza del Duomo. We were looking forward to seeing the Andrea Della Robbia lunette over the central door of the Cattedrale di San Zeno, but were thwarted by the perpetual need to repair and restore almost everything in this ancient country. The doorway was shrouded in plastic and pipe scaffolding, *in restauro* for the season. But inside there was another story, a Verrocchio tomb, and the silver altar for St. James's relics that was assembled over two centuries, some of the later work being done in the fifteenth century by the young Brunelleschi. The holy water font is thought to be by Nicola Pisano, the progenitor of that wonderful family of sculptors. This work here is fine, but Nicola's best work is in Siena, and next door in Pisa he signed his pulpit with an inscription claiming for himself the title of the world's greatest sculptor. His son, Giovanni, surpassed him, and so titled his work here in Pistoia. He carved a line on the pulpit in Sant'Andrea, saying that he had beaten the old man at his own trade, a sort of Oedipal competition in the years before Freud proposed that theory. There are several more Pisanos in the history of Italian art, but since the surname is merely an indication of their hometown, I can't be sure if Andrea and Nino are descendants or merely fellow countrymen.

The campanile next to San Zeno is freestanding, and was originally built as a civic watchtower from which the alarm bells could be rung to summon the citizenry to arms in the event of attack. Its rather severe architecture betrays this utilitarian purpose in the first hundred vertical feet of masonry. Above that rise three arcades of delicate Romanesque arches. Behind them are lofty porches lined with dark green and white marble layer-cake interior walls. Farther above rises a square crown and a slender pyramid that bring the whole tower close to two hundred and fifty feet. Next door is the octagonal baptistery, also striped horizontally in dark green and white, the trim and color scheme of many of the thirteenth-century churches in Pisa and as far south as Siena. The style of this one is distinctly Gothic and its date, around 1350, is consistent with the idea that it might have been built from plans drawn by Nicola Pisano. Somehow Florence's similar baptistery seems from a different era, which I guess it is; the building is several centuries older, and Ghiberti's later doors are contemporary with the kickoff of the Renaissance. Whatever its lineage, this one in Pistoia is a lovely building, trimmed around the upper courses with a lithe wedding-cake colonnade of tall, slender Gothic arches.

We navigated by the excellent map the tourist office at the station had provided, and found our way slightly downhill to the Church of Sant'Andrea. Here again we found the dark and light marble decor of the facade, but this one dates from 1166. The church is tall and severe in design, with narrow window lancets and only a little light admitted by the bullet window high up over the entrance portal. But our eyes got used to the holy gloom, and there was coin-in-the-slot lighting for the greatest work of art in Pistoia, the Giovanni Pisano pulpit.

The date of completion of this elaborate and wonderfully human creation is 1301, almost exactly the same as Giotto's frescoes in the Scrovegni Chapel in Padua. Of the two I would pick out the pulpit in Sant'Andrea as being the opening trumpet blast of the Renaissance. Or, perhaps, it sounds the first harmonious chords of that most fruitful period of Italian accomplishment.

The pulpit is hexagonal, perched six or eight feet in the air on seven dark marble pillars, three of which stand on the floor. The other four rest on saddles on the backs of a cheerful pair of lions, and a twisted and perhaps tortured figure of a man who may represent Adam, the archetypal sinner in us all, and a *grifone* which holds up the center support. Above this spiritual menagerie are Gothic spandrels between a set of passionate sibyls, anxiously prophesying the coming of the new dispensation. The six scenes from Scripture that fill the panels around the top of the pulpit are crowded with figures in attitudes of the strongest emotion as they witness the crucifixion or the nativity. Perhaps most powerful of all are the soldiers following Herod's order to kill all the male children under the age of two in Bethlehem. Protesting mothers vainly try to protect their tiny sons. One soldier, tense with effort, holds a child by his feet, upside down, while he prepares to dispatch the child with a sword. For all the tangle of bodies (I counted at least thirty-two, including Herod himself scowling at the massacre), the sculpture is so provocatively realistic that you can almost hear the screams of the women and the crying of the baby boys. What a shock this tortured scene must have been seven centuries ago. It still rattles me even though we know that the story is much more likely to be a Midrash created by St. Matthew than a real historical event. Metaphorical truths are among the most powerful and the most likely to move our hearts.

Seeking lunch in Pistoia turned out to be a problem, since we had wandered into an area seemingly devoid of *pizzerie*. We did discover, however, a pair of lady *polizia urbana*, both of them blonde and charming despite their carrying twenty or thirty pounds of police gear, guns, radios, and suchlike on their belts. They understood our need for refreshment well enough, but seemed at a loss for locating a place for us to eat in the neighborhood. Finally they promised us a pizzeria if we would follow their instructions through a number of twists and turns uphill into yet another neighborhood. We obeyed, and in a scant fifteen minutes found ourselves quite lost along streets lined with wisteria and cherry blossoms, charmed but still hungry. We came across a *tabaccheria* and put the question of where to find lunch to the large and maternal tobacconist. She pointed us toward a municipal garden next door where there was a gate that admitted only children and grandparents. Inside, she assured us, we would find the senior center, where lunch was served daily at bargain rates. We found the simple cafeteria where there was an assortment of wonderful soups made from beans and various vegetables, served with crusty bread and butter. The nice woman ladling things out encouraged us to try the tripe, which was swimming in a sort of Neapolitan sauce of tomatoes and cheeses. Now we had heard that tripe is a Florentine specialty, so we plunged in and found it delicious (although it has a tendency to linger between the teeth later on).[14]

With our directions straightened out, we found ourselves back at the Piazza del Duomo and toured the handsome Palazzo Comunale

---

[14] There is a long tradition of institutional provision for feeding the poor in these Tuscan towns. In neighboring Prato, in 1410, a prosperous citizen named Francesco Datini left his considerable estate and adjoining lands to provide a "hospice, granary, and home [for] the perpetual use of the poor of Jesus Christ for their everlasting nourishment and emolument," provided that the hospice, granary, and home should never become the property of the Church, in no way subject to ecclesiastical authority or "Church prelates." Francesco's will sets up an elaborate system of lay trusteeship overseen by a committee of four, selected by the Prato city council.

and Museo Civico. If the paintings and sculpture there are not of the very first rank, they are surely far better than you could find in all but one or two of the greatest American museums. And some of the works of Gimignani and the "Master of 1336" are surely worth the trip from Florence if you aren't completely sated by the Pisanos. A block to the north is the Ospedale del Ceppo, a beautiful building with a loggia of delicate Renaissance arches protecting the original thirteenth-century building. It housed and cared for victims of the great plague of 1348. Later, a set of bright polychromed medallions and

a sprightly frieze showing the seven corporal works of mercy were added by Giovanni della Robbia in 1520. Della Robbias, perhaps in distinction from the Pisanos, really were all of the same family. They carried the beautiful blue grounded style of glazed terra cotta work through the years. As far as I can tell they are still at it; at least, there are stores which sell the brightly colored plaques at great price in Florence.

Pistoia has a splendid variety of architecture on display, the white-and-green layer-cake style of

Luca della Robbia   c. 1460

the twelfth century, the high Gothic, Renaissance, and Baroque. The late-fifteenth-century church of Santa Maria dell'Umiltà has a grand dome that looks like a miniature of Brunelleschi's triumph in Florence. This one was actually done by Vasari in 1560, over a hundred years after the spanning of the much-larger space in the big city next door. The influence of the neighboring town is everywhere apparent. In the Piazza della Sala, just behind the lovely baptistery, there is an elegant well surmounted by a lion that was given to the town by the Medici family in 1451.

But, recognizing that there were many more good things to experience here, we agreed that on a day trip such as ours, there was a limit to what we could accomplish. We caught a bus back to the station and within ten minutes found a train that brought us back to Florence in less than a half-hour.

Although at midday we had felt that the *trippa alla fiorentina* would satisfy our appetite for days to come, our taste for Tuscan cooking revived after a rest and a drink. Eight o'clock found us at the Trottarino Bordino, where Cathy chose the *vitello con funghi porcini* and I ordered up the *bollito misto*, steaming pungently in the trolley and accompanied by its sauce of mustards, both green and yellow. The house red wine was excellent. Our excursion to Pistoia was a mixture of history, art, architecture, and gastronomy, this last set of adventures being far from the least important. But of course, Italy never disappoints in any of these things.

XXIII.

SIENA AND LITTLE VAGLIAGLI NEXT DOOR

The village of Vagliagli consists of fifty ordinary houses, none of which seems to be possessed of any remarkable features. I don't quite know what gives it its undeniable Tuscan charm. Perhaps it is the color. The artist's pigment "raw sienna" is the color of the walls and "burnt sienna" is the hue of the roof tiles. There is an ordinary church here, a coffee bar, quite a good *enoteca*, a restaurant, and the other accoutrements of a proper Italian town. I think it lacks an elementary school but has a *scuola materna*. A bus will get you into Siena in about fifteen minutes to do serious shopping, or to attend high school or the university. We met at least one resident who had only once in a long life ventured as far away as that. Vagliagli contained everything he needed: a job, a pleasant place to live, and a girl to marry.

The secret thing about these villages in Tuscany is what's around outside them: green fields striped with the shadows of slender cedar trees planted in rows across the divisions of the arable fields and the pastureland. And up and down the curving flanks of the hilly topography are the vineyards. Here grapes grow in great profusion and produce one of the most famous wines in the world. For this is the district where the bottles bear the image of the Black Rooster, the symbol of the *Chianti Classico*, the best that central Italy has to offer.

Some years before I saw the town, I had befriended a young Italian couple when they visited the Mystic Seaport in Connecticut, where I was volunteering to explain catboats to sometimes curious tourists. Their obvious innocence compelled me to make their acquaintance, followed by lunch and a conversation in halting Italian. I learned of their plan to create a B&B from some of the ancient outbuildings of a family farm, vineyard, and olive orchard in the southern part of the Chianti in Tuscany. Because we were going to be in the neighborhood of Siena on our next Italian excursion, Cathy and I later communicated by fax to ask if the remodeling had been completed. The response was a sad negative; getting permits to remodel even an ancient stable in a country so conscious of its antiquity is a time-consuming bureaucratic process. But the gracious couple countered with a fax of their own, inviting us to spend a couple of days with them if we could "put up with" the environment of an eleventh-century castle. We pounced on the opportunity.

Federica and Enrico met us at the bus stop in Siena and, after a ritual coffee in the lovely, shell-shaped *campo* of that grand and dignified town, drove us the short distance to Aiola, a farm in the nearby countryside. We passed a sign that said we were entering the domain of the Black Rooster, the Gallo Nero area of Chianti. The original castle had been destroyed by the invading Germans and Burgundians who came through on their way to sack the city of Rome in 1527. But the foundation walls and the moat withstood the wrath of the avenging Protestants and, a century or so later, a large house was built where the superstructure of the fortification once stood.

We entered via a steeply sloping driveway that spanned the dry moat and brought us under an arch into the center of the building while still out in the weather. On a surprisingly cold weekend in early April, the massive stone walls had retained the temperatures of February and March. Design and construction of the seventeenth (or earlier) centuries did not provide for central heating. We ignored the rather grand parlor above and gathered in the stone-floored kitchen. There we found a fire built on a vast hearth set into the side of the high-ceilinged room. The actual fireplace measured a dozen feet across its opening and was seven or eight feet deep. A stone bench lined this space all around the open fire. We were actually sitting inside the fireplace while we sampled several of the prime wines of Aiola. It was a cheery beginning to a notable visit.

Conversation was mostly in English, with lots of helping out in Italian while Federica deftly dismembered a pheasant which she braised with mushrooms. We learned that her grandfather had been a senator in the 1930s, but had left Italy during the most oppressive period of Fascist rule and during World War II. He returned after the war and took up Aiola as a country retreat, as well as a commercial venture. What had been described as a "little farm" that made wine was actually a sizable corporation that employed an office staff of half a dozen, as well as a number of agricultural workers to prune the vines and harvest the grapes. Aiola makes, besides the famous *Chianti Classico*, another wine blended of several grapes called The Senator's Reserve, and a sweet, late-gathered *Vin Santo*, as well as several other wines and an amazingly alcoholic Grappa. They also gather and press thousands of bottles of prime olive oil each year.

Late talk and learning about wine and olive oil, as well as the life plans of the young couple, led us eventually to bed in a chamber with a fifteen-foot ceiling above an enormous bed heaped with blankets and quilts. We needed all of them. Tuscany really can be cold in the early spring. We were given strict instructions not to leave the propane heater on overnight lest we should suffer oxygen deprivation.

A sunny day of passable warmth ensued. We were wakened by a few shouts of the hired man's wife, who was berating him in the upper reaches of the castle for some deficiency of performance or character. This long-suffering man was always wreathed with smiles in spite of the acid consolation he received from his spouse. He built the fire in the kitchen, planted the flowers about the property, and generally maintained the livability of the four-hundred-year-old residence, along with working for the winery. Enrico explained to me that the hired man had been born in Vagliagli and once, when he was young, went to Siena to see the sights of the city. His money was stolen and he decided never to go back to such a wicked place. He had thus spent his entire life in the little town, and seemed perfectly content with this arrangement.

We spent the day surveying the famous cultivated hills of Chianti, visiting the neighboring village of Radda, and seeing Federica and Enrico's wedding church, a charming building of mixed architectural heritage that obviously had been begun many centuries earlier. In the process of being shown the winery itself at Aiola, we were overtaken by the arrival of a huge Mercedes busload of English tourists who were on a wine-tasting tour. Since we were all mingled together at the tasting session, there was no indication that we were with "the house" or merely other tourists. We commented enthusiastically on the wines, most of which we had sampled the night before, and recommended their purchase to our linguistic countrymen. Many took up our suggestions. Federica later joked about offering me a job as a wine salesman.

But finding these wines in America is a chancy business. Commercial importing in quantity is in the hands of jobbers who seemingly have to work on a state-by-state basis through the local alcoholic beverage commissions. The bureaucratic snarls are probably a lingering aftermath of the Volstead Act and Carrie Nation's crusade against the disagreeable effect of drink. For whatever reason, the wines of Aiola are currently available only in a few states where I do not live. This is, of course, also true of many of the middle- to small-sized wine producers in Italy and other countries. As a result, we are denied the opportunity to try some of the choicest vintages of what has now become the largest wine-producing country in the world.

On our second trip to Vagliagli, several years later, we found a number of changes. Permits had been issued and the old farm buildings skillfully remodeled without changing the general appearance of the *fattoria*. There was a new *parcheggio* marked with a neat sign, proclaiming CASALI DELLA AIOLA, with three stars displayed to indicate its government-approved rating. The parking area was sylvan to an extreme, being carefully designed to fill in the space between the olive trees in the grove nearest the house. The old brick fodder garner had become a lounge that commanded a splendid view of the Tuscan hillsides. Below there, a breakfast room had appeared with eight tables under brick arches, a reception lobby, and a kitchen gleaming with new stainless-steel restaurant equipment. The eight rooms open onto opposite sides of a hill so that each has a ground-floor entrance. Immaculate bath and shower rooms were finished in elegant Italian tile work, and best of all, the beds were contemporary and the rooms provided with central heating.

But newest of all was the youngest member of the family, Leonardo, who had been born less than six months before. Enrico carefully explained that although the town of Vinci was a short distance away, he was sure that Leonardo da Vagliagli would become a great mathematician or painter to bring fame to this town.

Casali della Aiola provided lots of good services, including directions for exploring Chianti and reservations made at a number of local restaurants. First among these was the local *enoteca* in the village. An *enoteca* is more of a wine store than a restaurant, but all of them serve food as well as drink. In Chianti they provide a great selection of local wines, and many from more distant vineyards. The menu is simple: salads and mostly vegetarian fare, except for a hot thick soup, or perhaps gnocchi in a fresh tomato sauce as a *primo piatto*. Their chicken salad was delectable. Such relatively inexpensive food is always appealing to students traveling on a short budget. We were well settled at a comfortable table when a group of thirty young Italian tourists arrived and filled the little restaurant to capacity. Ten minutes later, a pair of young American men whom we had noted at breakfast at Aiola arrived; they were in the process of being turned away by the *proprietario* when we interceded and asked that they share our table. When traveling in a strange land, wayfarers from your home country are a fine entertainment at dinner.

We made a number of trips about central Tuscany in the next several days; first of all, to Siena. The *centro storico* is well equipped with parking places, mainly around the soccer stadium, which nestles inside the medieval walls close to the church of St. Dominic, the founder of the sometimes intolerant but always intellectual Order of Preachers. San Domenico is a vast, austere church that contains, among other wonders, the ghoulish and rather badly mummified head of St. Catherine, the holy *fanciulla* who is credited with persuading the pope to return his residence to Rome from Avignon. The rest of her anatomy is in Rome, but Siena is her hometown, and the head is enclosed in an iron-grilled reliquary here for the veneration of the faithful. I wondered which awestruck member of the religious congregation was assigned the task of decapitating the corpse of the holy girl. Preoccupation with parts of the bodies of the sanctified may remain one of the least-attractive diversions of Catholic Christianity, but it still holds a great attraction for Italian churchgoers.

Recent work on the huge church has uncovered some wonderful ceiling frescoes in the sacristy. They had been plastered over, presumably because they were too damaged to restore a few centuries ago. Newly revealed, even though fragmentary, they are brilliantly colored masterworks (although I don't believe anyone is sure who painted them).

We lunched in the outskirts of Siena at a *pizzeria-ristorante*, the Fontebecci, in a somewhat improbable location across from a large Exxon petrol station on the Via Fiorentina. The dining room at the back of the gas station looked out over a steeply sloping valley; most things in Siena are on the verge of a ravine or mountainside. The tables were set with the characteristic pastel-colored linens, and the kitchen was ready to provide food at nearly any hour of the day. The pretty young waitress giggled at me when I ordered in Italian. Somewhat miffed at what I took to be a condescending attitude toward my use of the idiom, I switched to English. This brought forth more giggles. After a few moments of embarrassed confusion, we finally worked out that she was an Albanian refugee, didn't really know either language, and it was her first day on the job. By pointing and sign language we were successful in ordering an excellent lunch of *antipasto misto*, bread, butter, cheese, and wine.

The center of Siena is Il Campo, a large, shell-shaped depression in the middle of the city which faces the thirteenth-century *palazzo pubblico*. It is a space designed for mass celebrations and twice annually is the site of a hell-for-leather horse race around its stony circuit, Il Palio. The contestants are representatives of the seventeen precincts (or *contrade*) into which the city was divided centuries ago. Each has a colorfully decorated flag showing its tutelary beast, bird, dragon, lizard, or arthropod. Riders and their mounts are brought to the parish churches to be blessed and otherwise wished good luck by the local priest. Once the horses are under way, there are very few rules to inhibit the riders from disabling or otherwise eliminating their competition. The entire city takes the races very seriously, and the bragging rights enjoyed by the young men for the subsequent year can precipitate an occasional street brawl. But the Campo is usually devoid of horses or of testosterone competition. It is rimmed with

Siena Palazzo Pubblico
1288-1309

cafés and restaurants and is a sunny refuge in winter as well as a cool retreat in late-summer afternoons. The splendid slender tower called La Mangia rises three hundred feet above the town hall, where it stands as a thank offering to the Madonna for the remission of the visitations of the Black Death in the middle of the fourteenth century.

On slightly higher ground, two hundred meters to the southwest of the Campo, is the great Gothic cathedral of the medieval city, one of the most striking in all of Italy. Its pale gray, white, and dark-green stonework is accented by brilliantly colored mosaics in the pointed arches of the facade. Inside, the columns are made of drums of alternating black and white stone that give a zebra-striped look to the crossing. The great pulpit is one of the early works of Giovanni Pisano. Giovanni and his father Nicola were among the first to reintroduce the themes and forms of classical sculpture to Italy in the fourteenth century. Gods and heroes, nudes and angels are mixed together seemingly without any theological conflict. This work is one of the precursors of the great stylistic changes that we think of as the Italian Renaissance. The Pisanos stood on the brink of that rush of creative innovation while still seeming a part of the Gothic age that preceded it.

The mid-fourteenth century was of course the disastrous period when the Black Death swept through Europe in multiple plagues starting in 1348. Siena had been preparing to enlarge this cathedral to become the largest in the world, when a loss in a war with Florence—and the death of half of its population due to the horrible disease—brought a halt to all projects in the prosperous little city. Thereafter it stagnated for a number of centuries, and only began to grow again in the modern era. As a result, this city remains largely a Gothic town, while Florence to its north is a Renaissance city, and Rome to the south is a huge mixture of

Baroque and classical architecture.

But like all such generalizations about the Italian environment, there are plenty of exceptions. One is the Piccolomini Library, which is actually a midsize wing off the nave of the cathedral. Enea Silvio Piccolomini was one of the very archetypes of the humanists that flourished in Italy during the fifteenth century. He was born in 1405 in Corsignano, and grew up to be a freethinking intellectual and an enthusiastic ladies' man. He wrote poems and plays for the entertainment of the nobility, and took to the study of Greek in order to pursue Platonist philosophy. He served as lay secretary to an antipope and as court poet to the Holy Roman emperor. But he had a change of heart and decided to leave this *dolce vita* shortly after his fortieth birthday. He submitted to the more legitimate pope, became a priest, and was shortly advanced to become the bishop of Siena, and then cardinal. He negotiated treaties between warring princes and wrote an autobiography.

In 1458, in the flood tide of the Renaissance, he became Pope Pius II and moved far enough to the radical right of the church to declare it a matter of formal heresy for Catholics to believe that a church council could supersede the pronouncements of a pope. While occupying the Holy See, he redesigned his hometown as a community of Utopian perfection, renaming it Pienza to commemorate his pontificate. He built a grand palazzo there as a vacation home. But his mind continued to grow narrower as he aged. Besides eschewing the dissolute life of his youth, he focused all of his energy on mounting one more crusade against the Turks. He badgered leaders from all over Europe to join him, and, when sick and old, led the way to Bari for embarkation to the Holy Land. Almost no one showed up to join him.

This was the period in which the Ottoman Turks, having already taken Constantinople, moved north through the Balkans and settled the present Muslim population in Kosovo, Croatia, Bosnia, and Serbia. Pius died trying to fan the flames of that conflict back to life. After he breathed his last, the few reluctant warriors who had showed up for the embarkation simply returned home. It seems a disappointing end to a career that began with such style, liberality, and brilliance, but I suppose those qualities are not necessarily what one is supposed to be looking for in a pope. He remains the only one of the supreme pontiffs to have written an account of his own life.

Piccolomini's nephew succeeded him and took the name of Pius III. He built the library in Siena as his uncle's memorial, and commissioned Pinturicchio to cover its walls with eight large murals depicting the significant events of the earlier pope's life. The room is a stunning piece of late-Renaissance decoration. Today it has a wonderful set of manuscripts on exhibition around the lower walls of the great room and, in the center, a most marvelous triple statue of the Three Graces of pagan Rome, nicked and battered, but supremely graceful in their classical nudity. They are a wonderful reminder of the pope's humanistic background, when he was one of the scholars who felt that the proper study of mankind was not only God, but also man and woman.

Following Federica's instructions, we set out one evening to locate a nearby restaurant called Trappola. The sky was dark and riven with flashes of lightning, the weather threatening to break into a storm at any moment. We made one wrong turn along the way but recovered and eventually found the restaurant in the middle of an unpopulated countryside, where we were welcomed by an enthusiastic non-Italian host who wore a single earring and presided over a candlelit dining room. Electrical power was out for the nonce, but the candles were bright and the stove was fueled by wood. The Easter lamb was redolent of rosemary, and the *cantucci* for dessert were studded with fresh almonds. Eating well in Tuscany is no great trick—there are lots of good places—but it is pleasant to have a native like Federica give you authoritative direction and make the reservations for you.

Vagliagli is well situated for visiting cities and towns all over southern Tuscany. We made a daylong journey to the east to Arezzo, one of those places that is quicker to approach by the longer route because of the precipitous zigzags of the mountain-crossing roads. Nevertheless, the direct and sometimes breathtaking route gave us a series of wonderful Tuscan views as we progressed through one winery and woodland after another.

Arezzo was the hometown of Giorgio Vasari, the first art historian as well as a fine painter in his own right. His little city bulges with artwork of the fifteenth and sixteenth centuries. He was also a young disciple of Michelangelo, and the principal architect for the later Medici in Florence. We had read much about the great paintings here, but unfortunately, found the greatest of them—frescoes by Piero della Francesca—to be almost perpetually *in restauro* during our visits. Piero lived in nearby Sansepolcro and did much of his finest work here. The church of San Francesco in Arezzo houses his *Legend of the True Cross*, which had been scheduled to be unveiled after many years of careful restoration in the spring after our visit. Cimabue's great crucifix had been taken down for similar repair, but in its place, in the church of San Domenico, there was an excellent photographic reproduction on a full-scale wooden mounting, which gives a pretty good idea of what it should look like when the work is completed on the ten-foot cross and figure.

The writing, contorted figures of Christ on the Cross that Cimabue created have a power and sympathy that differentiates them from the idealized iconography of the Middle Ages. Although earlier even than Giotto (who was probably his pupil), they too are part of the beginning of the age of humanistic art that became the Renaissance. The town also has works by Luca Signorelli, who greatly influenced Michelangelo with his crowds of naked figures, as well as other *quattrocento* masters and Vasari. The houses of both Petrarch and Vasari are conserved as small museums here. The latter is decorated with a number of paintings Vasari collected, as well as some that he painted. It is a worthwhile visit. At the very least, reading an abridgement of Vasari's monumental *Lives of the Artists* is almost required background for touring about Italy.

We stopped for a leisurely and interesting chat with a rotund Franciscan friar at the portal of his church, eventually discovering that he had come originally from America and joined the order in Italy. He was immensely affable and full of information, his helpfulness going far to make up for our disappointment in finding the frescoes still veiled in the canvas screens of the restorers. We lunched on *ribollita*, a delicious, thick Tuscan soup, at an upscale restaurant in the Piazza del Popolo, and started back to Vagliagli late in the day. This time we took the four-lane Autostrada northwest to the southern loop of the Florence ring road, and then turned south toward Siena to follow a longer but faster route home by going around the mountains. Although the elapsed time was only slightly shorter and the views were not as pretty, the speed allowed on the modern road gave us a feeling we were getting somewhere.

Early April mornings in Vagliagli are often lighted by bright sun on the hilltops, while the valleys are still filled deep with cloud. Exploring this contrast of blue hills and woolly white fog one morning on the high hill above the town, I came upon the local monument to the partisans who had died in the closing months of

World War II, after Italy changed sides and began to fight against the
Nazis. Just up the hill from the simple monument was the walled
village cemetery, a little paved garden of small wrought-iron crosses,
vigil lights, and glass-framed photographs of the ancestors of the
town. There were fresh flowers on some of the small graves squeezed
into the restricted space, plastic blooms on others. The whole had the
air of a much more frequented shrine than any American country
graveyard could ever have. We have wonderful cemeteries in New
England which exhibit more restrained monuments than these,
but ours are almost universally unvisited, perhaps because families
frequently move about our vast country, and few live any longer in
the vicinity of their grandparents' graves. The Tuscan countryside is
populated by an agricultural people who have remained in place for
many generations. In Vagliagli there were fresh flowers on the grave
of one woman who had died sixty years ago.

Traveling around the Chianti north of Siena, we often passed
signs directing us to Poggibonsi, a town evidently midway between
Siena and Firenze. We were intrigued by the name. I still don't know
what it means, although it may have something to do with the halyard
of a sailing vessel, a hill, or something cut off.

Passing the sign in a rental car, we decided to investigate. We
found a square of ample proportion in the center of town, with no
sign of a coffee bar at the uphill end of the steeply slanted green.
Asking along the way, we were directed to the railroad station where
there was a simple barroom serving simple fare. Such places in Italy
are often a delicious bargain, so we went in. Conversation between
the *barista* and a customer were in mixed Italian and English. We
joined in, and soon discovered that the blonde lady standing at the
bar was the American widow of an Italian commercial traveler who
used to telephone home and, when asked where he was, would

reply "Poggibonsi!" meaning sort of nowhere in particular. She commented that he implied that Poggibonsi was something along the lines of a gas station with two toilets and a bidet, but since she had never been there, she set out to visit the town, just as we had done. We both agreed that her late husband's summary was pretty much on the mark.

But you can't ever write off an Italian town. There is always something interesting just around the corner. In the case of Poggibonsi, it was a collection of castle towers on a hill beside the road. They were of assorted sizes, but two seemed larger than those adjoining. There were something like fourteen in all, joined by a fierce wall of uncut stone that completed a circuit of the fortified village.

Toward the end of our stay at Vagliagli, another trip into Siena itself gave us not only the opportunity to visit the painting gallery, the Pinacoteca Nazionale, but also to retrieve the laundry we had delivered there two days earlier. The shirts were nicely ironed, and the gallery's display of Simone Martini, Lorenzetti, and Duccio quite wonderful. Climbing up and down to the levels of the picture gallery was easy in comparison with navigating our way up and down the hills of Siena itself. Many of the cities that grew up on the ancient foundations of Etruscan strongholds are a series of steep streets and alleys leading ever upwards to the remains of an original fortress or castle. But Siena seems organized around several great depressions in the saddle of the mountains; the soccer stadium, the neighborhood of St. Catherine's house, and the Campo itself. To get from any one of these locations to another, hills leading to the rim of the craters must be surmounted. In comparison, Rome's seven hills are a rolling prairie and Florence is as flat as a billiard table. For all of the exercise it gives to the legs to get about it, Siena is one of the most beautiful cities we have ever visited.

We returned for a last evening at Casale della Aiola and teamed up with newly made friends there to go again to La Trappola for a final Tuscan dinner. Our earringed host welcomed us cheerily and served us well. In the course of the evening we learned that he had come from Austria and had just taken over the restaurant ten days earlier. We wished him buona fortuna, although his English was considerably more fluent than his Italian.

We were instructed by Federica not to walk in the old dry moat around the castle in the moonlight. *I cinghiale*, the wild boar, might be strolling there too, and could possibly resent our presence. I knew that *cinghiale* was a delicacy of Tuscan cooking, however indelicate the animal, and decided to keep to the lighted pathways in the olive-grove parking lot.

The next morning Enrico gave us proper driving directions for finding our way on the Via Salaria, the ancient Roman salt-trade route, how to reach Piccolomini's ideal town at Pienza and, eventually, how to get to Rome itself. The week in Tuscany had been a time of both pleasure and learning. We said farewell to Federica, Enrico, and Leonardo, and set forth to the south to find the Salaria and sights both newer and more ancient.

XXIV.

ITALIANS' OPINION OF THEMSELVES

Among the many amazing things about Italy is how it has digested the vast differences between the rich and the poor. Nowhere else, it seems to me, has there come down to the present day such a legacy of a spectacularly wealthy aristocracy juxtaposed against a peasant class of such abject poverty. Everywhere you go in Italy there are palaces and cathedrals built in the grandest possible manner, and houses with staircases a dozen feet across that were never designed to be trod upon by less than two or three courtiers at a time. There are castles with moldings around their windows, each one representing the lifetime earning power of a half-dozen or more of the servants of the master of the house. The churches from the sixteenth century up to the present time—beginning with the basilica of St. Peter in Rome and the wonderful church of Sant'Andrea delle Valle of the eighteenth century—are magnificent structures, no matter what we may think of their style or the theology that inspired them. What lavish expenditure of human labor and invention went into these buildings! As a percentage of annual gross national product, they would seem to compare with the pyramids of Giza.

But amazingly, it seems there has been little resentment on the part of the underclass through the centuries. Could it be that they are able to appreciate the beauty of this lavish architecture without any accompanying bitterness about their own more frugal lifestyle? Once, when I was chatting with a grizzled Sicilian peasant, he pointed out a country palazzo where un marchese had lived, with obvious pride in his neighbor's existence.

The French situation in the period that stretched from the fifteenth to the eighteenth centuries was different, but the French felt that the inequity could be solved by literally severing the heads from the bodies of the privileged class. In Italy, violent reaction was sometimes focused on the French, as in the Sicilian Vespers of the thirteenth century, and later, during the nineteenth-century *Risorgimento*, when they banded together to eject the Austrians and the French who protected the reactionary Pope Pius IX. The partisans who executed Mussolini and his mistress as the Nazis exited Italy at the end of World War II were more cold-blooded than filled with any sort of bloodlust. *Il Duce* had already made one comeback to power under the protection of Hitler; his captors simply wanted to ensure he didn't have a second recrudescence.

Campagna, Puglia, Calabria, and Sicilia were prosperous in the time of Frederick II in the twelfth and thirteenth centuries, but were impoverished in the more modern periods. Yet in the Baroque Era, the wasteful aristocrats were able to build palaces of grand proportions and exquisite workmanship. Many of them are museums today. The whole city of Lecce is the very model of Baroque splendor.

Sicily has its Mafia and the Camora is the curse of Basilicata and parts of Puglia, but both seem to be based on a sort of free-enterprise theory of profitable crime rather than vengeance against the oppressors of the masses. The Red Brigades have been a popular exception in the last century.

The Italians are historically accustomed to being abused by their rulers and have recently come to a sort of national agreement that crime should be suppressed and the poor assisted; other than these essential exercises, government is deemed largely irrelevant. They are grateful for the legacy of Mussolini in that the trains run on time; the Ferrovia dello Stato is actually a national treasure that the United States could emulate, to our profit. The glorious uniforms of the *carabiniere* reflect the national pride in aesthetic matters, like the uniforms which the Swiss Guards of the Vatican wear today, nearly five hundred years after they were designed by Michelangelo.

By and large, Italians are a gentle people, and certainly much less racially prejudiced than Americans. The horror of a black prisoner being sodomized with a mop handle by a pair of white policemen in the U.S. is unthinkable in Italy. Perhaps the exhibition of cruel death in the amphitheaters during the age of the emperors sated their taste for blood and gore. Even the despised *zingari* (gypsies) are more often pitied than censured. There is no history of lynching in Italy. Perhaps the Catholic tradition of forgiveness in this country trumps the American habit of seeking vengeance.

In 1902, Alessandro Serenelli murdered twelve-year-old Maria Goretti, and was sentenced to thirty years in prison. Upon his release, he retired to a monastery where he spent the balance of his life in prayer and penance—surely a better conclusion to his crime than our rewarding a prosecutor for racking up another death-penalty sentence.

Black prostitutes who come to Rome as immigrants are usually unmolested, except for the rare "Jack the Ripper" type who sets forth to correct the morals of the city by murdering some of these impoverished women. As a rule, Romans are kind to criminals, prisoners, the destitute, and the mentally ill, including the schizophrenics who wander into bars looking for a handout. Proprietors usually give them a cup of coffee. The old gypsy ladies posted at church doors with their baskets more often receive small coins from local citizens than donations from the affluent tourists rushing by on their way to view the lavish displays of Baroque art.

I guess it takes all types to build a civilization designed to exist for several thousand years.

"Schifanoia" c. 1470

PART V

CENTRAL TO THE EAST OF ITALY
ETRUSCAN COUNTRY

XXV.

VITERBO:
A Summertime Resort for the Popes

We came to Viterbo on a gray day, a chilly spring day of the sort that is common in Italy in March, hoping for better weather of the sort we had found in Umbria farther north. It is a small city, a repository of much of the history that encrusts the boot of Italy, reaching back to the Roman period and to the second millennium before our common era. If what we see today is architecture of the Gothic and pre-Renaissance styles, the bowels of the town are darker and earlier than that. There are few signs of Roman construction here, and many of its thoroughfares are medieval. Alleys and streets that thread about its hilly topography occasionally turn into extended stairways. These streets were quite surely laid out for people or horses to walk upon, and only minimal accommodation has been made for the automobile. Some look to be too narrow for American-sized cars. The ever-present Italian scooters seem to get around well enough, occasionally bouncing down the low-rise stair steps.

Much of what is presently visible in the old *centro* of Viterbo was built in the twelfth and thirteenth centuries, even though the town goes back several millennia before that. Like most towns in this part of Italy, it is of Etruscan origin and was one of the legendary twelve cities that formed their defensive league. In the third or fourth century BC, it was taken over by Rome, a scant sixty kilometers to the south. The decay of Rome and subsequent collapse of its defensive perimeter led to frequent troubles with marauding Saracens and, in early medieval times, turned out to be of help to Viterbo. Being farther inland, it was relatively safe from seaside attack, although the Langobards overran it in the sixth or seventh century. Their conquest of Italy was a permanent one, and although we don't have much information about who was who in these times, the blond-bearded and -tressed northerners took women of the late Roman people here and left behind descendants of blue-eyed Italians who are still part of the population. Charlemagne's Carolingian steamroller came through on his way to Rome at the end of the seventh century, and the doughty French emperor made a present of the town to the pope. For a time it served as a refuge for the popes when things became too disorderly in the shattered old capital.

We arrived after a circuitous rail trip from Florence, which included a change of trains at Orte, and eventually found ourselves at one of Viterbo's two rail stations, Stazione Porta Fiorentina. The usual courtesy of European students had provided us with places to sit on the crowded flyer. A quartet of Spanish kids on their way to Rome simply crammed the four boys and girls cozily into three seats with the smallest girl stretched across the knees of the other three friends, thus making space for us on the other side of the compartment. Cathy said later that they curled up like a litter of bear cubs in their den.

Although there was no *posteggio* for taxis at the station, we were picked up by a helpful driver who zigzagged up and down hills to deposit us at the Hotel Tuscia, a small, modern *albergo* that made up in comfort and efficiency for its slight lack of historical and local color. Perched on the side of a hill on the Via Cairoli, the location of the Tuscia presented us with the alternative of walking down into a valley to seek our *aperitivo* or climbing up to the plateau above. We first found our way upward under glowering clouds and thence back down and up on the other side via a narrow alley paved with damp, black, diamond-shaped cobblestones to a *pizzeria-trattoria* that gave us a full measure of local flavor. No other tourists here, only *Viterbesi*. We dined on *acqua cotta*, a hot broth of a great number of vegetables, bread, and a pitcher of the local red wine—just the thing for a chilly evening with the rain beginning to fall.

In the morning the Tuscia provided a much more modern array for *colazione*, a copious spread of cereals and sweet buns, zwieback, honey, and a few foil-wrapped cheeses and jams. The usual steam-brewed Italian coffee came in the form of cappuccino. We headed downhill to the Piazza dei Caduti, the place sacred to the memory of those fallen in the wars that have beset Italy in recent centuries. This green patch with a mysterious tub-shaped building in its center is the terminus of a broad avenue named for Guglielmo Marconi, the proud son of Italy who invented the radio and ushered in the age of modern communication. Halfway up the hill on the other side we came to the Fountain of the Lion, first of a series of such waterworks which, I suspect, reach back in origin to the ubiquitous hydraulic engineering of the Romans.

There is plenty of available water here among the lakes and the Tiber itself. Fountains at significant street junctions are a specialty of Viterbo. There must be a dozen of them around the town. From here we climbed again and took a pleasant walk across the brow of the hill toward the Cathedral of San Lorenzo, a stark Romanesque building that could be said to have benefited from being bombed in World War II. Most of the Gothic and all of the Baroque accretion of the centuries was shattered and simply carted away when restoration got under way. It is a handsome building, uncompromising in its shape and decorated only by the horizontal bands of brown and white stone that ornament the tower, accenting its four tiers of Gothic lancets in the belfry. It stands next to a building that was used for the papal conclaves when the popes ruled from here in the thirteenth century. A lovely series of delicate Gothic arches form an arcade between it and the Palazzo Papale. The arches are all that is left of an imposing building, half of which simply fell off and dropped into the valley below in the fourteenth century. The open loggia that remains is rather like a Victorian folly, pure ornament to delight the eye.

There is a story of great antiquity and reasonable veracity that says when the cardinals meeting here were unable to decide on a candidate for the next successor to St. Peter in 1271, their deliberations went on for close to three years. Eventually the townspeople grew so impatient with the quarreling prelates that they tore the roof off the consistory chamber, locked the cardinals in, and put them on a starvation diet. Hunger and cold worked to settle political differences, and within days the selection of Pope Gregory X was announced. The fact that Gregory was a layman and away on a pilgrimage to Acre in the Holy Land seemed to present no problem. He (either in Palestine or back in Italy, I cannot determine which) was speedily ordained a priest, consecrated a bishop, and in a few months installed as pope. Four days later he summoned a general council at Lyon and set about reconciling the Byzantine and Roman churches. A notable arrangement was worked out, but unfortunately it didn't stick. Gregory died on his way back from the council, just two years after he took over the papal throne.

At the hour of our visit to the cathedral, we found it vacant, and we had to seek out Mass at a small modern building nearby. It seemed to be the focus of a lot of devotion. It was the church of Santa Giacinta (Saint Hyacinth). We were unfamiliar with her life and legend but decided that her name was charming and that she probably did much good in this world. The celebrant was young, black-bearded, and looked Ethiopian. A screen behind him supported a circular silver tabernacle door that outlined his head like a halo. The effect was striking. Was he supposed to be standing in the place of the Lord? The open grillwork behind him revealed fifteen or twenty nuns of some cloistered order of Franciscans. They sang with that compelling sweetness that is characteristic of choruses of women in religious orders. Although most of the nuns were middle-aged or more so, there was one young postulant in a white habit among them. Out in front of the altar where we were, there were several nuns in different white habits who we guessed worked in a hospital nearby. Habits on nuns are far from outmoded in Italy, and their useful and compassionate work with the sick and unfortunate continue in the pattern as old as the buildings of Viterbo.

Heading back toward the center of town, Cathy spied a stationery and magazine store that had racks of postcards in its doorway. We shopped extensively and discussed various works of art in the display. The young man at the counter spoke and understood English easily, and was interested in our focus on his town.

"The people of Viterbo," he commented, "don't know their own history and aren't interested in it."

We responded that their lack of interest in the past was similar to most people in any small city. He asked if we would like to see some of the earlier history of Viterbo.

Slightly apprehensive, we were ushered through a dark opening to a stairway that led down damp and shiny stone steps to a space and time of earlier centuries. Our host lighted a few bulbs and we descended through arches cut out of the primordial tufa and down to a second subterranean level, where there was a large room with a long trestle table set with tankards and candles. He explained that this underground *taverna* was the site of medieval meals served to the cognoscenti when they came together to discuss history on Friday nights. We progressed yet farther down and discovered that there were a total of five underground levels in the ancient rock directly beneath the magazine and souvenir shop. The chambers had been quarried out well over a thousand years ago and are professed to be hiding places originally constructed during the Langobard invasions during the sixth and seventh centuries. Maybe so, but the idea of crouching in such an underground space while bloodthirsty pagans were clanking about overhead seeking candidates for slavery gave me a severe attack of claustrophobia.

Our host and guide was both voluble and welcoming. His shop had a number of nice reproductions of Etruscan plates and vases, but we felt we could not safely pack the fragile pottery for our trip home. This is always a mistake. We find ourselves back in the New World regretting that we didn't bring back one of those red and black vases or little bronze figures to help us remember the place and the generous and knowledgeable proprietor.

Among the number of fountains in this town, some, like the Fontana Grande, are quite beautiful. There are five or six indicated on the advertising map handed out at the hotels. There may well be more. It would be a pleasant jaunt to make the circuit of the town on a sunny afternoon and visit the full set of them. But we had only a short stay in Viterbo due to bad planning, and only had the time to visit one of its three or four museums. We skipped the National Archaeological Museum and the Museo della Macchina di Santa Rosa, which displays the towering constructions that are carried around the town by teams of robust young men from time to time to celebrate the feast of Saint Rose.

Instead, we chose the Museo Civico, which is just outside the walls of the old town in a converted convent. The size of the institution makes me wonder at the number of women and girls it must have housed when it was an active nunnery. There are two or three floors, starting with a pretty cloister garden studded with Etruscan figures and sarcophagi. This is a first-rate collection started by a young man named Danieli, who recognized the extraordinary wealth of Etruscan grave goods in the neighborhood of Viterbo, his hometown. He managed to start a society for their preservation (and further excavation) before he died prematurely at the age of forty-two. His work persisted and the collection continues to expand even today.

Painting galleries upstairs (there is a modern elevator!) have a number of interesting works by fifteenth-century painters, as well as a few we recognized, such as Lucca Signorelli. This is a very worthwhile explore for many of its statues and rescued wall paintings, but the pride of the collection is a striking *Pietà* by Sebastiano del Piombo. This sad Madonna is starkly and realistically outlined against a deep blue background. It is a sixteenth-century painting but looks much more modern to my eye. The style reminded me oddly of Norman Rockwell.

We eventually returned through intermittent rain to the same Pizzeria Sarda that we first found in this hilly town. It was warm and dry, and one of those wonderful Italian waiters took us in hand, providing antipasto and an excellent pale pink ravioli followed by a tart with cheese and honey.

Because of the drizzly weather we experienced during this visit, I'm afraid we missed much of Viterbo. The excellent Cadogan guide to Italy suggests a number of churches and *piazze* that are worth a visit, as well as villages in the hinterland, some built in the Middle Ages and now deserted since the really notable *terremoto* of 1971, others crushed by the wars of Guelphs and Ghibellines five or six hundred years earlier. And of course, the prevalent stonework and burial mounds of the Etruscans in this area serve as testimony to the civilizations that were so fully developed here more than twenty-five hundred years before our time. Quantitatively, the span of the Roman Empire is only a brief episode in the history of Viterbo.

XXVI.

BOLOGNA:
Most Medieval of Italy's Modern Cities

Even in the distant view from the railroad windows, you can catch a glimpse of an asparagus patch of medieval towers that sprouts from the center of this town. There are stubs of at least twenty of them still standing, and two are of magnificent height: the Garisenda of more than 150 feet, and the Asinelli of 319 feet. No one is quite sure when they were built, but before the year 1000 is a pretty firm guess. Such towers were commonplace in late medieval years, and no one bothered at that time to note the precise moment of their construction. The towers were places of safe haven in periods of strife inside the city, but they were also important for showing that the wealthiest families were superior to others whose constructions were shorter. These two lean a little to one side or another. The Garisenda used to be quite a lot taller than it is today, but a number of years ago it began to tip alarmingly to one side, and a hundred feet or more of the masonry was removed to stabilize it. They are rooted astride the Via Emilia, the ancient Roman road that connects all the classical-age cities of the Po Valley. Their charming alignment stands as a symbol of this city, which is also famed for its arcades, its learning, and the richness of its wonderful food.

Among the other charms of Bologna is a tidy, modern, and people-friendly airport named for Guglielmo Marconi. British Air flies between Bologna and Gatwick several times a day, and German Wings sometimes connects it with Cologne. Clearing customs and getting on or off a plane is a vastly simpler exercise here than it is in Rome or Milan. Better yet, the airport is a scant fifteen-minute taxi trip from the very center of Bologna and costs a modest handful of euro.

When one comes to Bologna, it is essential, even for a few days, to abandon all notions of health food or a low-fat diet. I don't know if the cardiac surgeons of the old university do a particularly brisk trade scraping out the arteries of the citizens of this butter-clogged town. I have a hunch that the longevity of its citizens is not greatly different from all of Italy. I also know that they live very well in the meantime. Since it was here that the English physician William Harvey received his education in medicine (before he discovered the function of the heart and the circulation of the blood), it would seem that modern Bolognese cardiac specialists ought to have learned something about cholesterol and triglycerides. I guess I am grateful that I follow the diet of Bologna only during infrequent foreign voyages.

Besides its towers, Bologna has miles of arcaded sidewalks, about a half-million residents, and perhaps the oldest university in the world. Today there are about 65,000 students in town. The university started back before the year 1000, perhaps even around the time of Charlemagne, who came through Bologna on his way to Rome to get his European empire legitimized in the year 800 by having the pope crown him. As civilization and trade began to revive long after the decay of Rome and the depredation of the Goths and Langobards, someone decided that law was too important to be left to casual recollection. Students began to hire the best lawyers to teach them what was remembered of the Roman laws, which had once been engraved upon twelve tablets in the forum. Groups of students from various European countries established colleges in Bologna. From this grew the first university in Europe. Schools of medicine, liberal arts, surgery, and mathematics were added in the thirteenth and fourteenth centuries. This is where the famous Thomas à Becket, the martyred archbishop of Canterbury, took his bachelor of laws degree.

It is hard to find the site of the university today, since it has no real centralized campus. Northeast of the Due Torre, along the slightly downhill course of the Via Zamboni, is the student quarter, where there are a number of academic buildings as well as ice cream shops, bookstores, and the Teatro Communale. There are also fascinating buildings to visit scattered around the center of the town. The Archiginnasio is an old university building that is now the city library. We wandered in under the arched ceilings and found them emblazoned with the coats of arms of many hundreds of titled young aristocrats from all over Europe, who came here over the last three or four hundred years and left these mementos of their happy undergraduate days as decorations of walls and soffits.

The dissection theater of the medical school has been restored since it was bombed during World War II. Here doctors of medieval Europe strove to catch up to the Arabs and the Persians who, besides their own inventiveness, had the advantage of the texts of the Greek scientists of the third and fourth centuries BC to build on. Learning anatomy when the church forbade dissection was difficult, but a compromise was worked out, allowing the bodies of executed criminals to be used for study. But the popes grumbled over this and outlawed the practice from time to time. In any case, medical education was far from a hands-on experience. The anatomical theater must have held over a hundred students in three or four elevated circles. They probably didn't see very closely whatever the professor was excavating from the criminal cadaver at hand. There are also wonderful wooden statues of "skinned men" that probably taught the neophyte doctors how to do a mercifully swift amputation on the battlefield or in hospital.

"IL GIGANTE" - BOLOGNA 1563

We have stayed in Bologna several times and have a favorite small hotel right in the center of town, the Albergo Centrale at the Via della Zecca 2. It is entered from the street through a gloomy outdoor vestibule to the iron gates of an old-fashioned cage elevator that lifted us at a leisurely pace past a series of offices to the fourth floor (called the third in European fashion). Here we came upon the tidy little lobby of a perfectly modern hotel with pretty rooms and contemporary bathrooms. All of this at less than the price of a Holiday Inn Express on I-95, which is, as always, my standard of comparison for the cost of quarters.[1]

---

[1] Most of the estimates of Italian prices in this book (when given in dollars) must be increased considerably since the recent elevation of the euro in comparison with American currency.

Around the corner is the Piazza Maggiore, the great open square in the center of Bologna. Here is Giambologna's fountain with the statue of Neptune prodding his pet dolphin with his toes, perched high up above a set of mermaids whose breasts spout allegories of the great rivers of the world into the basin below. Neptune is a tall and shiny bronze fellow, called *Il Gigante* by the Bolognese, who leans lightly on his trident.

He stands just below the windows of the suite of rooms where Enzo, the natural son of Emperor Frederick II, was held imprisoned as a hostage for most of his life in the thirteenth century. His father had made him King of Sardinia, but the fortunes of war made him a captive in a battle with Bologna, and he served as a safeguard for the city forever after. Frederick tried to ransom him back for "enough silver to circle the walls of Bologna," but the shrewd townspeople reasoned that a live royal hostage was a great way to protect their town. They locked him up in dignified if limited quarters and kept him there for the rest of his life. He was, however, allowed some royal prerogatives. Once when from his window he spied a pretty girl feeding the pigeons in the piazza, he requested an introduction from a member of the tower-building Asinelli family, who was in charge of keeping the royal prisoner in all reasonable contentment. When the young king met the young lady, he is said to have blurted out: "*Anima mia, ben ti voglio!*",[2] an expression of a rather enthusiastic and joyful proposal. The family that sprung from this union came to be known as the Bentivoglio, and in subsequent centuries became the strong men and rulers of Bologna. They managed the town for

---

[2] "Upon my soul, how I desire you!"

about half of the fifteenth century, until the warlike Pope Julius II conquered Bologna. But the Bolognese have never taken kindly to the strong central government, and through the latter half of the twentieth century, the town was the center of Italy's homegrown sort of Communism. They still vote for the leftist parties today.

After paying due deference to Enzo, the imperial bastard and his illegitimate descent, we made a circuit of the Piazza and looked up to pass Niccolo dell'Arco's sculpture of the Virgin and Child set in a shallow niche high up on the ancient brick wall of the next building. Here the Virgin Mother is a perfectly lovely young lady holding up her perfect baby for all to acknowledge. She reminds me of the *studentesse* crossing the square on their way to lectures at the university. The date on her pedestal is MCDLXXVIII, which, in Roman numerals, works out to be 1478. Niccolo carved her just fourteen years before his contemporary, the Genoese explorer Cristoforo, discovered America . . . or at least discovered the islands of the Caribbean.

We settled in under a characteristically Bolognese arcade where a cheery waiter served us *tramezzini* made of prosciutto and mozzarella with a glass of white wine. It was a lovely afternoon, and there were plenty of children and pigeons to watch in the piazza. All the ages of man are reflected in the interaction of pigeons and people in the great public squares of Italy. Pre-ambulatory infants sit in the midst of the flock and smile. Toddlers lurch about trying to catch them. Five-year-olds run to make the flock fly up in a burst of fluttering wings. Preteens on bicycles do their best to run them down, seeming to know that they will not succeed. Hand-holding adolescents are usually too interested in each other to pay much heed to the birds, but the elderly stand in their midst and scatter scraps of stale bread to attract great gatherings of these imported descendants of the Asiatic rock doves that have adapted so completely to the environment of towers and open squares in the cities of Europe.

The south side of the Piazza Maggiore is formed by the facade of the Basilica of San Petronio, the patron of the city. It is a huge Gothic church that was constructed in stages over at least four or five centuries. Only about the lowest quarter of the facade is clad in marble; above that, the severe brickwork of the understructure still broods over the great square. Lots of the Renaissance churches in Italy have half-finished facades and still look impressive. Better an unfinished masterpiece than a second-rate work of art. The sculpture around this central doorway is one of the treats of the town. There are a dozen five-by-five-foot marble frames containing sculptured images of the Creation and fall of man in high relief. Jacopo della Quercia carved them at the very beginning of the fifteenth century (the *quattrocento*) when Italian artists were beginning to come out of the Gothic age and rediscover the figure modeling of the Greeks and Romans.

The Pisano pulpits in Pisa, Siena, and Pistoia do come first by a century, but here, della Quercia's Adam and Eve are much more in the style of classical statuary. He shows them proud of their naked beauty before the fall. They're not a bit like the medieval statues at the great cathedrals of Germany, England, and France. Eve presents the forbidden fruit (it looks rather like a pear) quite seductively. Their expulsion from paradise is a heartrending affair, with Adam ineffectually trying to ward off the angel's sword while his wife is obviously in tears beside him. (Perhaps Masaccio's painted Expulsion in the Carmine of Florence was inspired by this sculpture.) But our first parents seem to have cheered up a bit in the scene where Adam has begun to dig in the stony soil outside of Eden, and Eve admires his industry while she herself holds up a distaff heaped with new-spun wool. Her two sons, little more than toddlers, clasp their mother's knees and seem to be begging for a treat.

Inside, San Petronio is a vast church fashioned from great Gothic arches forming a huge nave with two gigantic organs on either side. The great structure lacks transepts and an apse. If these had ever been added, it would have been the largest church in the world, surpassing even St. Peter's in Rome. Apparently, the Renaissance popes who conquered Bologna called a halt to the construction of the basilica for a century or two, and it has stayed truncated but magnificent ever since.

A pale, cream-colored marble stripe runs at an angle across the red marble floor of the nave. It traces the local meridian, laid out by the astronomer Cassini, who found the rings of Saturn in the seventeenth century.

Across from the church, on the north side of the great square, stands the Podestà, the original site of the city's government. Part of it is still called the Palazzo Enzo for the captive king who lived there.

Exploring a modern Italian city or an ancient one can produce both appetite and some fatigue. But fortunately, in Bologna, you are never far from a *pasticceria* where you can retreat and restore yourself in the late afternoon. You can choose either in Italian fashion (whipped cream on the pastry or *gelato* with slivered almonds), or the more American way, with gin and tonic or a dry martini (be sure to specify your own proper proportions for the cocktail).

Later, we explored the wonderful Feltrinelli bookstore, a chain that is the Italian equivalent of Barnes & Noble, or perhaps better. Modern Italians are intensely literate, and pursue both their own classics as well as Italian translations of books that were written in English, French, German, or Russian. Bookstores are always crowded, and people in buses or on park benches always seem to have a book in hand. We took to book-browsing for translations of books we had already read in English as a means of improving our Italian while we waited for 7:30 P.M., the earliest possible opening of a respectable *ristorante*. I discovered a text of T. S. Eliot's "The Waste Land," which was presented together with the original version (in English) that Eliot had submitted to Ezra Pound for editing into the form in which I had read it in college a half-century ago. Pound excised close to half of what Eliot had written. In his introduction, Eliot dedicated the poem to him as *il miglior fabbro*—"the better blacksmith." The exercise in deconstruction across the language barrier was instructive and fun.[3]

On the east side of the Piazza Maggiore is the Palazzo Communale, where there is a slightly less than world-class collection of pictures. It is worth the visit for the papal collection of paintings, but also to experience the climb up (or perhaps better, down) Bramante's gigantic stairway to the galleries of the commune and the Museo Morandi, where the output of this hometown painter is on exhibit. Altogether you can spend a long full day in and around this great central square, perhaps two. And in the evening one can stroll the arcades and inspect the brightly lighted shop windows that display the latest fashions.

After our experience with art and literature, we stopped into the most logically located *pizzeria-ristorante* on our way back toward the Albergo Centrale. I think you can hardly go wrong in Bologna, the capital of Emilia Romagna, the province generally conceded to

---

[3] I was pleased to learn that the barman's call for the closing of "hours" in an English pub—"Hurry up, please—it's time"—is rendered Sbrigatevi, per favore, si chiude. Eliot's Cockney dropping of the initial "H" is not indicated, but the Italians are less likely to assign social class to regional pronunciation.

have the best food in Italy (if not the most dietetic). We thus came to Zia Caatarì where we had a wonderful *primo* of tortellini, followed by a delicious fillet of buttery fish with Emilian spinach liberally treated with garlic. Wine and all, our dinner for two came to 77,000 lire—about $43 at the time. Food in Bologna is more than just the derivation of the name of mortadella sausage.

I have heard it said that Bologna has no suburbs; everything is within the compass of the central city. The vast network of arcades makes it especially easy to traverse. Even if it rains.

XXVII.

FORLÌ:
Just Down the Via Emilia from Bologna

Forlì is typical of many of the places discussed in this book: smaller than many in this densely populated country, full of art and history, pleasant in all seasons of the year, not far from the beach towns, ornamented by an airport that will deliver you to Rome or Sicily, and measurably less expensive than the more-famous tourist sites of northern Italy. We would never have found it at all had it not been for the invitation of Cristina and Alberto Mazzoni, whom I had shown about the Mystic Seaport the prior summer. We put up at the Vittorino, a very pleasant small hotel that provided an excellent restaurant, almost deserted at night but bursting with happy and well-fed *Forlese* in midday. Knowing how all Italians value their luxurious lunch hour, we rightly interpreted this as a strong commendation of the chef. The Vittorino also has the advantage of being in the very center of town where Cristina presides over a successful business and tax-consulting "studio." Her husband, Alberto, is largely retired and focuses mostly on a deep and even passionate interest in music and art. They had already promised us a concert in their neighboring town of Imola, where a famous conductor of J. S. Bach, Helmut Rilling, was scheduled to present the "Mass in B Minor" with a chorus and full orchestra of soloists, singers, and instrumentalists he would bring from Stuttgart. German—and even Hungarian—music is almost as popular in Italy as their own homegrown compositions. It also fills in the season when the Grand Opera is not in session.

Bach was wonderful, and Rilling was a startlingly small man of great energy, snow-white hair, and energetic shoulders. Cathy pointed out later that his downbeats seemed to be on the upstroke, but his chorus and orchestra followed his every requirement with total precision. He has come occasionally to music festivals in Oregon and in other parts of the United States. The great Gothic church in Imola, however, was one of those beautiful and acoustically perfect spaces that only recovers from its winter chill by July, and we were there in mid-May. Cristina and Alberto had warned us to wear sweaters, coats, and perhaps even woolly hats. Warmed by the great music, we ignored the temperature. The next night we had an excellent dinner and a fine bottle of *Chianti Classico* at the converted monastery of one of the medieval orders of Knights Templars halfway between Imola and Forlì.

Forlì is typical of small Italian cities in that it was organized around a great central square, the Piazza Saffi. The tall and very slender bell tower of the Abbey of San Mercuriale was built here in 1180. Elegant if rather severe, it stands on the east side of the piazza, not far from the Pinacoteca Civica, which was eclipsed during our visit by a special exhibition of the work of Marco Palmezzano at the Musei in San Domenico. Palmezzano was a hometown boy, and the city is justly proud of him. Many of his greatest works had been brought together from all over Europe and the United States to help celebrate his residence in this city when he was at the top of his productivity, five hundred years ago. Only a few of his paintings are permanently in Forlì, but several of these are choice. *The Baptism of Jesus* is a starkly human, almost naked representation of the Savior standing modestly in front of a rather scruffy Baptist on the rocky shore of the West Bank. An unidentified young man seems to be washing his own feet nearby. The painting, done in the later years of the *quattrocento*, seems to me to be the very essence of the top of the *Rinascimento*, before Signorelli and Michelangelo ushered in the mannerist paintings of the sixteenth century. On the other hand, Marco's Saint Catherine of Alexandria is one of those pale northern beauties who is ready to worship the infant Christ. The baby toys with a wedding ring on his index finger, and doesn't seem to be paying much attention to the beautiful girl who is pledging fidelity to Him in the presence of a chubby John the Baptist.

"Saint Catherine" - Marco Palmezzano - c. 1530

On another day, our enthusiastic hosts took us east to the Adriatic shore. We stopped off at Cesena to visit the earliest public library set up since the collapse of the Roman Empire. Malatesta Novello had built and endowed this remarkable hall in the latter half of the fifteenth century. It is still in use today, but since the books are of ancient content and rare condition, the place is quiet and uncrowded. Desks in ranks like church pews have generally one book per sitting space. Usually the volume is chained to its shelf, not to keep the faithful from making their own interpretation of Scripture, but to preserve the books from the hands of thieves, perhaps a precaution that the Beinecke Library of rare books at Yale might have copied for their map collection. This midsize library is a perfect symbol of the great explosion of knowledge and learning that took place in the post-Gutenberg age and began after 1450, about the time that Malatesta Novello extended this Franciscan Monastery to embrace a public library. It contains a unique collection of manuscripts from the early 1200s to the subsequent age of printed books. Some of the hand-illuminated parchments are of classical Greek and Latin texts, and a unique set of seven are Hebrew books.

Milano Marittima is, curiously, nowhere near Milano. Early on, it became the vacation town for prosperous Milanese who wanted to visit the Adriatic shore for a cool and breezy vacation in the summertime. We visited the tidy little getaway where a three- or four-item visit to the local supermarket provided all Cristina needed to whip up a delightful lunch before we undertook an exploration of the locale. In the adjoining town of Cesenatico, there are a half-dozen ancient fishing boats rigged with colorful sails that are moored in the canal-harbor that has served this tiny port since early times. In the early sixteenth century, the lord of Romagna was Cesare Borgia, brother of the famous beauty, Lucrezia, and son of Pope

Alexander VI. He had become a cardinal at age twenty-two, and was a capable warrior who served his father as captain general of the papal armies. He had the good sense to hire Leonardo da Vinci as his military engineer shortly thereafter. Polymathic Leonardo's plans for the improvement of the canal and harbor of Cesenatico are still extant in the Paris Library.

Forlì and its environs are among the small treasures of Emilia Romagna. This area, besides being down the way from Bologna, is just between Ravenna, where the great Byzantine mosaics are, and Rimini, the most famous of the Adriatic beach towns. There is much more to be visited to the south and west as well, but as tourists ourselves, we know you can't see it all at once, and are thankful for every fleeting visit.

XVIII.
THE ADRIATIC COAST
AND ASCOLI PICENO:
The Marche, the Home of Fried Stuffed Olives

The Piceni were contemporary with the Sabines, wherefrom the descendants Romulus and Remus found their brides and, according to Livy, carried them off after an athletic game party to fill the aching void left by their own lack of women. It might be likened to a group of college thugs inviting the boys of the opposition team to bring their sisters to a postgame party and then keeping the girls for the rest of the weekend in their dorm rooms. Livy spins the event into a charming tale of romantic warfare that has provided the subject for a number of neoclassical paintings: the brothers and fathers of the Sabine girls making war on the Romans to rescue the young women and take them home, only to have the kidnapped girls thrust themselves between the warriors in order to break up the battle. They wanted to stay with their new husbands, and also to protect their fathers and brothers from harm. Whether the Piceni were part of this ancient affair is a matter of conjecture for my fertile imagination, but the two tribes were at least contemporaries. Whatever events actually took place, these peoples occupied the same part of Italy, got over their hostilities, and intermarried. Eventually, Rome governed the whole area of the Adriatic coast.

To reach Ascoli, we came down that eastern coast of the boot of Italy, visiting several beach towns and the great ferry terminals where the big boats push off for Serbia, Greece, and even Turkey. Like many tourists we had neglected the central Adriatic coast of Italy and had much to learn. Searching Google for affordable *alberghi*, we came south from Padova where we had stayed at Tibet House, a B&B run by an intellectual Italian lady who was enamored of the Far East, and found one in Rimini.

Although our departure by rail was inhibited by a brief bomb scare for a few minutes after we boarded the train, we were happy to have planned this entire trip by railroad and enjoyed peering at the sea through the clean windows of the rapid (although local) train of the Ferrovia dello Stato as it bore us along the shore. Rimini is the largest and most venerable of the Italian beach towns. Villas and villages decorate the shoreline, and even in March there were a few sailboats cruising off the coast.

We put up at the Napoleon, a simple but comfortable hotel obviously named to attract the French tourist trade, since the late emperor of France was never a favorite of the locals whom he abused at his pleasure for the greatest part of his sojourn in Italy.[4] We chose it because it was close to the station and we had to haul our bags from train to hotel. Anyway (*dunque*, as the Italians say), the whole town is strung out along the seaside, so everything is close to the water. The ingratiating concierge did not protest at my rejection of his stale martini vermouth, and didn't even seem surprised that I, an American,

---

[4] The one blessing the little Corsican tyrant conferred upon Italy was the universal adoption of the "metric system" of weights, measures, volumes, and, eventually, all scientific quantification except for the Babylonian "base 12" of hours and degrees of angle that measure the depth of the starry universe.

insisted upon such a generous measure of the new bottle added to the gin of my cocktail. He helped us locate an adequate restaurant where the hard-shelled langustini in the *antipasto al mare* seemed a bit too tough. The wife of the *proprietario* made up for this by pressing on us a semi-fredo mango cheesecake with a small glass of *Limoncello*, gratis. If the supper was mediocre, the dessert was splendid.

We set out for the seashore in the morning. There were a number of rather elegant houses along the way, but none of them old in the proper Italian sense. But there is one magnificent five-star hotel, The Grande Hotel, which would seem to be a late-nineteenth-century pile of luxury that had survived several world wars and sheltered the Fascists in the late thirties and early forties of the last century. I didn't inquire about the tariff, but a fair guess would be that the immaculately restored palace required something in excess of 500 euro for a night's lodging. Even the usually restrained upper-class Cadogan Guide rates it as "luxury," and mentions that the hotel supports its own full-time orchestra. I resolved a night or two there would reward Cathy if one of our books sells in excess of a hundred thousand copies.

Italian beaches are clogged with little bath houses and orderly ranks of *ombrelloni* set on three-meter centers or closer. Each family has its own ten-foot-square patch of sand for its exclusive use, generally crowded under their own bit of shade. The umbrellas are set up and struck at day's end by *il bagno*, usually a strong and handsome young man who does his best to entertain and flirt with the teenaged daughters of the family. Everybody has a good time, what with minimal bikinis, sun, sand, and an occasional swig of ice-cold carbonated orange juice, the *aranciata*.

A hundred yards along the beach we came to an imposing dolphinarium. The Mediterranean *delfine* are smaller than their

Atlantic cousins, but no less capable of learning to do tricks for the tourists and a horde of schoolchildren. They were led through their paces by an athletic and very pretty young swimmer with a pale blonde pigtail. The little whales would lift her out of the water on their backs and toss her in the air, boosting her 110 pounds with a mere shrug of the head, while her foot was supported by their snouts. It was a good show and the schoolchildren squealed their approval.

Another touch of civilization along the beachfront was a large aluminum and canvas shelter that housed an extensive bookstore. Italians are voracious readers of books and magazines. We gathered the impression that adult Italians spend most of their time at the water's edge reading under an umbrella rather than splashing about in the Adriatic Sea. The other great and popular occupations of a visit to Rimini are dining on the really fresh seafood to be found in the local restaurants and inspecting the plethora of Roman remains and early Renaissance buildings that surround you. The great Roman road from the sea to Cisalpine Gaul began here, the Via Emilia, which connects all of the old Roman centers: Forlì, Faenza, Bologna, Modena, Reggio nell'Emilia, Parma, Piacenza, and, eventually, Milano. The emperor Augustus erected

ARCH of AUGUSTUS   RIMINI

a triumphal arch where this road met the north-south road that led to Rome itself.

Still standing in place after a couple of thousand years, the elegant arch was later crowned with three or four feet of medieval machicolations, added for defensive purpose six or seven hundred years after the original construction. People and vehicles, shuffling peasants, ranks of briskly marching soldiers, as well as wagons of animal fodder, new-milled grain, and the fruits of the vine have passed through this portal since the first emperor built it and dedicated it to the gods of his people.

A few hundred yards away to the east we found a neoclassical temple, the Tempio Malatestiano,[5] where the medieval lords of the country might have prayed, or received the sacraments of the Roman church. But it doesn't seem to have been a place to be married or to celebrate any other religious rites. Sigismondo Malatesta remodeled an earlier church in the classical style and buried Isotta degli Atti, his much-loved mistress, here in a white marble sarcophagus. The rest of the building is in the classical style of the sixteenth century, pure and reserved in design, a successful re-creation of the *putti* and garlands of the old Roman burial coffins in this newer and still brutal "civilization" by the edge of the sea. Since the Malatesta were among the most brutal warriors of the fifteenth century, this, their family chapel, is of the very essence of the Renaissance: bloody battles, lofty works of art, and an infusion of the thought and art of the latter centuries of the pre-Christian era. It all seems to come together in Rimini where there are centuries' worth of old olive trees growing

---

[5] The name Maletesta means "headache," probably the condition he inflicted on those who opposed him.

in the interrupted traffic circles of the modern city. Not far away in the same area of the Marches is the small Renaissance city of Urbino, where ruled Federico da Montefeltro.

We had supper at Il Giordini's, a pleasant garden spot in back of an old church where we dined on pizza *caprese* and (for me) stuffed tortelloni. Our habit has usually been to order the house wine, but here that choice was faintly sour and I complained about it. The waiter swiftly removed the carafe and returned in a moment with a nice new bottle of an excellent Sangiovese, which he uncorked in our presence and poured generously into large wineglasses. Neither of us ordered dessert, but a nice plate of cookies appeared

Piazza del Popolo
Ascoli Piceno

unbidden with my coffee. Altogether a very good experience with a low-priced restaurant.

The train on to the south dropped us off at San Benedetto del Tronto, another beach town, where we changed to the ten-mile shuttle rail service directly inland toward the mountains in the west where Ascoli Piceno nestles. The town presents a splendid jumble of medieval towers and churches in granite, as well as a couple of lovely Renaissance *piazze* in travertine stone and a few *palazzi* of almost contemporary vintage. We had reserved at a B&B in the northwest quarter of the little city. Marilena Piccinini, our hostess, descended one long flight to greet us, explaining that reconstruction at street level was regrettably slow. We were grateful that two burly laborers looked up from their cement mixing, seized our bags, and trotted up the two flights of great stairways to her apartment, each of which reached up beyond the fifteen-foot ceiling heights of the palazzo.[6] Lightweight Italian women seem to keep in shape by running up and down magnificent stairways. We also marvel at their ability to walk in the highest of heels on ancient cobbled streets.

The apartment was large and elegantly furnished. Of the two bedrooms, one was her own (she moved upstairs to a smaller room when she had paying guests), and the other was called "The Blue Room," which had a bathroom en suite that presented a tub of such vastness and depth, we were both afraid it was one from which we would never be able to emerge. The mistress's bath had a shower, but the entry to the room was protected by a portal around a corner undecorated by a closable door. Once we got used to it, we decided

------

[6] When booking a room in Italy, remember that our first floor is their piano terra and their first floor is our second, etc.

that the whole place was charming and there was, of course, some style in the view of a third-century Roman bridge over the Tronto from the window in one direction and a pair of the eight or ten neighborhood towers visible in the other.

Ascoli has two principal squares and a half-dozen minor ones. The original, and still the seat of commerce, is the Piazza del Popolo, where medieval buildings have been surrounded and augmented by Renaissance ornamentation and graceful modern adaptations of Romanesque and later styles. There are also two splendid bars diagonally across from each other: a very modern one called Eight and a Half, and the other, more famous one, Caffè Meletti. The latter is about a hundred years old and was the favored watering place of Ernest Hemingway and Jean-Paul Sartre. It is most famous for an anise-flavored liqueur named for the Meletti, which we passed up because of our affinity for Gordon's gin after five o'clock in the afternoon.

Eight and a Half has no such aristocratic descent. It is all clear plastic, colored glasses and globes, imitation Eames chairs, and small, black Formica-topped *tavolini*. We tried the two cafés in both rain and sun. In the long run we preferred the modern one dedicated to Federico Fellini and Marcello Mastroianni's first great film. It strikes me as odd to note that both Fellini and Hemingway flourished in the same century.

The other great center in Ascoli is the Piazza Arringo, the gathering place of the citizens when the city became a free commune in the twelfth century. Somewhat more severe than the nearby Franciscan church, the cathedral of St. Emidio closes off one end of the Piazza Arringo. It is named for a bishop about whom little is known, except that he was martyred in 303 shortly before Constantine made Christianity legal. He is quite usefully invoked for protection from earthquakes.

One side of the Arringo is occupied by the art gallery, the Diocesan Museum, and the city library. The collection is rich and staffed by a proper rank of conservators. The director was in conversation with the ticket taker, and we took the opportunity to ask what we hoped were a few sensible questions in limping Italian. The learned gentleman listened intently and then turned to the girl at the counter to say (in English): "Tell my secretary I am taking the rest of the morning off." He then devoted himself for the next two hours to escorting us through the galleries and inspecting painting, furniture, and sculpture of the past half-dozen centuries. If the collection rates perhaps only four of a possible five stars (like Florence or Rome), it rates well into the second rank, especially because of the jewel-like paintings of Carlo Crivelli and members of his school which have been the ornament of Ascoli since the *quattrocento*.

We were out of season to witness the *Quintano*, the ritual and athletic jousting that takes place during July, and especially on the first Sunday of August. Gorgeously costumed combatants and gorgeous girls strut their stuff in the great squares, rigged out in the latest fashions of the Middle Ages, in competition for the *palio* which confers undisputed bragging rights on the representatives of the winning neighborhood team. In winter there is also a Mardi Gras celebration that features outdoor performances of Commedia dell'Arte characters mocking the eternal relationships of lovers, braggarts, charlatans, shepherdesses, and their loyal swains. For the next trip maybe. Ascoli is such an agreeable town, and the olives ascolana are *cosi* sinfully delicious.

XXIX.

PERUGIA:
Where the Chocolate Comes From

The queen city of Umbria is a high, jumbled collection of buildings spread over the ridges of a small mountain in the "green heart of Italy." Approaching it from the south gave us a good idea of what the rivers and Apennine Mountains required of Italian travelers, both ancient and modern. There are simply no direct routes among the mountains and the torrents. The rail line from Firenze goes past Lake Trasimeno, two or three valleys to the west of Perugia, and then comes to rest at the small city of Terontola, where a locomotive is hooked on to what had been the last car to start east again through an interconnecting vale to the valley of a nascent Tiber. There the city sprawls above its rugged and sizable hill with some remarkable views in all directions. Most of the sprawl is of this century, and quite a lot of it has taken place since World War II. The *centro storico* is arranged along the upper ridge of the small mountain, still largely surrounded by much of its medieval wall. But Perugia is a lot older than the masonry we can see today. The town seems to have originated with the Umbrians, the pre-Etruscan people who dwelt here before the first millennium BC. Sometime after 800 BC, the area was either invaded by or gradually reformed itself into an Etruscan city set on top of the hill, as almost all Etruscan cities were. By 300 BC, it had been taken by the Romans.

Though Roman ruins abound in Italy, the hegemony of the republican city and the emperors actually was relatively brief, if quite complete. In this case the town was Roman for about seven hundred years of the three thousand it has been populated. Yet when Hannibal came through on his way south after his famous Alpine crossing, the Perugiani remained faithful to Rome, which had been their overlord for a little more than a century. The town was prosperous in later Roman times, but fell to the Langobards by the sixth century, and didn't manage to acquire any degree of self-government until after 1100. But then a wonderful period ensued when the arts and commerce of all of Umbria poured through the little city.

Very little of this history save a ragged skyline was visible to us from the train as the track swung through a gradually ascending curve to approach the town. It came to rest at the Piazza Vittorio Veneto, still a long way downhill from the nearest portals of the ancient wall. A characteristically obliging cab driver piloted us up through steep drives and switchbacks to find the Hotel Iris on the Via Guglielmo Marconi. Our course reversed a full 180 degrees at least four times as we progressed through rather modern streets named for modern heroes: the universally revered twentieth of September (the date of liberation from Nazi control), and, eventually, the Street of the Hunters of the Alps (*Cacciatori delle Alpi*), whose history I was unable to determine, although there are crack mountain troops in the Italian army. (They wear jaunty alpine hats with spiffy badger-brush ornaments.)

We wound around the soccer stadium before the road plunged through the Tre Archi, a triple portal which seems to have been started by the Etruscans and more or less finished by the Romans. The current communal government was giving it a major repair job when we visited. Reversing direction once more just short of the archway, our driver explained that because so many of the streets were *senso unico*, he would have to leave us at the foot of a midsize stairway that led to a terrace above a group of stores where the hotel was located. The day was growing later. We shot out the handles of our wheeled luggage and did the last flight on foot.

The Iris, chosen because it was a bargain, was pronounced, of course, with the long Italian I's, "Eerees." It is a venerable building that once hosted Richard Wagner for at least part of the winter of 1880. A plaque giving witness to this remarkable event was on the uphill rear side of the building where it was quite invisible to anyone using the front entrance. I eventually figured out that during the last century, the periodic remodeling of the building and redirection of the streets of the town had resulted in turning the original back of the Iris into the front when the modern motorcar required a considerable regrading and lowering of the neighboring streets.

Our room for the first night had an elegantly domed ceiling frescoed with cupids, flowers, and birds done in blues and reds on an ochre background. The bath was nearly contemporary. But the bed—a large-sized version of what the Italians call *un grand matrimonial*—had been stiffened with a large sheet of particle board that had cracked in the middle and formed a valley that thrust its occupants downhill from each side into an enforced intimacy that largely precluded sleep. Always test the beds before accepting the room in an *albergo* of less than three stars. Demanding better quarters the next day produced a splendid bed but an unadorned ceiling. On balance, the Iris, not a tourist palace, was a good value, but we recommend rooms 20 and 21 for their remodeled bathrooms and (at the moment) firm and modern beds. The little restaurant has quite acceptable food, and the breakfast provided was just fine.

Perugia has taken modern means to ameliorate the steep climb that is necessary from virtually any part of the town to get to the center of the old city. There are two multistage *scale mobile*[7] which climb to the level of the *prefettura* and the cathedral. The one that approaches from the south has four or five spans of moving stairs, each one raising us to the height of two or three stories. They travel through stone chambers vaulted with ancient ceilings, and are paralleled by stairs, just in case. As we approached the upper reaches, we realized that we were traveling upward through parts of a filled-in quarter of the town, through massive military architecture of an earlier time. We later discovered that the structure was the result of the end of the city's life as a free commune. Pope Paul III Farnese sent one of his well-endowed nephews to conquer the town, which had been a bit rebellious concerning the salt tax he had imposed sometime before 1540. Paul III is perhaps better known for his role in calling the Council of Trent, where he got a start on defining all Protestant groups as burnable heretics, and built the grandest papal *palazzo* in Rome before he died and went to whatever reward his maker had prepared for him. This political and religious resolution helped sharpen the conflicts of the wars of religion that drenched sixteenth-century Europe with blood, and perfumed it with the stink of the smoldering bodies of those judged to think incorrectly about the church's magisterial authority. He also employed Michelangelo and lured him away from Florence to

---

[7] This seems to me a far more sensible name for the device than our more highfalutin' use of "escalator."

Rome. His home is now considered by many to be the best of the Renaissance palaces and, except for the Pitti Palace in Florence, would appear to be the largest. The welfare of his family was ever in his mind, perhaps as central to his attention as the preeminent authority of the chair of Peter.

In Perugia, Paul commissioned a fortress at the brink of the south-pointing ridge. Designed to hold the town in subjugation after it was taken by his nephew, Pier Luigi Farnese, this large complex of buildings was known as La Rocca Paolina. How did those Renaissance building contractors move those huge stones to such towering heights! It stood as the symbol of papal rule until the time of the revolutionary changes of the mid-nineteenth century, when the city finally rebelled successfully, fought hard for its liberty, and gleefully demolished the architectural symbol of papal authority. The remaining understories are still called by the original name.

After the *Risorgimento*, Perugia became the capital of Umbria, and rejoiced in the new freedom of being rid of church control. One of the great paradoxes of modern Italy is the wonderful depth of feeling both for and against the pope that Italians have to this day. He is *their* Papa, and they are proud to have him in Rome. On the other hand, they have generally paid much less attention to the strictures of his teaching than American or even Irish Catholics do. They positively resent the church poking its institutional nose into their political affairs. Papal interference in Italian politics is forbidden under the terms of the concordat that established the modern relationship between the Republic of Italy and Vatican City. The kinds of statements that some American cardinals feel free to make about political campaigns would be either widely unpopular or against the law in Italy.

As we ascended through many levels of the underworks of the

former castle, we found (between the escalators) small art shops, secondhand book stalls, and a midsize exhibition of both ancient and modern ceramics of Umbria. The tradition of making pots and bowls out of glazed, baked clay is many millennia old in Italy, and some of the best examples of the potter's art have always come from this area. The famous pottery town of Deruta is only a few kilometers from Perugia. Each century seems to produce new designs, new styles, and new colors. The difficulty of transporting a large bowl in hand luggage and the expense of professional packing and shipping kept forestalling our desire to bring some of it back from Perugia or Florence. We eventually settled by purchasing one small but very beautiful blue and yellow bowl.

Mounting the final escalator, we eventually emerged in a pleasant city square, more than a hundred feet above the level of our hotel and nearly twice that high above the railroad that clung to the side of the hill below us. Beyond, the pleasant hills of Umbria, brown trimmed with many different sorts of green, stretched to a near-blue horizon of modest mountains. A profusion of early March flowers studded the beds in the green lawn that surrounded the Giardini Carducci at the brink of the cliff in front of the *prefettura*, and the equally manicured Piazza Italia behind it. The name of this pretty square struck me as obvious at first, until I stopped to realize that "Italia" as a country and not just the name of a geographical area is still a recent phenomenon here. The names of Mazzini, Garibaldi, and Cavour, who brought it into being, are still very much alive in the memory of a people whose national identity is far younger than that of the United States.

All Italian towns have their *passeggiata* in the late afternoon. Almost the entire population turns out for a stroll through the principal avenues and public squares of the center. In Perugia people swarm along the four-hundred-meter length of the Corso Vannucci,[8] from the Piazza della Repubblica to the Piazza IV Novembre in front of the cathedral. The members of the crowd were young, for Perugia has two universities and a proportionately large population of students. The broad *corso* was jammed with several thousand attractive *ragazzi* enjoying the early spring weather and each others' company. We worked our way north along the swirling patterns of the stone paving blocks in the direction of the cathedral, while at the same time seeking out a likely spot for our *aperitivo*. Along the way we got a first glance at the famous Fontana Maggiore.

Essential to the location of other Italian cities, including Rome itself, is a plentiful supply of pure drinking water. The aqueduct that feeds the wonderful fountain of Perugia was completed in 1278, and since that time there has been a perpetual flow of good water into the center of the lofty town, providing salubrious refreshment as well as a source of civic pride. It travels by gravity from Mount Paciano, five miles farther up in the mountains of the Apennine chain, where there is plenty of snowpack in the winter and lots of rain in other seasons. Celebration of the communal success of hydraulic engineering required an endpoint that was both handsome and instructive. The town commissioned the most famous sculptors of the age, Nicola Pisano and his son Giovanni, to carve the marble panels, and Rosso Padellaio of Perugia to cast the concentric bronze basins.

There are really two fountains, one on top of the other, surrounded by a casing of more than fifty bas-reliefs in two tiers.

---

[8] Pietro Vannucci (c.1450–1523) was an immensely talented painter of the quattrocento, as well as the teacher of Raphael. He is the favorite son of this town, but in the rest of the world of art he is known as the Perugian or "il Perugino."

These celebrate the city, the hand of God, and the mind of man.
There are reliefs of saints, allegories of virtues, representations of
Caesars and others from Roman history, as well as personages from
the past of the city itself. Philosophers, prophets, kings, and the
characters of Aesop's fables are presented in cream-colored marble
bas-reliefs in pink frames. The whole wonder was, when we saw
it, being cleaned and restored by scientific practitioners in white
laboratory coats, who work inside a large plastic dome that has been
erected over the whole fountain. The modern transparent cover looks
quite permanent, but I suspect that it will stay in place only for the
years necessary to complete the painstaking restoration and cleaning.
The Italians have had many, mostly unlooked-for opportunities to
practice the pleasant art of restoration, and they are surely the best
practitioners of it in the world.

From the piazza we retreated around the corner of the *Duomo*
to a welcoming bar and pastry shop to negotiate for a gin and tonic
and a martini made, as it always is in Italy, with lots of newly opened
Martini & Rossi vermouth. It has always seemed to me that people

who don't like a lot of vermouth in their martinis are probably suffering from the ill effects of using inferior vermouth (only Martini & Rossi will do), or from letting the stuff stand around in an open bottle until it has soured, or even, in some cases, turned brown with age. In Italy the *aperitivo* is as light and fresh as a spring day, and only requires a touch of good English gin to augment its virtues.

Besides upping the charge by a factor of two, among the nice rites associated with taking a table and being waited on in Italy (rather than standing at the bar) is that you are also provided with a bowlful of newly opened peanuts, potato chips, or small crackers. The glassware is often elegant, and a lace-trimmed paper doily is placed underneath it all. In its details the whole event seems more of a social ritual according to the pattern of afternoon tea.

We were joined in the bar, which might just as well be called a tea shop, by a pair of French college-age girls who were dressed in nylon windbreaker suits, one in blue and green and the other in peach, embroidered with green and white flowers. The *barista* had stopped serving long enough to make a call from the pay phone across from our table. He began by rattling a long-handled knife in the coin-return slot of the bright orange instrument, shaking out a couple of coins that were stuck in it. These he redeposited in the top of the pay phone and made his call. A few moments later, one of the French girls attempted to use the phone. Failing to get it to work, she asked the bartender for help. He approached with his special knife again, unjammed the telephone, and presented the coins to the girl who then made her call. It seemed to be the normal mode of operation.

The thirteenth, fourteenth, and fifteenth centuries were obviously a cultural high tide for this town before it was caught under the papal heel in 1538. Scholarship flourished in the 1200s, and resulted in the formal establishment of the university in 1308. Public buildings along the Piazza IV Novembre, such as the banker's clearinghouse, the Collegio del Cambio, and the Palazzo dei Priori present the grand style of Gothic public buildings of the fourteenth century, a period known in Italy as the *trecento* from the final three digits of its dates. The Palazzo dei Priori has a splendid Renaissance doorway that seems to be maintained more for looks than access. Another archway in the building next door led to the stair that took us up to the Galleria Nazionale dell'Umbria. This collection is broad in time and deep in many examples, but it is a pity that so many of the finest paintings of Perugino himself are still in the Louvre, to which I think Napoleon stole them away almost two centuries ago. It continues to surprise me how such a civilized people as the French manage to keep much of the spoils of those wars for themselves. Perhaps they were eventually paid for, although I doubt it. Perhaps some were considered a payoff for the help Louis Napoleon extended during the *Risorgimento* against Austria in the later nineteenth century.

But the Umbrian National Gallery is still full of treasures. The notable early use of landscape painting that borders the icons of Umbrian saints is unique in the paintings of the fourteenth, fifteenth, and sixteenth centuries. Perhaps even more surprising is the work of the early *quattrocento* painters, such as Piero della Francesca. Arezzo and Sansepolcro, sites of some of his greatest works, are not far from Perugia, and there are some wonderful things in this gallery as well. Piero was one of the first Renaissance masters to subdue perspective to an exact mathematical discipline. There is a remarkable altarpiece here that presents a perfectly proportioned rank of columns and arches, which form a background for Gabriel and the Virgin in an elegant Annunciation atop a celebration of Francis, Anthony, Clare, and the Baptist surrounding another Madonna and Child.

Perugino and Pinturicchio are also well represented here, as is Domenico Alfani. For me, the most moving painting is Perugino's *Christ in the Tomb*, in which Jesus displays his wounded hands in a contorted gesture that makes the naked body seem all the more bereft of life. The background of this painting is almost entirely black and undecorated, a pattern which seems to underscore the depth of despair and permanence of loss in the human death of the crucified, but at the same time presents him as divine. The figure, for all its starkness, looks forward to resurrection.

But the most famous, elegant, and delightful of Perugino's works in this collection is his amazing *Adoration of the Magi*. It is an immensely busy pictorial space with plentiful detail of hills, rocks, trees, a lake, and a distant ocean. The royal astrologers have a half-dozen attendants, and they are all gorgeously arrayed. The oldest of the three kings has presented his gift and is on his knees, his gaze wide with astonishment as he looks at the child. The baby, held on his mother's knee, gestures with his right hand as though he were giving the old man a blessing in the form of the still-distant cross. The other two kings present a mixture of motives. The youngest is magnificently arrayed in the latest fashion of a very short padded kilt and long, orange, skintight hose; he also has a brilliant scarlet cloak looped around his arm. He holds a silver ciborium in the tips of his fingers and reaches out in the direction of the child and the mother. I couldn't tell if it contained incense or myrrh. His face is boyish and a trifle supercilious. The third traveler seems of middle age and regards his younger colleague with something like reproach. The painting is the only presentation of the Magi that I have seen which suggests a variety of motives for the great journey the three undertook. They do not all seem to have come with the same point of view. One of the attendants appears to be looking toward the viewer (or the artist) with a glance of worry or suspicion.

Perugino was born in Perugia but moved to Florence in search of instruction at an early age. According to Vasari, he was so poor when he first came to Florence that he slept in a box, although he studied with Verrocchio. Later his work was in demand all over Italy and in more distant parts of Europe. He did a considerable fresco in the Sistine Chapel, but a bit later Pope Paul III, surely no friend of the Perugiani, had it chipped off the wall to make way for the later work of Michelangelo—an example, I guess, of a bad thing leading to a better thing.

While wandering the center of the town, we had seen modest posters for a string quartet concert to be presented in the Sala dei Notari, a public hall built in the fourteenth century to house the gatherings of what must have been a guild of rather grander functionaries than public notaries are today. These fellows got to have their coats of arms painted on the walls and ceilings of a grand, polychromed, well-lighted hall that would accommodate three or four hundred lawyers or real estate brokers at the same time. I could imagine the room buzzing with business as deals for farms and city houses were being closed, loans recorded, and credits exchanged that would later be redeemed in the Sala del Cambio next door.

On the night we visited it, the hall of the notaries was set up comfortably with armchairs for several hundred who gathered to hear three quartets of Bela Bartok played crisply by the Hungarian Quartet. I sat studying the armorial bearings above the musicians and wondered what the Renaissance Italians would have made of the complex harmonies and folk themes of these descendants of the bloodthirsty invaders from central Asia, who were here in Perugia now dressed in costumes derived from eighteenth-century English evening clothes, playing in such a civilized fashion on exquisite fiddles that were almost surely made in Italy.

We sat near an English-speaking couple and chatted with them during the intermission. They seemed to have lived in a number of Italian cities and gave us good recommendations for restaurants in several of them. I asked what his profession was and got the reply that they moved about while he lectured for a few months each in a number of Italian universities. I joked that this sounded like a cover for the CIA. He came back quickly that it was a cover for having a good time. Still, his answer was so quick, almost rehearsed, that I thought for a bit that I might have accidentally hit on a sensitive nerve. They seemed less interested in talking to us after that exchange, and we didn't see them on the way out of the concert. (I still wonder . . .)

Seeking to attend mass on the following morning, we wound around the long way up the hill from the Iris and came to the church of Sant'Ercolano, presumably built on the very spot where that sixth-century bishop was beheaded as a result of his attempt to negotiate with the invading Goths. His church was built on a small patch of land near an Etruscan arched portal, and was designed as a delicate little octagon. But the small footprint was not allowed to diminish the significance of the building. The angled facade is approached by a splendid double stairway, and the building itself rises above, easily three times as high as it is broad. Inside, the vertical extent of the building seemed even more pronounced. While mostly Gothic on the outside, the decoration of the interior is Baroque.

Attendance on Sunday morning was greater than in most of the churches we visited in Italy. Dignified young women acted as lectors and read the lessons in carefully enunciated Italian. The parable of the prodigal son is moving in any language, but hearing it from the elderly priest in almost lyrical speech nearly made me cry. *Il tuo fratello era morte, e poi vive!*

We spent the balance of Sunday morning at the Cavour, a small restaurant on the *corso* of that name. Gnocchi cooked in sage and butter and a *zuppa verdure* were accompanied by fresh bread dipped in a small puddle of wonderful olive oil and sea salt. We divided an orange and a spicy chunk of pecorino, and fortified ourselves with an espresso for the afternoon. The whole, with a glass of very good white wine and a reasonable tip, came to $12 per person.

Thus ballasted, we set forth for the church of San Domenico and the Archaeological Museum, which is built into what had once been a huge Dominican Cloister. Here we found the mysterious presence of the Etruscans once again. Perhaps the most telling of their artifacts was a boundary stone bearing a clearly incised inscription. Although only thirty or forty words in length, it is the longest-surviving inscription in their language. The paucity of such texts shows the effectiveness of the Roman linguistic domination. Augustus made it a crime to write Etruscan or to speak it in public. The language was pretty well exterminated before the second century BC.

This visit to Perugia, like most of our trips about Italy, was much too short. Perugia contains much more than we were able to see, including more than twenty churches ranging from the Romanesque to the Gothic, the Renaissance and the Baroque. Perhaps best of all is the presence of the Università per Stranieri, to which people from other countries come to study Italian. So, promising ourselves a future stay to perfect our skills in that agreeable language, we acquired a couple of boxes of the famous chocolate *baci* which bear the town's name and took a train north to Florence.

XXX.

AGRITOURISM IN UMBRIA
and Getting Acquainted with the Etruscans

We had heard a good bit about "agritourism" in Italy but had always avoided it because of the lingering bovine aroma of a Welsh B&B in the UK many years before. After all, our trips were generally planned to be among the sophisticated cities of the *quattrocento*, the towns of the Renaissance, or the modern metropolises of the north, not among the fertilizers of the dairy farms of central Italy. But surfing the Net brought me into contact with the proprietor of an establishment called Poggio del Sole on the very borderland between Tuscany and Umbria, "The Green Heart of Italy." The owner's name was Enrico Dionisi, which had a nice classical ring to it, and the pictures on his website revealed a pair of sturdy stone farmhouses with exterior stairs to apartments above. A late-March rental for a two-room apartment with a well-equipped kitchen was quoted at a cheerful bargain price of around $350 a week in the current worth of the euro, probably a bit more now. We booked by e-mail well in advance to be sure of a place to light over the crowded Easter holidays.

Finding the *poggio*[9] was an adventure only in making our way

---

[9] Poggio means "hillock."

out of Rome. Our plane arrived in Fiumicino early in the day and we easily found the speedy, half-hourly train to Roma Termini. A hundred-yard walk towing our bags through the vasty station got us to the Auto Europe office, where we were presented with the keys to a very small but economical Citroën. I shouldn't mock French engineering, but in comparison with the Italian and German cars we had chartered on other trips, this was a lousy car: little space, virtually no pickup, and a trunk that could be easily looted by any lad with a Swiss army knife. Fortunately, we had no such disagreeable encounter, and I must admit that the little beast drank very little petrol.

But our next project was to head out of town and find the Grande Raccordo Anulare, the ring road that encircles metropolitan Rome. The map indicated various routes, but the Viale Santa Margherita turned out to be one of the longer ones. Not to worry; the day was young, and we had only three hours to drive. Eventually we found the Salaria, the modern version of the old Roman salt route that brought that important savor down from the north two or three thousand years ago. Thence, the high-speed A1 Autostrada led us through the opening spring of central Lazio to the north. We paused for lunch at an Autogrille and rejoiced again in the quality of Italian fast food in comparison to Denny's, McDonald's, and Roy Rogers back home. We branched off at the Chiancia-Chiusi exit to take the broad secondary road toward Castiglione del Lago and the pleasantly hilly countryside around Lago Trasimeno, where Hannibal slaughtered so many Roman soldiers in a foggy cavalry ambush more than two thousand years ago.

Poggio del Sole was well signposted, and our rooms were far more spacious than what we had become accustomed to in three-star hotels. Enrico Dionisi settled us in and showed us how to call up heat on demand (and at our own expense). The establishment was equipped with a rack of bicycles, a bocce court, pleasant green lawns, and a splendid swimming pool (unfortunately too cool to use in March). We unpacked and later repaired to the neighboring village of Sanfatucchio, about a mile away over the elegantly grooved Umbrian landscape of newly tilled fields. The little settlement supported a magnificent walled cemetery, a coffee bar cum trattoria, a dozen and a half houses, two churches, and was reputed to have an *alimentare*. In spite of some searching in so small a place, we were never able to find this store, so we pushed on to Castiglione del Lago, five miles away, to find a proper market.

The little city is laid out along an avenue straight down the center of a peninsula and projects into the lake. The *castello* is large and severe, straddling the middle of the town center, raised a hundred feet or more above the surrounding houses. Provisions were available at the Co-op. In the tradition of the modern supermarket, the Co-op was on the near periphery of Castiglione, where it is really only approachable by car. Conventional shops, *panifici, macellare,* and *fruttivendoli*[10] were arranged around a more traditional piazza a half-kilometer farther into the *borgo*. The Co-op isn't quite as big as a Stop & Shop or a Harris Teeter, but it stocked an even wider variety of merchandise. In the familiar task of pushing our cart through the aisles, we found standard varieties of breakfast food, freshly squeezed orange juice, Gordon's gin, Martini & Rossi vermouth, fine Sicilian lemons, and other accoutrements of the civilized life. The store would have provided socks, underwear, umbrellas, and popular Italian fiction if we'd had an immediate need for them. But Cathy, having been up and stirring for close to twenty hours by this time, elected not to

---

[10] Baker, butcher, and greengrocer.

initiate her project of learning how to cook in metric just yet.

We stocked up on the basics and went back to the village restaurant in Sanfatucchio, the Pizzeria Nanni, for an early dinner. Because the Nanni was also the village bar and coffee shop, it was open from seven in the morning until after nine at night. The waitress was agreeable and very helpful, although on another visit she confessed that working a fifteen-hour day was a bit much for her. She provided us with minestrone, salad, and a delicious bit of *assino stracatto*—braised donkey—a succulent dish that we had first met with in Pavia several years before. We then collapsed into the new time zone and went to bed to sleep off our jet lag.

We were back at the Co-op on the following day for proper shopping and, in a search for fresh garlic, met up with a very attractive young couple who spoke excellent English. It turned out that they had spent a year in the States perfecting their command of the language. We were later surprised to discover that they were Jehovah's Witnesses; having never met one before that was not in the act of proselytizing, we ended up with a far more positive opinion of that sect than we had entertained heretofore.

We later climbed partway through the Tuesday open-air market under the brow of the castle. I perused the items for sale, a wonderful helter-skelter collection of hardware, vegetables and dry goods, shoes and herbs. I came away with a small sack of *carciofini*, a lovely head of new lettuce, and a bunch of parsley that the vendor gave to me as a welcoming present. We found a neighborly bar on the way back down the hill and secured a *panino caldo* (a hot sandwich) and a glass of a pleasant white wine for lunch.

A couple of days later we began our exploration of Umbria by taking a back road over the *poggio* to Chiusi. Sitting stolidly on top of its hill in characteristic Etruscan fashion, the town was easy to find, although it proved more difficult to get out of later on. The central irregular square was bounded by a building in the style of a Greek temple, a Romanesque church, an Art Deco–style Mussolini Fascist municipal and telecom center, and a tidy green park. A number of teenagers were draped decorously on the steps leading to the classical building. The church has some nice mosaics, but the prize of the town is the temple, which turned out to be a museum of Etruscan remains. Most Americans are surprised to learn that Tuscany is named for these shadowy and almost mysterious people who dominated central Italy for a thousand years before Rome overran and submerged them.

A museum guide with a nametag inscribed *Sylvana* approached us and asked if we would like to visit a pair of Etruscan tombs that were open today, the Tomba Leone and the Pellegrina. There being more tombs than guides or guards, the ancient places are on display in a weekly rotation. Sylvana hopped into our car and gave us a lecture in shrill and speedy Italian, of which we understood perhaps 20 percent. She guided us out of town to a hilly patch of farmland where she deposited us on a gravel road next to an oversized barrow in the side of a hillock (*poggio!*). A few stone steps led down into the earth, where we said farewell to Sylvana before being welcomed by another guide. A half-dozen electric bulbs gave pretty good illumination to the cool interior which, mysteriously, did not have a musty odor. The ceilings were painted in abstract patterns of yellow ochre, dark red, and blue. The Etruscans laid out their dead on stone beds and left the bodies to decay naturally, until there was nothing left but the skeleton, which could be pushed aside to make room for the next generation of the family. It must have been a fearful smell for the first few months after Grandmother's death.

Two tombs later, we returned to the museum and wandered about, reading labels and studying pottery and statuary for the better part of an hour. It is an extraordinary collection guarded by Sylvana and her colleagues, who shadowed us discreetly from area to area, keeping an eye out for antiquity snatchers (or scratchers). This careful conservation is justified both by the riches and diversity of the collection, and the high prices pilfered first-millennium statuettes and pots can command on the illegal markets of Europe and America.

Leaving Chiusi was confusing at best. This turns out to be true of almost all old Italian towns. On the way in, there are signs bearing a bull's-eye of concentric circles and an arrow pointing to *il centro*. Unfortunately, there is no way of posting the roads which lead in dozens of directions on the way out. We ended up going down the hill on the wrong side of the railroad tracks and tried out a desolate little bar next to a petrol station, where the mistress looked to be in a drowsy sort of pout, but she brightened up when we ordered an *aperitivo*. She and an attendant trucker gave us somewhat conflicting instructions for finding Castiglione del Lago. We set out bravely and were eventually successful in getting back to town and seeking out the two *ristoranti* recommended by our guidebooks—L'Acquario and La Cantina—both of which were shut down for Holy Week. Farther along the Via Vittorio Emanuele we discovered the cheerful and pleasant Paprica, where we consumed *pasta e fagiole* and *vitella con funghi* with garlic-spiced spinach. When we emerged, the streets were almost empty and the oblong paving stones glowed with the reflected lamplight. The moon was full and helped us find our way home by several now-familiar landmarks.

The following day we decided to repeat the pattern of a day trip to an interesting site nearby. We got to Montepulciano in less than an hour, and started up the central street in the direction of the main piazza. Figuring that we were almost there, we seized upon a semi-legal parking place and continued on foot. This was an error in judgment. One should always explore beyond the goal and then walk back to it. The main drag of Montepulciano must be over a mile in length, and we had accomplished less than half of its gentle climb. This did, however, give us a chance to inspect the wonderful series of Renaissance facades and doorways that were attached to the medieval houses and shops of a few centuries ago. Many small *negozi* had bottles of the famous dark red wine made from the local Montepulciano grapes in their windows. They seemed a bit too heavy to buy and carry along, but we never found the noble wine at a better price.

Eventually, over the crest of our journey, we came down a gentle slope to the grand piazza. The Palazzo Pubblico is rather like a miniature of the Palazzo Vecchio in the Piazza della Signoria in Florence, and has a tower of the sort that Arnolfo di Cambio reared over his landmark center; not surprising in that Florence had beaten out Siena for making a "protectorate" of Montepulciano. Across the way is the *Duomo*, mostly Gothic, with the commonly found unfinished facade of raw brick like those of San Petronio in Bologna or on the cathedral in Padova. Inside is a good Madonna and Child by Duccio, and a wonderful altar screen by Michelozzo. For me, best of all was an Andrea Della Robbia *Madonna col Bambino* behind the baptismal font to the left of the entrance. It must surely add to the piety of any pair of parents to bring their newborn to such a place to be baptized under the peaceful gaze of that first-century Jewish maiden, as rendered by the skillful modeling of that most democratic of all Renaissance artists. Because Andrea and the followers in his family up to the present day worked in cooked clay, terra cotta, which was then coated in brightly colored glazes, these gleaming plaques were available at a fraction of the cost of the great marble sculptures of the Renaissance and subsequent centuries.

Descending from the high-altitude center of the town in half the time it took to get there, we were pleased to find that the little Citroën was unencumbered by a ticket or other evidence of the *polizia urbana*. There was a neighborly *pizzeria* close at hand, so we settled in for lunch. The pizza *caprese* was thin crusted and delicious with a red *vino della casa, Rosso di Montepulciano*.

We returned to our now familiar *poggio* and looked for a Holy Thursday celebration of Mass. We found one of the two churches open and set up with the necessary gear for washing the feet of twelve villagers standing (or rather sitting) in the places of the Apostles on the night before the crucifixion. A notice tacked to the door announced a service at 9:00 P.M., but an earlier mass would be held at a neighboring village. The church is simple and attractive, but rather startlingly decorated with a modern mosaic of the Holy Family, featuring an eight-year-old Christ quite stark naked, holding a child's hoop in such a way that his hands cover his genitals. The design was at least original, and Italian works of art are generally as often undressed as clad. In this case, the humanity of the youthful Savior was duly recognized but not totally exposed.

PART VI

THE SOUTH

XXXI.

THE REALM
OF EMPEROR FREDERICK

It is hard to know which people in what century brought the blessings of what we call civilization to this corner of Italy. There were early Greek settlers as well as Messapians here, where the Adriatic is in places less than fifty miles wide and the Albanian mountains are visible on a clear day. It would not require the services of a naval architect to devise a craft that could make such a crossing on a clear and windy day when the summer dawn is early and the sunset late. Surely the half-mythic Dorians were capable of such voyages, and the even earlier Minoan traders of Crete came this way in recent prehistoric times. Extensive colonies and indigenous people were here long before the Romans. Greek colonization was so extensive that the Romans called southern Italy and Sicily "Magna Graecia," in the way people in Manhattan call Westchester County "Greater New York."

There were scores of cities here, many whose names we do not know at all, and a few, such as Crotone and Sybaris, which are well recorded in Greek and Latin literature, but whose remains are shrunk to a few grassy mounds or hewn stones that project from a barren hillside. The Romans began their conquest of this part of their expanded realm in the half millennium before the time of Caesar and Christ. They brought law and order to the Salentine, but it was less than what we might consider civilized. Mass crucifixions were the standard form of civic discipline, repeated until the will to rebel or cause trouble was exhausted.

But we must remember that after the time of the Republic, the Empire of Rome itself only lasted five hundred years before it became a series of barbarian duchies and feudal principalities. Then the Greeks, this time Christians from Byzantium, came back. Roman temples were used as quarries or converted into churches. Later the detritus of minor-league wars filled the spaces in between, until the developing street level was as much as several meters above the original pavement.

Fifteen hundred years later when the bankers in Lecce set out to excavate a basement for a twentieth-century temple of finance near the central piazza of their town in 1938, they had not dug a meter deep before they discovered a complete Roman amphitheater under the skin of the medieval stone pavement. It had been, of course, a place of bloody combat put on for the enjoyment of the townspeople, of *retarius* and *secutor* armed with trident, net, and sword, who stabbed and hacked away until one of the bodies was reduced to helplessness or death while the crowds cheered the show. Half the amphitheater was carefully exposed, but not that portion which underlaid a monument to Saint Oronzo, a local medieval patron, the details of whose life I am still trying to discover.

Whatever Oronzo did in life, after his death or martyrdom he interceded with God to the advantage of several south Puglian towns. In the more or less Dark Ages, Brindisi too was grateful for his help, so much so that the citizens of the town gave one of their mighty leftover Roman columns to Lecce as a thank offering for the benefaction of the saint. These two columns (the other one still stands in Brindisi) once marked the terminus of the Appian Way, from which one could walk dry shod all the way to Rome some 600 kilometers north, a pleasant journey with the classical equivalent of B&Bs or inns to be found along the way. Dragging the great shaft from one town to the other must have been a chore for post-classical engineers, but it was erected in the market square of Lecce and surmounted with a large bronze statue of Oronzo, which presides over the town center of Lecce and the recently exhumed amphitheater. There are several cracks in the marble and a couple of metal bands holding it together.

Roman organization and administration were wonderfully efficient. Information and directives were dispatched rapidly over amazing distances, and a firm discipline held the empire together in a peaceful, if somewhat fearful society of armies, slaves, and country villas of the wealthy. It is also amazing how rapidly it disintegrated between AD 350 and 550. Those two centuries are a shorter period than the age of my little farmhouse in Connecticut, less than the time back to the presidential administrations of John Adams and Thomas Jefferson.

After the centralized strong government of Rome gave way to the quarreling feudal leaders of Goths and Langobards, the final destruction of the Roman world order was completed by the cataclysmic explosion of Islam in the late seventh century. Christian Europe really did not react to the new African and Arabic power for some time. Italy was in a state of chaos with some signs of new organization beginning to appear. The Goths took the northeast, while the Old Roman Empire, transmuted into Byzantium, tried to hang on to the far south, including Apulia. Sicily, the old granary of the Roman Empire, slipped rapidly into the hands of the Saracens. The Langobards, later more typically called the Lombards (now that their hirsute countenances seemed less unusual), decided to settle down and learn Italian. Their northern capital centered around Milan and Piacenza, but they also held two great duchies: Spoleto, north of Rome; and Benevento, well to the south.

Benevento eventually became a papal fief and debated with Byzantium over the governance—or, rather, the ownership—of Apulia and Calabria, the heel and toe of Italy. Sicily became a series of Islamic emirates, and the North African raiders pretty much had their way with all of southern Italy. It seems they never stayed for long after raiding Paestum, Naples, the towns of Apulia, or even Rome itself, which they sacked thoroughly in 827. The papal city seems to have shrunk to less than 20,000 inhabitants after having been more than a million a millennium earlier. The pope managed to hole up in the castle, constructed on the foundation of Hadrian's tomb, now called Castel Sant'Angelo. His successors would require this place of refuge many times in subsequent years.

Roman towns in southern Italy were late in being surrounded by walls, since the highly mobile legions protected the whole peninsula and the greater part of Western Europe as well. But as the organization fell apart, walls were thrown up around the Roman cities. Later, Europe became a land of castles, when it was discovered that only a strong point—fortified by high walls and equipped with a huge store of food and a well-protected water supply—could guarantee even a modicum of safety to the local baron and his entourage.

In the tenth century another sort of invasion came from the north, this time from a disciplined group of Christian knights, the Normans. Invited south to help the Lombards fight off the Byzantines and the Saracens, they arrived in small but effective numbers. Through an ever-shifting series of feudal alliances, they had an effect far beyond their numbers. Besides being the most disciplined foot soldiers, their mounted knights were the most effective cavalry in the area. Time and again, against unbelievable odds, a charge of Norman knights broke the formations of Saracens, Greeks, and even Lombards. There are well-authenticated records of a group of three hundred Norman knights, backed by perhaps twice that number of foot soldiers, taking on an army of ten thousand and putting them to rout. They were devout, cruel, treacherous, and fearless. These Lackland Normans of the tenth and eleventh centuries changed southern Italy and Sicily forever. The Salentine peninsula in particular flourished under their rule, even though their leaders changed sides with every other war.

An unusual thing about the Normans of southern Italy is that a great number of their leaders seem to have been descended from a single progenitor, the relatively modest Tancred de Hauteville, who begot a dozen adventurous sons and turned most of them out to make their own place in the world. His fief in Normandy was too small to support them. Almost all successfully sought their fortunes in a bloody conquest of the South.[11] And wherever the Normans went, they erected monumental stone fortresses and churches, from the Tower of London and the Cathedral of Caen to Durham in the north of England, even in faraway Syria at Crac des Chevaliers.

This last was a construction made during the most extraordinary and perhaps the most regrettable event in European history—the Crusades. It was a backlash of European adventurism against Islam, undertaken a thousand years before our time. Largely the result of

---

[11] A splendid account of the "other Norman conquest" was written by John Julius Norwich, whose huge scholarship is illuminated by his wonderfully colorful and often amusing language. It is available in a very thick Penguin edition entitled The Normans in the South and The Kingdom in the Sun, bound together as a paperback of 792 pages. Despite its bulk, it is, as H. V. Morton attests, the most readable account of this complex and fascinating chapter of medieval history.

the military demands of the bloody-minded Pope Urban II and the inflammatory preaching of St. Bernard of Clairvaux, this huge movement resulted in the creation of the realm of *Outremer*, a new Europe overseas with its own kings and noble warriors, sometimes rapacious pilgrims, and mysterious monk-knights who established hospitals and grew very rich. In spite of the southern Italians striving most often to stay out of rather than participate in these crazy bellico-religious adventures, they had a deep impact on the old Messapian land and the Salentine peninsula. Their dukes, counts, kings, and one emperor built almost fifty fortresses, large and small, as well as a garland of marvelous Romanesque cathedrals that rings the shore and ornaments its center.

Most of the best military architecture, but practically none of the ecclesiastical work, was the result of an amazingly capable young man who came to claim Apulia as his right in the earliest years of the thirteenth century. He succeeded to this realm as its infant duke, as well as king of Sicily when he was orphaned at the age of four. Frederick the Swabian was known as "the Second" because his paternal grandfather, Frederick "Barbarossa" Hohenstaufen, was the first of the tribe. That doughty crusading German emperor drowned while on the way to Jerusalem in the wholly ineffectual second crusade. Young Frederick's maternal grandfather was the Norman king, Roger Second of Sicily, surnamed Hauteville (or Altavilla, as they became known in Italian). He was the cleverest of the marauders who took charge of the triangular island in the sunny sea off the toe of the Italian boot. The Normans were amazing warriors who triumphed over staggering odds through good training, discipline, and marvelous bravery. The Swabian Hohenstaufens were equally devoted to belief in Christianity, but even more warlike in their desire to organize a realm that would rival the five-hundred-year-old memory of Charlemagne's world order.

These inheritances descended on Frederick II, who was born in 1194, elected king of the Romans in his infancy, and orphaned at four by the deaths of his German father and his Norman-Sicilian mother. He was left as a ward of Pope Innocent III, who paid little attention to the child at first. He was largely neglected by those who managed his theoretical realm to their own advantage. His Greek tutor, who is known by his Italian name, Guglielmo Francesco, seems to have started him on an extraordinary education which was augmented by playing in the streets of Palermo with the kids who lived in the neighborhood of the Palatine Palace and Chapel, built by his great-grandfather, the Great Count Roger. But it is reported that in these childish games he was always the king. At the age of eight he resisted a German knight who was attempting to kidnap him by brushing off his grip and crying out that it was sacrilege to lay hands on God's anointed king. His assailant retreated. He knew half a dozen languages by the time he was twelve, since Palermo was frequented by Sicilians, Italians, Byzantine Greeks, Jews, Arabs, and Spaniards.

When he was fifteen he was provided with a Spanish princess as a suitable bride, although she was ten years older than her boyish bridegroom. Although this match with Constanza of Aragon was inspired by politics rather than affection, it was dignified by loyalty and respect and was rapidly consummated to result in the begetting of Henry who, but for his untoward death eight years before his father's demise, might later have carried on the Hohenstaufen line into the future. Almost all of Frederick's later sons were illegitimate and, in the world of feudal loyalties, legitimacy of descent was the only sure way to pass on power without challenge.

By the time Frederick was eighteen, he declared his three-year-

old son Henry to be king of Sicily and, leaving him in the charge
of his mother as Regent of the Realm, crossed over the Strait of
Messina to the mainland to claim his hereditary duchy of Puglia. In
rapid succession he moved north through the provinces to take all
of Italy, and eventually lay claim to the Holy Roman Empire with
the blessing of Pope Innocent, who had rediscovered his ward and
not yet discovered what a threat to papal power he would become.
It was when he was traveling north to contest with Otto, then king
of the Germans, that that somewhat nervous monarch asked who his
young adversary from Sicily and Puglia actually was. An upstart, he
was told, to be sure. He was known as *Puer Apulia*, a boy of Puglia,
a mere child. When Frederick swiftly ousted the German king,
Frederick's young soldiers took up the phrase as a title of honor, the
lad from the south, the *Apulian Kid*. He soon earned the name of
Stupor Mundi, the Wonder of the World.

And a wonder he surely was. Besides being a brave and shrewd
leader in battle, he wrote a four-volume book on hawking that
stands as the first scientific work of ornithology. It is still in print
and unsurpassed. He befriended philosophers and mathematicians
such as the learned Leonardo Fibonacci of Pisa, the mathematical
geometer who worked out the sequence of integers that describes the
pattern of the seeds in the sunflower and, some say, the behavior of
the stock market. Frederick delighted in discussions with the masters
of all fields of study. He is reputed to have arranged a temptation of
Francis of Assisi by a beautiful courtesan while he checked on her
progress through a secret peephole. When the saint slept peacefully
on the stone floor after having wished the girl well and declined
her services, Frederick invited the little man in the brown habit to
lunch and discussed philosophy with him.

He decreed that all of his subjects should freely profess and practice the religion in which they had been born or brought up, Jew, Greek, Latin Christian, or even Muslim, reserving fiery punishment only for Christian apostasy or blasphemy, presumably because his right of kingship depended upon the ordination of God. When he heard of trouble from a number of Muslim bandits in the hill country back of Messina, he had thousands of them transported across the Strait and resettled at Matera in Puglia, where they were given the remnants of an abandoned Roman city. They became exemplary citizens and fiercely loyal to their liege lord. From their numbers he recruited the personal bodyguard who came with him when he went on crusade to contest with the Islamic emir of Egypt. Frederick settled that conflict by diplomacy and, in effect, drew closure to the whole sad and bloody business of the Crusades in the mid-thirteenth century. He succeeded despite the fact that the pope, who seemed to yearn for slaughter, excommunicated him—first, for not going to holy war, and second, for compromise in winning it.

Through the inheritance of his second wife, Yolanda of Brienne, whose deceased first husband had been "king of Jerusalem," Frederick claimed the title of king in *Outremer*. To spare papal wrath falling on any bishop who would crown him, he placed the crown on his own head. He sailed back from the Holy Land and faced the pope in a short but decisive war. He was excommunicated at least three, and perhaps, four times, but since he was always much younger than the keeper of Peter's keys, he outlived all his ecclesiastical adversaries and eventually died in the good graces of the church at the age of fifty-six, honored and bewept by his soldiers and subjects of all religious persuasions. Besides such straightforward accomplishments as becoming the first real European emperor in the thousand years between Charlemagne and Napoleon, Frederick promulgated the first code of laws since that of the emperor Justinian, seven hundred years earlier, called the Constitutions of Melfi.

Frederick was a fluent and accomplished poet who wrote love lyrics in the Sicilian language of his birth. He did much of the designing of the military strongholds that studded his realm from the far western corner of Sicily to the passes of the Alps. He differed from most such strong men in that, contrary to the later advice of Machiavelli, his subjects actually did love him. His severity was just and his lands prospered under his rule. Truly he was the *Stupor Mundi*, The Wonder of the World. His funeral was a great procession of flower-strewing women and weeping soldiers, both Christian and Muslim, across southern Italy and the Strait of Messina to Sicily, the land of his origin, where he was buried in the Cathedral of Palermo.

Among Frederick's three wives was also Joan Plantagenet, sister of King Henry III of England, granddaughter of the Lion Heart. But, less typically for a Christian monarch, Frederick also kept a

Federico's Castel del Monte, c. 1540

harem and dressed after the style of an Egyptian emir. He also was devoted to the dozen (or some say, fifteen) illegitimate children he sired along the way. These sons served him with mixed loyalty and treachery in war and peace. The daughters he married off to create advantageous political alliances. Besides the fifty castles he built in southern Italy, in Apulia he designed and constructed one relatively small octagonal one, Castel del Monte, near Andria, which seems to have been intended as a symbol of his realm, or a royal intellectual retreat, rather than a fortification. We visited it on a sunny spring morning and found ourselves among a sizable group of almost entirely Italian tourists. We were only able to park by seizing an illegal patch of gravel in the very center of the *parcheggio*, leaving the rented car there in the middle of the lot, hoping it would remain undamaged—indeed, that it would still be there—when we got back. Happily, it was safe and sound when we returned.

We walked up the hill to the strains of rather comic martial music and eventually came upon a three-piece band consisting of a snare drum, a piccolo, and a bass drum, accompanied by a large, sleepy dog. The little band got quite a lot of music out of the scant ensemble and lent a faint military air to the remnant of the historical emperor's country retreat.

Castel del Monte is an elegant if somewhat stubby piece of architecture. Its eight sides are joined at 135-degree angles, with small, octagonal towers at each joint. These tourelles contain stairs and, in a few cases, what may have been toilet rooms. There are only two stories and small and scanty windows in the sixteen rooms. There was evidently a cistern for gathering rainwater on the roof. The chambers have very tall ceilings and are arranged about a large interior court. A half-dozen of the rooms have fireplaces, their jambs now shattered. A few have rather elegant, double-arched windows that give onto the interior court. The ceilings are more than thirty feet high. It doesn't seem a very cheery place to pass a weekend in the country, but, of course, it currently lacks cozy touches such as Persian or African rugs on the stone floors, comfortable furniture, and tapestries on the walls. It was possible to imagine the philosopher king sitting at a banquet with his intellectual friends, served by the young ladies of the harem while the men debated the immateriality of the soul or the habits of the goshawk. We left his little bijou palace wondering how such an amazing man could be so largely unknown, even among the college-educated in America.

Cathy at Castel del Monte

XXXII.

RODI DI GARGANICO:
The Lump on the Calf of the Boot

Eventually we passed to the east of Foggia, Frederic II's favorite city in Apulia, and made a note that we should visit its famous *castello* and cathedral dedicated to St. Nicholas on our next trip to the far south. We soon passed the western escarpment of Gargano, where is perched the town of Rignano Garganico, known as the "Balcony of Puglia" from its position nearly two thousand feet above the flat, almost sea-level plain surrounding San Severo and Foggia. After traversing low Apennines and the hills of the Murge, this verdant plain is a surprise. Looking down on it from the western edge of the mountainous Gargano must be a thrill. But we pressed on until we saw signs indicating RODI DI GARGANICO, which directed us to our next destination.

The Gargano is the lump (or perhaps the spur) on the back of the heel of Italy's boot. It consists of a large mountain mass intersected by several high interior valleys. The upper ranges mount to nearly four thousand feet above the level of the surrounding sea. The closeness of the beaches to the tops of the hills makes the whole area seem even higher than it actually is. People have actually been climbing through and over it for thousands of years, and it became a site of pilgrimage shortly after the time of the Roman hegemony. We skirted its northern rim to find the odd little town of Rodi.

We passed a pair of large lakes to our left that seemed separated from the sea by a strand so delicate that it did not appear wide enough to hold off the winter storms of the Adriatic. Inland, on our right, there were little chalk-white villages perched on the flanks of the dark green hills. Beyond our way, the pale green of the shallow sea was embroidered with the lace of a series of white waves that chased each other toward the shore.

Rodi is a small town that we had selected more from its position on the map than from any promise of facility or cultural advantage. But one of the Italian travel guides awarded a small hotel there, the Villa al Mare, a distinguishing heart that promised it was "charming" as well as an off-season bargain. Our host Titino welcomed us in the little "reception," which also served as the bar. As I hoisted our bags up the stairs, I commented that there was good English gin on the shelf but no dry vermouth or *acqua tonica* at the bar. Returning after a short interval for a wash and a rest, we discovered that the children of the *proprietario* used the lobby as a living room, even to the extent of the eight-year-old boy practicing a few gentle soccer shots. We also discovered that Titino had gone out to acquire both of the ornaments for the gin and had broken out a bowl of ice cubes for us. There was a jolly fire in the hearth and Rita, his wife, was getting ready to serve us the dinner of our choice. The children by now included Donato, the seventeen-year-old boyfriend of Francesca, the older of their two daughters. Both girls were very pretty, but, in our experience, all fifteen- and seventeen-year-old Italian girls are almost breathtakingly beautiful. We were served our *zuppa di pesce* at a leisurely pace, since the kids were served first and the parents sat down to join them after our dinner was set out before us. Among several choices of dessert was a *crostata* filled with Rita's homemade *marmellata di arance*. After dinner they settled into conversation with us, half in English, half in Italian. We learned about the hospital that Padre Pio had built on the top of the mountainous peninsula, and the shrine of St. Michael, and learned that our hosts were devoted to both.

According to Lord Norwich, it was in AD 493 that a man, looking for his lost bull in a deep cave, had fired an errant arrow which turned in mid-flight to come back, wounding him in the thigh. News of the miraculous flight of the arrow prompted the local bishop of Bitonto to decree a three-day fast. He then visited the site of the miracle and was confronted by a vision of St. Michael in shining armor, who asked the bishop to declare the cave to be a shrine of Michael and all the angels. The site, along with Santiago de Compostela, Rome, and Jerusalem, eventually became one of the four journeys that would provide pilgrims with a plenary indulgence—a total remission of the pains of purgatory for any sins they had ever committed. A couple of generations ago, Catholic children were still being taught that the discomfort of purgation was just as bad as the fires of hell, only not as permanent. We would have done almost anything to gain a surefire plenary indulgence. If the good and encouraging nuns who taught us had suggested a trip to a mountain on the Adriatic coast of southern Italy, we would have attacked our parents with requests to make reservations right away.

Villa al Mare is about a mile east of the town of Rodi di Garganico. I bumped across the railroad tracks, drove to fetch a newspaper, and waited for the space of two cappuccini for the *edicola* to open. The proprietress eventually arrived and said that there would be no *giornale* that morning, since there was snow in the mountains and the delivery truck came over the hump from Foggia rather than by the sea-level route we had followed.

Our trip to this heaven-sent spot was, as is appropriate, a long and adventurous one. We first drove the perimeter of the Gargano to reach the pretty fishing village of Vieste, perched on a dissected rocky promontory thrust out into the sea. Everything to our right as we drove east was part of the Parco Nazionale del Gargano, a dramatic series of uplands and peaks that rise almost as high as three thousand feet. They aren't great mountains like the Apennines, but they look to be formidable hikes from the seacoast. In April there was no sign of vacation bathers on the rich, reddish-brown strip of sand that bordered the shore. The water was pale green and decorated with broad, lacy bands of midsize waves that moved shoreward in fifteen or twenty successive rows, marching from the dark blue of the deep Adriatic to the pale Hooker's green of the shallow water closer to shore. To judge the distance from the bottom of the water to the top by the color, I would guess that the coast off Rodi di Garganico would be a bad place for a sailboat on hard chances. Our host had explained to us the night before that Rodi had early become the exporting center for great crops of oranges and lemons that were moved to deepwater harbors by a small private railroad that still runs past his little hotel, now bearing mostly vacationing passenger traffic. The thriving lemon industry collapsed after World War I when the United States moved to aid the citrus farmers in Florida and California by levying a crippling import duty on Italian fruit.

We rounded the peninsula by way of Vieste, a simple town, devoted mostly to swimming and fishing, with an attractive cathedral that was locked tight in midday. The cold and the threat of more snow urged us on. There are splendid beaches here, both to the north and south of the town. The houses here also made our eyes blink at the brilliantly white hue that so stands out against the deep blue of the Adriatic. We made a brief exterior inspection of the cathedral and learned from our guidebook of still more beheadings of large numbers of men and boys by the Turks in the fifteenth century. We then found a warm little museum on the way downhill, back to the car. After convincing the guard that we were really senior citizens without showing our *documenti*, thus masquerading as European Union citizens and entitled to free admission, we examined a pretty collection of shell artifacts which were uniformly undated and generally unlabeled. A local *pizzeria* provided an excellent soup, their oven being as yet unignited for the afternoon's business.

Going up the Mount, especially with the April snow all about, is one of those precipitous ascents that makes me wonder how medieval or earlier peoples ever climbed it. But climb they surely did, for this two-thousand-foot summit has been a holy place since the time of the Greeks. But a couple of thousand years later, in the early eleventh century, a small band of Norman knights, perhaps forty in number, paid their devoirs to St. Michael here while on their way back from a pilgrimage to the Holy Land, a sort of trumping their own ace in the matter of indulgences. There they met a forlorn but still powerful Lombard who had been pushed out of his own Apulian fief by the then-regnant Byzantine Greeks. He told them that Puglia was a land rich in milk and honey, to which they could perhaps easily lay claim if they produced a sizable army and allied themselves with him. And so it came to pass. The Normans rode home through the length of Italy, through the passes of the Alps, and north through France to the lands given to the Vikings by the battered king of France two generations earlier. They told their story of the sunny peninsula around the winter fireplaces in dark castles of Normandy, and soon gathered a force of perhaps a thousand men, one third of them armed knights who were ready to go south in the spring.

The next two centuries were times of almost continual conflict in southern Italy, but I suppose the centuries preceding them were not conducted according to the manners of a Sunday School picnic. The amazing twelve sons of Tancred de Hauteville eventually dominated the land, principally under the joyful battling of Robert Guiscard, who sooner or later held all of Puglia, Basilicata, and Calabria by conquest or in fief from Pope or Antipope.[2] His somewhat more thoughtful kid brother Roger became king of Sicily and, for a time, of all the other southern provinces as well. There were wars with popes, wars by popes, wars with German emperors, and with the mercenary navies of the great commercial cities of Genoa, Pisa, and Venice. The Byzantine Empire was close to being knocked into the hazard more than once, and after the Seljuk Turks pressed west from the far edges of Asia Minor, the forces of Islam took over the Holy Land and precipitated the regrettable if temporary conquest of the Crusades. The arrival of the Normans in Puglia was not the only spark that ignited these conflicts, but their successes were a major part of them. They were brave and careless of personal safety. They fought with a discipline that the mob-like armies of the south had never seen before, and their leaders were clever and intelligent generals. These qualities enabled them to defeat armies of three to five times their numbers, using armored cavalry with skill and speed that Rommel, Montgomery, and Patton would have envied.[3]

---

[2] There were at least two popes at a time on several occasions in the Norman period. The one declared legitimate in the subsequent record books does not always seem the most convincing in the eyes of modern scholars.

[3] The best, although ponderous book on this subject is John Julius Norwich's The Normans in Italy, although it stops short of recounting the life and reign of Frederick II, great-great-grandson of Tancred de Hauteville, who eventually became Holy Roman Emperor.

With no such warlike thoughts in mind, we reached the summit of San Angelo, wind-whipped with snow all about. We soon found the entrance to the sacred grotto behind an ornamental entryway, bearing what Norwich called a "glutinous" representation of heaven's champion bearing his sword. We descended the eighty-two steps down into the damp bowels of the earth to pay our respects to the archangel, while listening to an echoing hi-fi recording of a group of monks singing modern hymns in the deep, echoing space. A large group of pilgrims joined in. We looked in at the bookstore and climbed back out to daylight, feeling a little unsure of the successful banking of celestial capital we might have accumulated by the visit and brief prayers we said. The snow started falling again and we decided to get ourselves off the mountaintop before travel became even more compromised. We pressed on through an area known as La Foresta Umbra (the Shadow Forest), which is a national park. We then traversed the breadth of the Gargano Peninsula and descended on the north shore, finding our way back to Rodi and the pleasant little hostelry we had left in the morning.

Through most of this trip we had been somewhat disturbed by a scraping noise issuing from the left front wheel of the reliable little Fiat. I discussed the problem with our host, who listened intently and pronounced the ailment to be one that would require the services of his mechanic. I followed him into the center of Rodi and abandoned the vehicle to a cadaverous and gloomy man who nodded wisely and said that he would deliver the car to us later in the afternoon.

He returned the car in about an hour, mumbling something about repairing the brake calipers. I drove him back to his garage and paid the bill of 52 euro, but when I asked for a receipt to present to Auto Europe, he said I would need not just a *ricevuta fiscale*, but a more complex document which was the equivalent of a notarized account, giving evidence that the job had really been done on the car. He drove away and returned in an hour with the more formal piece of paper in hand. This document almost defeated the clerk at Auto Europe in Rome, until he struck upon the solution of ignoring the reduction of the prepaid rental of the car and handing me the 52 euro in cash out of a drawer in his desk. This combination of spontaneous efficiency and complicated bureaucracy seems typical of the style of contemporary Italy. It also seemed an appropriate event on our first exploration of Puglia, so often an overlooked and delightful quarter of Italy. We'll be back.

XXXIII.

THE CATHEDRAL TOWNS
OF PUGLIA

Although they are all mostly of small size, there are at least a dozen cathedral towns in Puglia. On our first visit we managed to visit seven or eight of the most prominent: Trani, Barletta, Ruvo di Puglia, Bisceglie, Bitonto, Lecce, and Otranto, leaving Bari, Molfetta, Mola di Bari, Canosa di Puglia, San Severo, Manfredonia, and Foggia for "the next time." Every town has its unique example of a cathedral fashioned in the Norman Romanesque style. The cathedral of Bari is one of the oldest of the great Norman churches in Italy, and has a facade that might belong in Normandy itself. I wondered again about the nameless architects of these graceful buildings, the ones who had created the designs for these great facades and elegant clerestory galleries. Since the churches required up to a century to complete, none of them would have lived long enough to see their work through to completion. Although they were considered simple master masons by their ecclesiastical patrons, they must have been stirred by a passion for beauty that has ensured their preservation through the centuries—through storm, wind, and blowing sand, through wars and changing religious fidelities.

Of the towns we visited, Barletta has the distinction of owning

a sixteen-foot bronze statue of a Roman emperor in the center of
the town. The figure is something to behold, since it is the largest
bronze casting that has survived since the Classical era. The fact that
no one can figure out precisely which emperor he is detracts not at
all from his size and brutality. Since he wears barbarian boots (not
classical sandals) and carries a cross in his upraised fist, he is surely one
of the later leaders that came after Constantine. Evidently he was part
of the spoils that the Venetians were bringing back following their

A Roman Emperor, Rescued from the surf

rape of Constantinople during the later Crusades. The ship bringing back the famous bronze horses that grace the facade of San Marco in Venice made the trip with no trouble, while the one transporting this huge statue sank in a storm on the offshore sandbars of Barletta. Despite some anxiety as to the bad omens attendant upon taking on a shipwrecked emperor, the Barlettani eventually dragged his effigy ashore and set him up in the middle of town. We paid our respects to the towering ancient brute and passed by to visit the castle. The seaside third of the building was built by Frederick II, but the land side was completed by Charles V, who was the most active of the Angevin French who ruled here in the late thirteenth century. We climbed to the upper battlements, where we discovered a museum of oversized marionettes. Arranged in glass cases, these dolls are three to four feet tall and clad in gorgeous costumes, including coats of mail and full suits of armor.

On another level, we found a gallery of very fine paintings by the Italian impressionist, Giuseppe de Nittis, which occupied our attention so long that we tarried past the midday closing hour of the cathedral and had to content ourselves with looking at its Puglian Romanesque exterior. In the process we lost our bearings and were unable to remember where we had parked the car amidst the tangle of medieval streets and avenues that we had zigzagged through in the morning. Eventually we stumbled on the *Colosso*, now our friendly Roman emperor, and successfully retraced our steps back to the trusty Fiat Punto. We got back on the track toward Trani, but by this time, we were both tired and hungry, and began a search for a bar with chairs. This required a considerable circuit because Barletta is accustomed to patrons who stand belly up to the bar. We were eventually successful and settled into yet another splendid tuna salad with crusty, olive-oil-baked bread. We were surprised to find that they had no *vino della casa bianco*. They did offer to open a bottle of Prosecco, the delicious bubbly, dry white wine from the north of Italy that is the fashionable *aperitivo* in contemporary Italy. The combination was restorative and encouraging, and soon, we pressed on to visit our next sites of Norman Romanesque architecture.

These excursions on the Puglian coast put us in close proximity to the brilliant, dark blue-green of the Adriatic Sea, an extraordinarily limpid body of water which is bordered by sculptured cliffs of limestone that have been bleached chalk-white by salt and sun. Since the buildings are almost entirely made of this material, the brilliantly white towns stand in stark contrast to the greenery behind them and the blue, blue sea in front.

The southeasternmost of the seaside towns we visited was Otranto, on the very spike of the Salentino. Facing the strait that bears its name, Otranto is only fifty miles from Albania, just north of Greece, and is the easternmost extremity of Italy. It has always been closely related to the traffic that has sailed through the Adriatic and Ionian seas since the beginning of time, from the commerce of Rome and Byzantium to the savagery and gallantry of the Crusades. Horace Walpole's Gothic horror novel has nothing to do with the actual castle of Otranto or its neighboring cathedral, but the church has its own horror story. In 1480 the Turks took the town and offered the conquered men the choice of joining Islam or being beheaded. This was an uncharacteristic act for the Muslims, who generally left people to their own faith, but here—perhaps in revenge for some of the Crusaders' excess—eight hundred men and teenaged boys went to the block. What happened to the women and children is unreported. Inside the white limestone cathedral, there is a chapel with glass-fronted recesses that reveal the eight hundred skulls of the martyrs.

But the most unusual thing about the cathedral is a vast, primitive mosaic floor that includes the entire nave and sanctuary. Done in the mid-twelfth century by an untaught priest-artist named Pantaleone, it is a charming series of depictions that present the history of the world, from Adam and Eve and the first animals all the way to stories of the Bible and the legends of all peoples. Here are Greek gods and heroes mixed in with a tree of life that includes King Arthur, Alexander the Great, an expulsion from paradise, the tower of Babel, and zodiacal signs that present the twelve months of the year. Cain is taking a terrible whack at Abel with what looks like a primitive golf club, all the while with a sly sort of grin on his face. Noah's ark looks a bit like a chest of drawers. Since he and his sons are armed only with axes as shipwright's tools, the lack of a nautical sheer to their construction is perhaps not surprising. Although the Genesis figures are all quite naked, it is odd to find Diana letting fly an arrow at a deer while wearing an ankle-length skirt. There are also elephants, the Queen of Sheba, a huge serpent who seems intent upon devouring Eve (not a bad conceit, that), Jonah, a mermaid, a Minotaur, the gates of Hell, the Furies, and many of the damned squirming in Hell. While I was acquiring a booklet illustrating the mosaics, a priest pointed out to me that even the Muslims were included in Father Pantaleone's benign vision of God's creatures.

After a long look back at the lovely fifteenth-century doorway and rose window on the west facade of the cathedral of Otranto, we wound our way down from the battlement and moat-encircled center of the town. We came upon a small but civilized little restaurant with a shaded exterior, set with a half-dozen tables and bamboo wicker chairs. Here we sat quite accidentally next to a pair of Englishmen, who caused us to reflect that they and an English couple at the Regia where we had registered were the only non-Italians we had

encountered in Puglia; no Americans, no Germans, and no French at
this season of the year. The two turned out to be Church of England
clergymen, one retired and the other the Queen's chaplain at St.
George's, Windsor—or was it St. James Palace? The ability to strike
up a conversation with anyone who speaks one's home language
is one of the pleasures of foreign travel. We all dined upon *antipasti
di mare*, which we were a little startled to discover consisted of at
least ten dishes of cold and hot delights: breaded mussels, shrimp,
tender baby octopus, fresh anchovies, small whole fish of unknown
origin, chunks of other fish on skewers, broiled breaded shrimp, and
a creamed shrimp salad on radicchio leaves. The older of the two
priests said that he had discovered the breadth of the antipasto here
on an earlier trip, and had returned to experience it again.

We came back to Lecce after this extended visit to the thirteenth
century and felt a somewhat dislocating return to the more modern
style of the seventeenth century. Lecce is the heart and center of
a unique architectural style generally known as Lecce Baroque: a
crust of flowers, curlicues, and arabesques carved in the compliant
limestone beyond the capability of most of the quarries of Europe.
The material is soft, honey-colored to brown, and after it is exposed
to the air for a few years, becomes hard and durable. The graceful
ornaments of the seventeenth century are in excellent repair today. We
walked among them for an afternoon and early-evening *passeggiata*,
in search of a *ristorante* named Atenze, which was supposed to be
near the Hotel Patria. Wandering in search of it, we caught a glowing
nighttime view of the Basilica di Santa Croce, with its transept rose
window highlighted by golden floodlights of the current era.

Later, we found a curly-headed boy who told us in clearly
enunciated Italian that the Atenze was *inside* the Patria rather than
next to it. The experience proved again that getting directions from

the local kids is usually more reliable than from their elders, several of whom directed us in various wrong directions. The Atenze provided us with an extraordinarily served and very good dinner: *orecchiette* (pasta baby ears) with broccolini, *paillard de veau* (titled in French) with spinach timbale and braised leek, and the delicious *rognons de veau con carciofini* (baby artichokes) which are so seldom obtainable in America. The French are masters at putting an elegant sauce on a pancreas or kidney, whereas the Italians are best at cooking plain dishes centered around very fresh vegetables, tender young veal, and springy pastas cooked *al dente*, not too soft to be felt under the teeth. Both schools of *cucina* are wonderful, especially when alternated with each other.

Heading north the next day, we began to pass through the *trulli* country, an area around the somewhat excessively photographed town of Alberobello, which features those round, whitewashed stone houses with conical roofs. We passed a number of these odd constructions, said to be very old, and debated whether or not to visit the mother lode in town. Somewhat to Cathy's distress, I pronounced the *trulli* to be overly cute habitations not worthy of more than a passing glance along the highway, and a few photo ops through the rolled-down window of the Punto. When we reached home, the results were, to me, gratifyingly disappointing.

XXXIV.

A FOUR-STAR HARBOR TOWN:
Trani in Puglia

We had come to Puglia by car, driving from Fiumicino Airport in Rome to the coast on the Adriatic, a moderately long day's journey which we broke into two manageable segments by staying one night in a modern Jolly Hotel in Caserta, just north of Naples. This small city is the site of the great Palazzo Reale of the Spanish Bourbon Charles III, who ruled southern Italy in the seventeenth century, almost five hundred years after the time of Frederick. The palace of the kingdom of the "Two Sicilies" was built to compete with Versailles. Luigi Vanvitelli, the architect, was the son of a Flemish painter and wasn't quite equal to such a monumental task, but he did a fair job of batting in the same league as *Le Roi Soleil*. It is vast, but the Jolly does a bit better than either in the matter of bathrooms and an elegantly served dinner of nicely boned *orata* and spinaches adorned with garlic and oil. Even when the March weather is cold in Italy, there are fresh vegetables to enjoy. We wondered if they came from southern Sicily, or perhaps across the narrow bottleneck of the Mediterranean from Tunisia. After such a start at the *cucina*, we began to wonder what it was going to be like to experience the simpler real food of the *Mezzogiorno*, the south of Italy.

We need not have been concerned. Lunch at an Autogrille, along the Autostrada, maintained the high standard of Italian fast food—in this case, a salad of tuna and fava beans with really ripe tomatoes and small balls of mozzarella. A little farther north it would have been *pasta e fagiole*, hearty white beans and elbow macaroni swimming in a thick soup of tomatoes and other vegetables. Although we have come each time to Italy to experience the magic of the art and architecture, it is often the memory of the food that we recall most vividly.

We had made reservations at a hotel of good repute in the small city of Trani on the Adriatic coast of Puglia, a dozen kilometers north of Bari. The Hotel Regia was granted an impressive number of stars by the Cadogan Guide, and at 150 euro per night, was at the top of our range of accommodations. Information on the Internet said that it was on the Piazza Cattedrale. Driving directions from my computer at home were so detailed as to be hopelessly confusing. We drove into town and began to ask "*Dove il duomo?*"— since all cathedrals in Italy are so designated, whether they have a dome or not.

San Pellegrino

The Regia turned out to be on the oceanfront, a

recent conversion of an eighteenth-century palazzo that has but ten well-furnished rooms and an excellent restaurant. But its landmark neighbor church is more than eight hundred years old and is blessed with a stunning, startlingly severe facade with small rose windows in the western facade and the transepts. Converging flights of stairs lead from both sides of the western front to a central doorway flanked by rows of classical blind arches. Above all soars a magnificent campanile, a bell tower rising at least 180 feet in height. It is composed of eight lofty chambers with the traditional increase of open windows at each level as the tower rises. Besides giving the bells a greater range, this increasing fenestration with height takes a bit of the load off the foundation; in this case, an archway on which the campanile stands. The great tower is seated upon a seemingly delicate, small arcade which is attached to the eastern side of the church proper. The rank of blind arches across the facade is shown off by being raised on a broad, flattened arch that separates the double stair.

Like many Romanesque churches, the transept is higher than the nave, and the triple apse is higher (or surely as high as) the western facade. Its location on a broad stone piazza next to the sea gives it a fairy-castle air, even if the fact that the rear is higher than the front is a bit off balance. The strength and simplicity of form excuses the diversion from more expected proportions. There seems to be no record of the wonderful architect and engineer who drew its elegant design, but this is not unusual, since architects' names are generally unknown before the fourteenth century. Whoever he was, his is Norman architecture at its best. British students once voted Durham Cathedral, built in the same period (approximately AD 1150), the "second-best building" after the Taj Mahal. Although smaller, simpler, and less pretentious than either of those famous landmarks, I think the Cathedral of San Nicolo Pellegrino in Trani ranks right up there with the very best.

Actually, the present cathedral is the topmost of three churches built one upon the settled remains of another in this place. The second church now functions as the undercroft of the present church, and is actively used for mass most days. It is called the Crypt of Santa Maria. The image of the sad Madonna here is dressed in black and has a huge dagger, the symbol of her sorrows, lodged in her breast. The precise date of the forest of columns holding up the great burden of the cathedral above is hard to determine, but the undercroft was built as the Church of Santa Maria della Scala in the eighth or ninth century, above the lowest church, the little Chapel of San Leucio, whose relics were brought here from Brindisi in the sixth or seventh century; why, I have no idea.

We started through a side door to the middle level of this grand architectural sandwich. After a good deal of inspection of partially preserved mural paintings of the Madonna and Child and a Byzantine image of Saint Theodore, as well as an elaborate family tomb of the fourteenth century in the musty basements, we were able to work our way down to the Greek chapel of the sixth century. Later, it was a delight to finally emerge in the clear light of the great Norman nave of the upper cathedral, where the plain architecture is revealed by the light of the generous windows. The additions and decorations of the Baroque era have been stripped away, and the interior vaults and clerestory arcading are pleasantly revealed. The original center bronze doors from the west facade have been conserved here indoors where they can be protected. They were made by Barisano da Trani, one of the few twelfth-century artists who signed his work. The thirty-two panels present Christ in Majesty, an enthroned Virgin with Child, lots of apostles and saints, and rather startlingly, winged dragons, centaurs, sirens, and a number of characters from Greek and Roman mythology.

Outside, the slanting sun illuminated the detail of the few ornaments on the facade: an angel contesting with Jacob and a pair of cute elephants supporting the sill of the central window below the rose. Along the bright and breezy north side of the church there were a half-dozen preadolescent boys playing one-ended soccer, using a lofty, eight-hundred-year-old blind arch as a goal. They seemed as content and active on their flagstone pavement as they would have been on the green lawns of any New England school, or the meadows of Central Park, but they gave evidence of somewhat greater ball-handling skill than their American counterparts.

Later, thinking about these boys (and the girls they would soon pursue with all the passion and avidity they now focused on the soccer ball), I was struck by the fact that the church that was largely pulled down to make way for this wonderful cathedral was in itself a remarkable edifice, judging by the size of its foundation and the forest of columns still in place in the crypt. Yet no one has any idea of what it looked like during the four or five centuries when it served as the center of life in this town. Twenty generations of children born here were baptized, received communion, were married and buried here, and yet, we not only do not know the names of a single one of them, we also do not even know what their church looked like.

Even in so small a city as Trani, there is much to see and visit. The *castello* is around the corner from the cathedral, well restored to the level it attained just before the age of gunpowder when Charles of Anjou took it over from the early construction, which had been carried out at the behest of Frederick II. Military architecture evolved with the ages and with the growing inventiveness of engineers, who planned the breach as well as the construction of such fortresses. Today this one, like many ancient castles, has become a civic center, offering everything from art shows to rock concerts in their due season.[4]

But the area that truly defines Trani and first established its character is the harbor. A graciously curved indentation in the shore was early extended by moles, great rows of massive stone blocks heaped out into the sea. I suppose these huge and orderly piles of stone have been extended over many centuries. Now ornamented at their seaward ends by matching red and green lighthouses, they almost completely enclose a peaceful harbor where fishermen and yachtsmen seem to cohabit in happy understanding of the complementary roles of the two most profitable pursuits of these seaside towns: fishing and tourism.

Inside their embrace, the great crescent of the *darsena* (the municipal dock) is divided into ample areas for both fishing and pleasure boats. The commercial boats are out early in the morning and come back with their catch in the early afternoon, when the yachtsmen are getting under way. The fishing boats are tied up with their sterns toward the quay, and the crew offloads their catch to tables set up on the shore. They put on a sometimes melodious hard sell in hawking the seafood, but only with the lightest of pressure. Their customers are largely housewives who prefer their fish only a few hours from the sea, and restaurateurs who are selecting the menu for the semicircle of *ristoranti* that rims the harbor. We tried several, and concluded that La Rosa di Vente (the Wind Rose), only a trifle pricey, was as good as anyone could ask. The *orata* was splendid.

---

[4] A current list of these events may be found at www.traniweb.it, which provides not only information (in Italian) about upcoming concerts and films, but also pictures of the town's elegant buildings and pretty harbor.

Inland from the nautical bustle of the harbor there is a tangle of ancient streets that eventually can be penetrated to reveal a tidy, good-sized rectangular park that is surrounded by lots of shade trees and a number of shops, several of them featuring fashions that would do credit to Rome, Milan, or Turin. Best of all, we found a stylish *gelateria* that was actually combined with an elegant cocktail lounge. Such a happily discovered place is always an essential recovery stop after a strenuous afternoon of tourist walking, especially giving deference to the later-than-eight-o'clock opening hour of many Italian restaurants.

XXXV.

NAPOLI:
Beautiful Despite a Bad Reputation

When we first approached Napoli, we had defended ourselves with a slightly better grasp of Italian than we felt was necessary in the northern cities. After all, the time-honored expression "See Naples and die!" might even have been interpreted as something more ominous than a statement of the effect of the beauty of the famous bay or on the fulfillment of life itself. We studied the map and guidebooks at length, debating locations before deciding on a hotel near the *Duomo* or the *questura*, balancing the possible safety to be found in divine or human protection. We were also warned to accept the services only of taxis painted white, with meters, although many others might offer their services. The Cadogan Guide states flatly that all Neapolitan cabbies are criminals who will overcharge and take you for *un giro*—a long ride, that is.

We had no trouble with the Stazione FS, although it is famous for pickpockets. Outside we found a gleaming rank of white cabs. I gave the name of our hotel, the Orchidea (on the edge of the somewhat infamous Spaccanapoli), using my finest Tuscan pronunciation and my coolest attitude. The driver sped off in what seemed to me to be a direction 180 degrees from the hotel. It wasn't the fact that I was giving him the benefit of the doubt that kept me silent; I just didn't want to appear to be as much of a rube from the country (*un forestiero* in Italian) as I actually was, possibly putting us in even greater danger. But after a rapid circuit of the Piazza Garibaldi, following the one-way arrows, we reversed direction and rocketed down the Corso Garibaldi to a point across from the front door of the Hotel Orchidea on the neighboring Corso Umberto. He then executed a perfect and obviously illegal U-turn with a flourish. I liked his style and gave him a generous tip. We also liked the hotel, which was just short of the Piazza Bovio and a great bargain by Roman standards, at 140,000 lire (about 85 euro) for a night. It was also a short walk from the Stazione Maritima, whence we planned to depart for Sicily in a few days' time. Although the hotel lacked a breakfast room, there was a splendid café around the corner where we found excellent pastries in the morning and cocktails in the late afternoon.

Spaccanapoli is the "split" of Naples, the divide that separates the warren of streets on the east from the somewhat less unruly area to the west. A more exact crease in the center of town is formed by the Via Roma and the Via Toledo, which name recalls the fact that the Spanish ruled this busy town for more than half a millennium. They seem to have governed it for their own pleasure, building several palaces for themselves but doing little for the tough common people, the Lazzaroni, who were unaccountably loyal to them when the theoretically republican French came to town after their revolution.

We followed the main streets by bus up the long rise to Capodimonte, where Charles III Bourbon had started out building a hunting lodge and ended up constructing an art gallery of huge proportions in which he could enjoy his great collection of paintings. He inherited these from his mother, Elisabetta Farnese, heiress of the family that reared the great palazzo used today as the French embassy in Rome. The collection is fascinating enough to be worth the trip up the mountain, if only to pursue the hagiography of seeing St. Ludwig place the crown of Naples on the proud if bowed head of his brother, Robert of Anjou, who was the first of the French misrulers of the two Sicilies. There is a luscious Mary Magdalene by Titian, a stark Masaccio crucifixion, and any amount of elegant porcelain, much of it portraying frivolous figures of courtiers, courtesans, goddesses, and miniatures of the animals the upper classes spent their time hunting before the revolutionary upheavals of the late eighteenth century.

On the way back down the hill from Capodimonte, we passed a poster that advised us that at the Conservatorio della Pietà dei Turchini, there would be a concert that very evening. We pounced upon the bargain tickets, dined in a neighboring *ristorante*, and simply walked in. The auditorium had been constructed in a modern style from the remnant of the hall that had survived a bombing toward the end of World War II. It is amazing to contemplate the inaccurate scattering of high explosives that attended that period, in spite of the elaborate top-secret Norden bombsights and the highly trained bombardiers that figured so largely in those battles.

The concert presented a trio of young musicians, violin, piano, and cello, which produced a balanced mixture of music by Brahms and Vivaldi. The evening, a few yards from Spaccanapoli, seemed to us to be the very essence of civilized living.

On the following day we quite inadvertently found the CTS travel agent which we discovered while walking toward the Castel del Ovo on the waterfront. We were soon to depart for Sicily, so sought the advice of the pretty *impiegata* whose desk was in front of a large photomural of Mount Etna. She explained that there were no first-class cabins available for the next few days, but was sure we would be comfortable if we took all four berths in a second-class cabin. She was right; although the cabin was small, the lower berths provided a place for our luggage and the cost was about the same as the two-passenger accommodation in first class.

Vesuvio is visible from almost anywhere in Napoli. It erupts frequently, but not with the violence that destroyed Herculaneum and Pompeii in 79 BC, which was accurately described by Pliny the Younger and took the life of his father. Another acute observer of the explosive mountain was Sir William Hamilton, British ambassador of King George III of England at the time of the French Revolution and the Napoleonic Wars. Hamilton had climbed Vesuvius during a mild eruption, as had Cathy's great-grandfather somewhat later, in 1843. He, John Williams Lewis, was nearly brained by flying volcanic rocks during his descent, and had to flee headlong down the slope to the point where they had tethered their horses to escape.

Hamilton seems to have had no such close call with volcanism, but he did have an adventurous time with his second wife, the ravishingly beautiful Emma Hart. Emma was the daughter of a British blacksmith and the previous mistress of Hamilton's own nephew (although all the young blades of London had also been in love with her). George Romney, one of the greatest portraitists of the age, painted her almost a hundred times. Portraits of Emma, Lady Hamilton, can be found in most of the great art galleries of Europe, and also in the Frick Collection in New

Emma Hamilton

York. Although her spelling in English was unreliable, she learned to speak Italian fluently and became the confidante and advisor of Maria Carolina, Queen of Naples. As her husband became older, she became the de facto ambassadress of Great Britain in the Mediterranean. The heroic one-eyed and one-armed British admiral, Viscount Horatio Nelson, also fell hopelessly in love with her, and the story of their scandalous relationship is one of the great star-crossed love affairs of the nineteenth century. Their illegitimate daughter was named Horatia.[5]

Horatio Nelson

We made several walking tours of downtown Naples, visiting the glass-and-cast-iron mall, and the great San Carlo Opera House. We were unable to get to a *spettacolo*, but the house itself is a spectacle, and we were able to hear a considerable lecture about it in rapid Italian. The docent was gracious about answering questions in English, but then quickly lapsed back into her mother tongue. Oh well ... we were able to get some of it.

---

[5] I have long assumed that Horatia also had an illegitimate daughter, who would have been named Emma Nelson, who grew up and emigrated to New York in the nineteenth century. If so, and also if the young lady lied about her age (by four years) when she married Alexander Hume in 1848 (not an improbable fib for a girl a few years older than her intended husband), she was quite probably Emma Nelson, my great-grandmother. The given names of the participants and my father, Nelson Hume, all match perfectly. In an age before reliable birth certificates, such juggling of birthdays was common among Victorian ladies. I am indebted for much of the research for this information to my cousin, Professor Joan Carson of the College of New Rochelle.

We took a tram along the waterfront, the Mergellina, almost as far as Posillipo around the loop of the bay. We walked back past a chain of parks, yacht anchorages, and ice cream vendors. There were plenty of baby carriages, toddlers, and small children in evidence. This face of Naples is sunny and unthreatening. It forms a seaside border to the fashionable Vomero, the residential quarter reached by funicular cable cars that rise from the teeming city below. Naples is Italy's second-largest city, and its millions include not only some thieves and desperate prostitutes, but also the honest and prosperous, and a fair number of millionaires as well.

We departed for Sicily in the evening on board one of the great Mediterranean ferries from the Stazione Maritima. Sailing away from the romantic city of love songs, the sunset silhouetted the irregular cone of a currently passive Vesuvius. As we passed between the two islands of Ischia and Capri that serve as sentinels of the Bay of Naples, we reflected that the ancient Romans who made this place a site of holiday homes had gotten it just about right; the beauty of the Bay of Naples really is to die for.

We had an elegant dinner in the first-class dining room: delicately sautéed pesce spada in butter, served by white-jacketed waiters with pink roses in their lapels. We reflected on the real meaning of the old expression, *Veda Napoli e poi morire!*

By morning we would be in Sicily, ready for another adventure among the less-touristed locations in Italy. We were again ready to be inspired by the fascinating variety of this volcanic country, its ancient civilizations and mountain masses, its natural beauty, its art and architecture, and, not least, its friendly and hospitable people.

Finis

Author's Note

This book is a collection of essays written over more than a decade of adventures in Italy. Many good friends have contributed to it. Jeremy Townsend even suggested a subtitle: *Searching Italy for the Perfect Martini.* Various members of my family have voiced the opinion that my writing included too much of this or too little of that. Helene Billera, generous reader, managed to prune some of the excessive conjunctions from my accounts. I am even indebted to U.S. Airways who, despite occasional bankruptcy, have provided us with several free trips to Rome and back as their "frequent flyer" patrons. Most of all we fondly thank the good new friends we have met in this country or in Italy who have subsequently greeted us again on our travels and taught us much about their agreeable homeland and helped us become a little more intelligible in their flexible and dignified language: the Caldarella family, who we met first in Sicily and then pursued to Germany; Federica and Enrico Campeli, their son Leonardo; Cristina and Carla Alberto Mazzoni whom I adopted at the Mystic Seaport in Connecticut, and thence were taken in at Forlì and exposed to much of the best of Emilia Romagna, as well as some first-rate J. S. Bach in Imola next door.

But beyond the formal dedication, I want to record the great contributions of Catherine Hume, who kept careful journals of our travels and thus is responsible for all that is good and savory in this book. Errors of fact, history, or Italian orthography are mine alone.

—DDH
Salem, Connecticut
Wilmington, North Carolina

Index

About the Author

David and Cathy Hume have enjoyed traveling to Italy every year since David's retirement as headmaster of Saint David's School in New York City.

When not exploring the art and culture of Italy, the Humes divide their time between Connecticut and North Carolina. David Hume's previous book, *About Sicily*, is available from J. N. Townsend Publishing.